Economics: A Business Management Approach

Ashutosh Tripathi

authorHOUSE®

AuthorHouse™ UK Ltd.
500 Avebury Boulevard
Central Milton Keynes, MK9 2BE
www.authorhouse.co.uk
Phone: 08001974150

© 2011. Ashutosh Tripathi. All rights reserved

No part of this book may be reproduced, stored in a retrieval system, or transmitted by any means without the written permission of the author.

First published by AuthorHouse   2/28/2011

ISBN: 978-1-4567-7040-2 (sc)
ISBN: 978-1-4567-7063-1 (hc)

This book is printed on acid-free paper.

Foreword

The book written by Dr. Ashutosh Tripathi is to promote economic literacy and is a strong piece of work. George Stigler, a Nobel Laureate in economics, probably stated it best almost three decades ago. In Stigler's view, economic literacy is special because it contributes to two classes of knowledge. First, it serves as a "means of communication among people, incorporating a basic vocabulary or logic that is so frequently encountered that the knowledge should be possessed by everyone." Second, it is a "type of knowledge frequently needed and yet not susceptible to economical purchase from experts."

Economic literacy certainly contributes to the first class of knowledge. People like to think and talk about the economic issues that affect them as consumers, workers, producers, investors, citizens and in other roles they assume over a lifetime. Economic literacy also gives people the tools for understanding their economic world and how to interpret events that will either directly or indirectly affect them. Nations benefit from having an economically literate population because it improves the public's ability to comprehend and evaluate critical issues. This understanding is especially important in democracies that rely on the active support and involvement of its citizens.

What this means is that each person must ultimately serve as his or her own economist in making many economic choices, whether those choices involve buying a product, getting a loan, voting on candidates and economic issues, or something else. Economic literacy improves the competence of each individual for making personal and social decisions about the multitude of economic issues that will be encountered over a lifetime. Knowing what determines prices in a market economy and accepting the outcomes are two different things. If demand or supply conditions change, prices in a competitive market will rise and fall. Having a basic understanding of how markets work does not always mean that people will like price changes, especially if prices rise, but it should increase the probability of accepting the market outcome.

The development of basic economic literacy is an important goal for a democratic society that relies heavily on informed citizenry and personal economic decision-making. To achieve that goal will require that significant gaps in the economic education of youth be closed by giving economics a more central place in the school curriculum. More economics coursework at the precollege level sets a foundation for economic literacy, but it is only the beginning. As, George Stigler reminded us long ago: "We shall have to combine vast efforts and creative experimentations if we are to produce the first economically literate society in history."

As technological advances continue to expand the range of financial services available to consumers, money management becomes increasingly complicated. Helping consumers navigate this sea of financial products is important. When households are capable of building wealth, they are also capable of building more economically stable neighborhoods and communities. That's one reason economic education is vital to the future health of any nation's economy. In **"Economics: A Business Management Approach"**, the author, Ashutosh san outlines the interrelationship between economics and business management in a simple way to promote economic education which is most needed in our ever more complex world.

Dr. Machida Kazuhiko, 町田和彦

Acknowledgement

First and foremost I would like to express my deep and sincere gratitude to Professor (Dr.) Bishwanath Singh, Head of Economics Department, Magadha University and Dr. Shivendu, Professor, Department of Economics, University of California, Irvine (USA). They supported me throughout my writing and in the end with critical review of the work. I am indebted to their encouragement and effort and without them this book, would not have been completed.

I am also thankful to Dr. Gopal Tripathi (Founder Director IT-BHU & ex-Vice Chancellor Lucknow University) and Pt. Vachaspati Pathak (doyen of Hindi literature) who have inculcated and imbibed in me the seed of writing. Their enthusiasm and motivation has been instrumental in going through this journey.

It is also an honor to show my gratitude for Dr. D.N. Tewari (Chairman Planning Commission of India Chgh. & ex-Director General ICFRE) who instilled in me the art of living and re-kindled the flame of continued education through his sheer dynamism and never say die attitude.

During this work I have collaborated with many colleagues for whom I have great regard and I wish to extend my warmest thanks to all those who have helped me with my work such as Dr. V.P. Singh (India), Dr. Ulf Osmers (Germany), Dr. D. Desai (Germany) and Mr. Hans Kroeppelt (China), Mr. Ronald Gentsch (Germany), Mr. Yong Yuth Limpa – Amara (Thailand), Dr. Machida Kazuhiko (Japan), Dr. Athiwat Prachaseri (Thailand) who constantly encouraged me to not to give up.

I owe my loving thanks to my wife Dr. Arti Tripathi and my daughters Aditi and Anika. They have lost a lot due to my research at various places and long visits abroad. Without their encouragement and understanding it would not have been possible to complete this work. My special gratitude is due to my sisters Dr. Archana Dubey and Dr. Alpana Shukla and their families.

In the end, I dedicate this book to my parents Late Smt. Mala & Shri Prem Chandra Tripathi.

Preface

A lot has happened to the business landscape in the last few decades since regressions and depressions created interest in the study of economics. Several years of steady but unspectacular economic growth culminated with the dot.com bubble and a subsequent global recession. A broad-based recovery enabled many firms in both the Old and New Economies to enjoy unprecedented profitability, only to see profits dry up in the wake of a credit crunch and rising energy costs.

Through it all, the strategy gurus have been quick to remind us that "the rules of business have changed." The French have an apt rejoinder: *Plus ca change, plus c'est la mˆeme chose*. (The more things change, the more they stay the same.) Consider the fate of managers and investors who followed the latest fads of the last decade without paying attention to tried-and-true economic concepts. Dot.com businesses sold identical products (pet food, toys, you name it) and discovered the perils of perfect competition. Movie studios followed the mantra of convergence, creating entertainment super giants that failed to overcome the risks of extensive vertical integration. Banks ignored basic economic principles of asymmetric information and loaned billions of dollars to home buyers who could not repay them.

These catastrophic mistakes reaffirm what was preached since day one: There are a set of business principles that apply at all times to all sectors of the economy. Sound strategic management requires mastery of these principles, not blind adherence to the *"strategy du jour"* Managers who ignore these principles do so at their own peril.

By their nature, principles are enduring. But they are not always well understood.

In view of the above, this book has been written for anyone who has the desire to know how an economy functions and the invisible hands of market mechanism, but, is not comfortable with lot of analytical theories using algebraic and logarithmic mathematics involving linear and non-linear equations which are normally interesting to academicians only.

It would be a great pleasure if this book helps in improving the understanding of the world we live and also benefit the readers in managing their financial affairs. Effort has been made to simplify the economic theories without usage of jargons. The book has been organized in a traditional way and has been divided into the following parts:

1. **Introduction:** This includes historical background, business economics, economic environment, business dynamics, economics and finance. This will provide the foundation for the complex subject and prepare the readers for further complex mechanism of economics.

2. **Framework of Economy:** This includes economic system, planning, controls, imbalances & fluctuations, development and growth. This will provide the basics of system structure on which economic principles operate. It is said that planning is important for successful execution to elevate business performance.

3. **Functioning of Economy:** This includes economics of money, indicators, conditions, policies, stabilization, and institutions. This will provide the working of economics and its measurement with highlights on economic upheavals and remedial actions. International organizations playing important role in economics and finance also have been introduced for broader understanding.

4. **Economics & Business Scenarios:** This includes economics, business & industry, foreign direct investment trends, new business investment arena. This part would provide an insight of the economic developments which have taken place in view of changes in consumer desires and also changes in the world economic structure with rising BRICs and CHINDIA poised to take control of the world economic order in the near future.

5. **Glossary & References:** This includes the glossary of economic and business management terms with additional inclusion of financial ratios normally used in business management. This part would be more as a ready reference, should there is a need. This is primarily to highlight the importance of financial ratios to constantly monitor the health of the companies in the wake of adverse economical environment. In the end, references and bibliography has also been provided in case the readers would like to go deep into any particular topic.

The book is liberally interspersed with real-world examples that bring the economic models to life. The examples are drawn from throughout the world and cover business practice from the eighteenth century to the present day. The business world is ever-changing, and by the time this book hits the market, some of our references to organizations and individuals will be obsolete. We hope that the lessons learned from them will endure.

We believe that this book can be used for general reading. Nevertheless, this can also be utilized as a text either in a core economic course or in a business management course that focuses on the economics of industry and business management of the company.

Ashutosh Tripathi

Contents

Foreword	v
Acknowledgement	vii
Preface	ix

Part A. INTRODUCTION	**1**
A.1 HISTORICAL BACKGROUND	3
A.2 BUSINESS ENVIRONMENT	12
A.3 ECONOMIC ENVIRONMENT	26
A.4 BUSINESS DYNAMICS	40
A.5 ECONOMICS & FINANCE	53
Part B. FRAMEWORK OF ECONOMY	**64**
B.1 ECONOMIC SYSTEM	65
B.2 ECONOMIC PLANNING	86
B.3 ECONOMIC CONTROLS	104
B.4 ECONOMIC IMBALANCE & FLUCTUATIONS	113
B.5 ECONOMIC DEVELOPMENT	129
B.6 ECONOMIC GROWTH	142
Part C. FUNCTIONING OF ECONOMICS	**154**
C.1 ECONOMICS OF MONEY	155
C.2 ECONOMIC INDICATORS	165
C.3 ECONOMICS CONDITIONS	173
C.4 ECONOMICS POLICIES	188
C.5 ECONOMIC STABILIZATION	207
C.6 ECONOMICS INSTITUTIONS	216

Part D. ECONOMIC & BUSINESS SCENARIOS   246

    D.1 ECONOMICS, BUSINESS & INDUSTRY   247
    D.2 FDI & BUSINESS TRENDS   257
    D.3 TRENDS IN BUSINESS INVESTMENT   269

Part E. GLOSSARY   283

    E.1 ECONOMICS & BUSINESS MANAGEMENT TERMS   285
    E.2 ECONOMICS & BUSINESS MANAGEMENT ACRONYM LISTING 327
    E.3 BUSINESS MANAGEMENT: FINANCIAL RATIOS   332

Part F. REFERENCE/BIBLIOGRAPHY   337

PART A
INTRODUCTION

A.1 HISTORICAL BACKGROUND

Starting from Homo habilis to Homo erectus with an on-going progression to Homo Neanderthalensis and finally culminating to Homo sapiens; the nature has tried to refine the human race. The process still continues with man trying to improve his material well being, sometimes at the cost of nature and most of the time at the cost of other human beings primarily because human behavior is a relationship between ends and scarce means. With the growing population and desires the available resources became insufficient. The usage of brute force for accumulation got subdued and alternative means surfaced in various areas spanning from business, politics, religion, family, war etc.

Economics began to develop even before the Middle Ages notably in the Nile Valleys, India, and China. Some of the earlier important economic philosophers were - Xenophon, Chanakya, Wang Anshi, and Ibn Khaldun to name a few. Economics started to develop as a behavioral science studying individual choices and more broadly societal choices in choosing scarce resources. It like this, planning a function or planning a leisure trip – all is about doing economics. Human desire is unlimited. However, the resources available to satisfy these desires are virtually limited or scarce. Hence, Economic choices arise from scarcity. In nutshell, the need to manage scarcity resulted in the evolution of economics – to understand and facilitate making choices, constructing economic structures, market mechanism to produce and distribute and try to maintain them in a smooth & efficient working.

Over the centuries, the world witnessed strange phenomenon of regional shift in riches (# GDP share %) which can be seen from work of economic historian Angus Maddison:-

Sl. No.	Region / Country*	Century(s)							
		1	1000	1500	1600	1700	1820	1998	2007
1	India	32.9	28.9	24.5	22.6	24.4	16.0	3.1	4.72
2	China	26.2	22.7	25.0	29.2	22.3	32.9	4.6	10.78
3	United States	-	-	3.4	0.2	0.1	1.8	22.0	21.10
4	Russia	1.5	2.4	3.4	3.5	4.4	5.4	9.4	3.19
5	Africa	6.8	11.8	-	6.7	6.6	4.5	3.3	-
6	Japan	1.2	2.7	3.1	2.9	4.1	3.0	7.7	6.54
7	Germany	-	-	3.3	3.8	3.6	3.8	5.9	4.17
8	UK	-	-	1.1	1.8	2.9	5.2	4.2	3.13
9	France	-	-	-	4.7	5.7	5.5	4.3	3.15
10	Eastern Europe	1.9	2.2	2.5	2.7	2.9	3.3	3.4	-

- *Political boundaries of present day nations may differ.*

#: *estimates from the I st century to 1998, with figures in millions of International Dollars.*

Please note that Maddison's data is based on the detailed economic data collected and it is considered as a herculean task. Commenting on the accuracy of data, economist and journalist Evan Davis praised it as fantastic publication and that —"One shouldn't read the book in the belief the statistics are accurate to 12 decimal places".

From the above data table is evident that the world started to witness a significant amount of economic turmoil around 1700 AD. This attracted the attention of several thinkers who tried to explain – how economies work and how economic agents interact. Some of the notable academicians who contributed from 1770 to 1870 are Adam Smith, Thomas Malthus, David Ricardo, John Stuart Mill, and Karl Marx.

The momentum was set with the publication of Adam Smith's *The Wealth of Nations* in 1776, which has been credited to have given birth to economics as a separate discipline. The main factors of production and contributors to a nation's wealth were identified as –

1. Land

2. Labour

3. Capital

Adam Smith's approach to explain economic issues was called political economy and later classical economy. In his view, the ideal economy is a self – regulating market system that automatically satisfies the economic needs of the populace. He propounded the concept of "invisible hand" that motivates all individual to pursue their own self – interest in order to benefit the society as a whole. Interestingly, he argued that competitive markets tended to advance broader self interest although driven by narrow self interest. Basically, he keenly observed man's behavior and its outcomes and tried to explain it all. The economics which came into existence with the advent of his book was a mix of sociology, politics and philosophy. At a later stage, the same was refined and specialized to the present day form.

Continuing with works of the persons who laid the foundations of the subject, it is worthwhile to understand the work of David Ricardo who emphasized on the distribution of income, while Smith tried to explain the production of income. Explaining the distribution of income among landowners, workers, capitalists; he observed an inherent conflict between the landowners, labor and capital. He put forth the theory of that due to fixed supply of land, the rent increases while wages and profits thin down with the growth of population.

Thomas Robert Malthus focused on the fact that population increases geometrically, outstripping the production of food which in his opinion increases arithmetically. As the land is fixed; the growing population amounts to a diminishing return. This results into chronic low wages which prevents most of the population from rising above the subsistence level. Contrary to this simple algorithm, 1998 Nobel Laureate Dr. Amartya Sen tried to explain in Poverty and Famines, that famines occur not only from a lack of food, but from inequalities built into the mechanisms for distributing food. Amartya Sen pointed out a number of social and economic factors, such as declining wages, unemployment, rising food prices and lacunas in the food distribution system resulted into starvation among certain groups in society.

Coming back to the theories of Malthus, who was Professor of History and Political Economy at the East India Company College, we see that he went to the extent to say that "The power of population is so superior to the power of the earth to produce subsistence for man, that premature death must in some shape or other visit the human race."

Later Karl Marx argued that Malthus did not fully recognize the human capacity to increase food supply.

Malthus even proposed moral restraints (postponement of marriage until people could support a family), coupled with strict celibacy until that time. Malthus stand on public assistance to the poor is also interesting as he proposed gradual abolition of poor laws as this would have acted against the long term interests of the poor by raising the price of commodities and undermining the independence and resilience of the poor.

Malthus evolutionary theory: population pressure stimulates – productivity stimulates – population growth, has had great influence both on biology and in social science. Referring to Malthus, even Darwin recognized the significance of competition between populations of the same species, as well as the importance of competition between species. He also blamed economy's tendency to save too much may give rise to unemployment – a theme that was revived by John Maynard Keyes in the 1930's.

In the beginning of nineteenth century came John Stuart Mill, who was the son of James Mill, the writer of *History of India*. John Mill's *Principles of Political Economy* which was first published in 1848, was one of the most widely read books on economics in this period. He pointed out that the market has two roles – allocation of resources and distribution of income. However, the market may be efficient in allocating resources but not in distributing income, necessitating society to intervene.

Karl Marx, who was greatly influenced by Adam Smith and David Ricardo, published *Das Kapital* in German in 1867. Marx focused on the labor theory of value and exploitation of labor by capital. According to labor theory, the value of a thing is determined by the labor that went into its production. This is in contradiction with the modern understanding that the value of a thing is determined by what one is willing to give up obtaining the thing. Marx assumed that human nature involves transforming nature. He used the term "labour" for this process of transformation and "labour power" for the capacity to transform nature. Marx considered this as a simultaneous act between physical and mental capabilities:

"A spider conducts operations that resemble those of a weaver, and a bee puts to shame many an architect in the construction of her cells. But what distinguishes the worst architect from the best of bees is this, that the architect raises his structure in imagination before erects it in reality."

While analyzing history, Marx focused on the organization of labour and drew distinction between:

1. The means / force of production, literally those things such as land, natural resources, and technology, that are necessary for the production of material goods; and

2. The relations of production, in other words, the social relationships people enter into as they acquire and use the means of production.

On the basis of modes of production, Marx tried to distinguish historical eras. He observed that European societies had progressed from a feudal mode of production to a capitalist mode of production. He was a firm believer that capitalism was instrumental in changing the means of production more rapidly than the relations of production. From his point of view, the mismatch between economic base and social superstructure is a major source of disruption and conflict. Marx tried to define classes in terms of their accessibility to resources. As different classes would have different divergent interests, this gives rise to another source of social disruption and conflict. He regarded conflict between social classes as something inherent in all human history:

"The history of all hitherto existing society is the history of class struggle."

Marx was a firm believer that capitalism can stimulate considerable growth because the capitalist can and has the incentive to reinvest profits in new technologies and capital equipment.

Application of mathematics to Political Economics had already started during the Victorian Era and the logical inputs gained prominence with William Stanley Jevons's *The Coal Question* (1865) in which he drew attention to the gradual exhaustion of coal suppliers. He proposed that technological progress that increases the efficiency, with which a resource is used, tends to increase the rate of consumption of that resource. In other words, improved efficiency lowers the relative cost of using a resource – which increases demand. This is known as **Jevons Paradox**. In his book, he observed that England's consumption of coal soared after James Watt introduced coal fired steam engine. Watt's innovation made coal a more cost effective power resource. This resulted into increased usage of steam engines, and hence, increases use of coal.

Broadly speaking, a decrease in the price of good or service will increase the quantity demanded. Thus with a lower price for work, more work will be "purchased". The resulting increase in the demand for resource is known as rebound effect. This increase in demand may or may not be large enough to offset the original drop in demand from the increased efficiency. In 1992, the economist Harry Saunders revisited this hypothesis –

1. Increase energy efficiency makes the use of energy relatively cheaper, thus encouraging increased use.

2. Increased energy efficiency leads to increased economic growth, which pulls up the energy use for the whole economy.

Considering the resource petroleum which has been continuously on the economic front due to steep fluctuations, we can see that increased efficiency usually reduces fuel usage. However, faster economic growth may still offset it. Taking the argument forward, even if the fuel efficiency does not reduce the total amount of fuel used, this may still have an effect on price hike, shortages etc. Hence, this necessitates government intervention for promoting ecological sustainable activities in order to check the spiraling increase in the usage of energy resource.

Coming back to the prosperous Victorian era massive industrial improvement and large educated middle class; the economic fluctuations was minimal. However, the end of Edwardian Period saw high levels of unemployment – a phenomenon which was difficult to explain with the positivism theory. It was John Maynard Keynes who in his the *General Theory of Employment, Interest and Money* (1936) challenged the economic paradigm by stating that as societies develop, people's behavior undergo changes and the relationship between input and output become imprecise and unpredictable. Keyes tried to highlight the importance of emotions in the economic system & the importance of feel good and feel bad factors which drive public emotions at large. He advocated the use of fiscal and monetary measures by the government to balance economic meltdown, recession, depression, boom etc.

In his book Keynes tried to explain to variations in the overall level of economic activity, similar to the one observed during the Great Depression (1929). Similar to GDP concept, he defined total income in a society by the sum of consumption and investment; and in the state of economic downturn resulting unemployment and surplus production capacity the only viable way out is financial injections for enhancing investing and consumption. The book suggested investment as an economic policy by the government especially in times of high employment. The book is viewed as a foundation of modern macroeconomics.

By the end of World War II, Keynes proposed the creation of a common world unit of currency and new global institutions. Keynes envisaged these institutions managing an international trade and payments system with strong incentives for countries to avoid substantial trade deficits or surpluses. The two new institutions were founded and would be later known as World Bank and International Monetary Fund (IMF). Keynes is considered as the most influential economists of the 20 th century. Even Bertrand Russell named Keynes as one of the most intelligent people he had come across.

With this brief historical background, we see that economics as a subject has been developed over a fairly long period with significant inputs from various thinkers. Modern economics has been substantially refined and can be broadly divided into two main streams:

1. **Macro-economics**: attempts to explain the average level of all prices in an economy and changes in that level. In other words, it deals with the total output produced by a country and changes in the level of that output. Also, variation in the levels of employment and unemployment.

2. **Micro-economics**: attempts to explain the behavior of the individual components of the system.

Basically, an analogy may be drawn with the body as a whole (macroeconomics) and body parts (microeconomics). In macroeconomics, the behavior of the whole macro economy is greater than the sum of individual actions and market outcomes. Macroeconomics is widely viewed as providing a rationale for continual government intervention to manage short – term fluctuations and adverse events in the economy by suitable adjustments in monetary policy and fiscal policy. Broadly speaking, macroeconomics is the study of long term growth whereas, microeconomic focuses on the amount of output the economy is capable of producing as given. In macroeconomics there is much wider role for government by way of fiscal policy and monetary policy, but surprisingly, in microeconomics government intervention in the market usually leaves society worse off.

To make it clearer, microeconomic examines the aggregate behavior of the economy i.e. how the actions of all the individuals and firms in the economy interact to produce a particular level of economic performance as a whole e.g. overall level of prices in the economy (how high or how low the prices are relative to prices last year) rather than the price of a particular good or service. Microeconomics, on the other hand, focuses on how decisions are made by individuals and firms and the consequences of these decisions e.g. how much it would cost for a university or college to offer a new course – the salary, facilities, class materials etc. Based on the overall cost estimation the school or college can then weigh whether it would be viable to offer the course or not.

Now we will try to ask some questions to bring out the subtle differences clearly –

Sl. No.	Microeconomics	Macroeconomics
1	What determines the cost to a university or a college of offering a new course ?	What determines the overall level of prices in the economy as a whole ?
2	What government policies should be adopted to make it easier for low – income students to attend college ?	What government policies should be adopted to promote full employment and growth in the economy as a whole ?
3	What determines whether Standard & Chartered bank opens a new branch in Pattaya ?	What determines the overall trade in goods, services and financial assets between the US and other countries ?
4	Go to the business school or take a job ?	How many people are employed in the economy as a whole ?
5	What determines the salary offered by ICICI to the brand ambassador ?	What determines the overall salary levels paid to workers in a given year ?
6	What determines the manufacturing cost of a new BMW model for optimum sale price ?	What kind of cash injections are required to stabilize the car industries in US ?

In the beginning, we have seen that the need to manage scarcity resulted in the evolution of economics. Broadly, two ways can be discussed to manage goods in short supply:

- Invisible hand

- Command system

A market economy uses price to allocate scarce material. The invisible hand works on the basis of transaction between willing buyers and willing sellers. The seller will decide on the predetermined price based on various factors such as manufacturing cost, profitability desired whereas, the buyer will decide whether the predetermined price represents a good value for the money. Thus the invisible hand ensures buyers and sellers exchange goods for mutual benefit.

Therefore, the role of mutual benefit is paramount in driving the economy. In the command system, the central decision making authority states what the population should have and other state machinery to work accordingly. This type of economic system is viable in the initial stages of development to generate momentum however, lacks sustainability because of the absence of motivation concerning individual mutual benefit. In the coming chapters we will see the measurement aspect of economics with respect to business dynamics as well as financial environment.

A.2 BUSINESS ENVIRONMENT

Generally speaking, buying and selling of goods may be thought of as business. However, this concept is not valid in the context of present day modern economic sense wherein, the entire gamut of activities involving raw material, production, distribution and even after sales is considered as business. The scope of activities is gigantic and involves finances which were unthinkable before. From a simple subsistence economy to corporate business models with revenues as big or even bigger than some of the countries has made economics and business an inseparable and most talked subject of today.

Single thing which differentiates between a business and a non-business activity is the profit motive. Here, activities which do not conform to the law of the country is not considered as business activities although, these do have profit motive. The complexity of business nature increases with the increase in quantum of revenues and also on the nature which has a bearing on cash flow cycle. Modern business may be best described as oligopolistic in nature, which is characterized by small number of firms engaged in selling homogenous or a wide array of differentiated product. One of the important features could be that the interdependence among various sellers in the network is recognized.

Numbers of factors influence the emergence of oligopolistic nature of business such as, large financial requirement, economies of scale, cost advantage, acquisition and merger and product differentiation as well. However, the most common feature of this nature of business is collusion. This can be categorized into – cartel and price leadership. When business firms combine with an objective to minimize competition, they form a cartel. Normally, formation of an open collusion is not permissible and the companies avoid entering into any kind of enforceable contract. But secret collusions are common in business world. In nutshell, cartels are formed with the view to maximize joint profit as well as optimizing market share with a combined effort to tackle competition. In order to avoid conflict of interest, a common understanding regarding quota with non-price competition is adhered to. It may be visualized that oligopolistic markets do create a certain degree of uncertainty due to a closed market scenario which lessens the dynamism. This often gives rise to price leadership which is a subdued form of collusion when compared to cartel. In a relatively new market, firms often resort to price wars to facilitate penetration at an early stage. This helps in creating a space for the firm. An example from cheap Chinese products amassing the markets is easily understood. Nevertheless, with increase in maturity of the firms, such price wars decline as consumers gradually develop their own preferences. Therefore, as the market matures, firms are less interested in market penetration by way of pricing strategy alone, and they substantiate it with product differentiation.

There are several methods to differentiate products. Minor changes in design, which are often known as *'facelift'* to attract different segments of consumers, even different levels of quality to suit the expectations of consumers who wish to pay matching their requirement concerning reliability and usability. On top of these advertising prepares the ground for consumer awareness and often it is observed that there is a sudden surge of sales if the things are handled properly. However, this does not mean that the surge in demand is likely to be for a long time as other companies also retaliate with more improvements. That is why we often see – *'New'* or *'Improved'* labels on various brands wherein the base product remains the same. Such activities which lead to product differentiation is good both for the producers as they may give rise to sales and at the same time benefits the consumers due to industrial research.

As discussed, product differentiation provides leverage to companies to play within a constraint which can boost the business in an incremental way. However, corporate enterprises who would not like to confine their scope to a single commodity opt for diversification. This has normally two modes – Concentric or Horizontal diversification. When a company wants to add the product line of the similar type like BMW which keeps on adding new series of cars or Microsoft for operating and application software, this is called concentric diversification. In this a company may also takeover another company which matches its product line and is likely to strengthen the brand further. For example TATA taking over Land Rover & Jaguar and Mittal Group taking over Arcelor Group to further strengthen their brand equity. In contrast, when the companies decide to grow overtime by way of adding unrelated products in their portfolio, then this is called Horizontal diversification. On a bigger scale, when big business houses expand their activities by way or adding or takeover pertaining to a specific product line i.e. a combination of horizontal diversification in concentric way, this is called conglomerate diversification.

The sustainability of any business decides which diversification is best suited to the brand in the context of product and services. Economic recession witnessed during 2008 / 2009 showed that uncontrolled diversification – either horizontal or concentric may lack sustainability, on the contrary at the same time; this period sees major activities concerning acquisitions and merger as well. Except for few highly diversified big conglomerates, normally the trend is to expand businesses in case of surplus resources in area with similar competencies. The reluctance to diversify comes from the fact that consumer acceptance in most of the cases is observed to be brand – product specific. Therefore, recessionary phase would not provide adequate solid ground to foray into new businesses. However, in some cases, it has also been observed that conglomerates takeover another business not from the point of long term perspective but from the point of selling them at a profitable gain. This happens with liquidity infusion and better management practices which pull these companies from the brink of red zone. One interesting point which holds true in majority of the diversification is that weak brands tend to prefer horizontal diversification whereas, strong brands tend to go for concentric diversification or even convergence by offloading less competitive businesses of the same product line.

In the modern global scenario, political boundaries are becoming less important and economic spheres are gaining recognition. In pre-liberalization era the companies felt more secured to conduct businesses in domestic market, however, with globalization the multi-national culture is becoming a normal trend and this is measured by the *'Index of Trans-Nationality'*. Conglomerates originating from smaller countries have higher index of trans-nationality as they rely primarily on exports due to less scope of consumption in the domestic market. Therefore, countries having export driven economy are more susceptible to recessionary fluctuations or downturns. This was seen during the 2008 / 2009 economic recession which affected the smaller European nation badly and resulted into large scale stagflation. So far, the majority of global fortune 500 companies come from the bloc comprising of USA, European Union, Japan. However, gradually companies from South Korea, Singapore, India, China, Hong Kong, Taiwan, Thailand, Malaysia etc., have started spreading the operations beyond their political frontiers.

In spite of the increasing globalization, an interesting observation is that primarily production, sourcing and distribution activities which are spread with a view to tap local market to achieve the optimum revenue. The research & development activities are still rooted to the mother country. In nutshell, majority of expansion across the border is to increase the revenues, assets and flow of capital. The basic reason is to increase the sales. However, as the tax structure makes the import significantly costly rendering it non-competitive to the local producers, hence a manufacturing base is also established. This normally starts with import content to offset the competitive price gap keeping in view the volumes of production and market off-take. Some reverse examples may also be noticed, wherein brands trying to establish themselves in the international arena tend to takeover foreign design houses in order to match the product with local taste and also to enrich the expertise of the local research and development to the levels required for being transnational. This activity also provides a multi-national facelift to the local organization planning to foray into foreign boundaries.

Another fast track approach which is nowadays seen is a kind of convergence in the sense that companies' take-over existing companies in order establish themselves in the country with already existing consumer base with plans to gradually broaden that base with product differentiation. Hence, acquisitions and mergers are becoming fiercer. It is also interesting to note that it is not always that in corporate world a bigger fish eats smaller fish. This is determined more by the liquidity situation and not merely by the total turnover. In scenarios of hostile takeover, it is the shareholder gain that decides the fate of the future owner coupled with the sustainability capacity of the bidder.

During the last three decades the market has seen a sea-change in terms of consumer products. From food processing to electronics and even to entertainment; one can see quantum changes in telecommunication where 3D and touch screen are in thing. The packaged food once considered to be a worst resort has got significant acceptability from the nuclear families having working couples. Therefore, one can see the impact of technology in today's business. In manufacturing, processing or even service industries the concept of quality has also undergone a sea-change. Zero – defect is considered to be a desired standard. Even in consumer white goods complicated button panels have been replaced by fuzzy logic control system which decide an array of combinations based on the basic standardized requirements. Innovations in order to have an edge over the competitor are an important factor. In automobile sector the burning example can be seen in the case of hybrid technology which has been the basis for product differentiation and led to few takeovers as well to facilitate technology transfer. This innovation led product differentiation has increasingly benefitted the consumer and science as a whole.

The importance of research and development has been well understood by the corporate world and more and more investment is being poured into this segment. Technology creation in itself has become a large industry and majority of Joint Ventures are formed on the basis of technological advantage of the partners in terms of sustainability and adaptability. Since, research and development activities are quite expensive; hence, sustainability and adaptability of the industries are important factors to evaluate the effective life of the business. However, sustainability depends on demand and continuous demand. This can be either due to non-availability of comparable product or by market penetration. Similar to the human body the longevity of the business depends on constantly finding ways to keep up the optimum or at least break-even demand. This means a constant proactive approach to replace or change products and service with the likings of consumers. This activity becomes vital considering reducing brand loyalty due to standardization of basic design requirement as mentioned before and cut throat competition.

If we go a bit deeper, it becomes clear that nowadays, the market is driven by our basic requirements. It is combination of our normal basic requirements which is strongly bonded with synthetic needs created by the companies via product differentiation or innovation – strong enough to overlap with our basic needs. These synthetic needs are normally misused as is the usage of mobile telephones. Due to counter strategies these synthetic needs, have a short shelf life, hence, the companies need to formulate strategies to increase brand loyalty of their customer bases. For brand image to be of high esteem, the strategies need to be dynamic and progressive with focus on constant up gradation of their capacities to deliver products and services in line with purchasing power and expectations of the respective customer segment.

With the breakdown of the erstwhile USSR and increasing influence of capitalism, economy has acted as a catalyst towards reduction of government controls in business in terms of regulations and liberalization was instrumental in globalization. It would be wrong to say that absolute abolition of government regulatory controls would favor the market as it would lead to *'laissez-faire'*. Hence, government regulation in business is acknowledged primarily to control monopoly, pollution. Even the great economic recession of 2008/2009 saw significant stimulus packages being forwarded by the respective government to boost economy by increasing expenditure in capital expenses. Government controls are sometimes implemented from the point of protecting the market as well so as to provide some lead time to the domestic industries to develop till these are capable of facing stiff competition posed by comparable multi-nationals. However, it is normally seen that absence of competition normally limits the fighting or competitive spirit of these companies and they start to focus more on manufacturing rather than putting equivalent effort on research and development.

The business environment of the country is largely shaped by the government regulations and controls exercised. The ease of starting a business is mapped based on these controls, but not necessarily depicts the sustainability of the business. For example, most of the countries which are ranked among the top 10 countries having highest ease of starting or doing business do not find their place in highest growing economy. For example the BRIC countries (Brazil, Russia, India, and China) do not belong to the group of countries with highest ease of starting business yet are among the leading economies with highest GDP growth rates. It is normally seen that smaller economies have less complicated procedures than bigger and stable economies. One of the reasons could be the tight fiscal and monetary regulation exercised in countries having stable economies that are undergoing growth in order to ward off any instable market condition such as 2008/2009 which is also known as European and American recession. This clearly showed resilience of the Indian, Chinese and Brazilian markets against all odds in spite of the fact that most of the robust economies of America, Europe and Japan went into a recession in no time.

Capitalism is closely associated with privatization, however, in any country the government tries to control, in varying degrees, goods or services which are directly related to public in general. This could be in hospital sector, infrastructure sector, defense, banking, law & order and public transport system. The reason is that these goods and services cannot be created for the purpose of profit maximization. Therefore, production or creation of public goods is not delegated to private enterprises and this varies from country to country depending on the administrative control the government would like to control and also its willingness to participate in this exercise.

As the human personality is influenced by both internal and external environment i.e. the way socialization has taken place. Similarly, any business irrespective of its origin is also affected by the internal and external environment. These two do have an impact on shaping the business strategy for sustainability. Some economists have also divided the external environment into *'micro'* and *'macro'* environment for the purpose of clarity of impact it has on the business. Analogous to the family, organizations also have their formal management structure, technological capabilities, financial resources, mission & vision, strategic planning etc. These various constituents put together make the internal environment of the organization which culminates into a specific organization culture. Even though the basic objective of all businesses remain the same i.e. profit maximization, still these different value systems which evolve during the passage of time shape the internal environment.

One of the prominent factors which have a pronounced effect on the internal environment is the management fabric i.e. family controlled or professionally managed. Majority of European business houses are family controlled even though nowadays, the priority is shifting towards professionally managed companies – due to increase in size, increase in complexity of business which necessitates faster decisions and expertise in strategy implementation to counter the competition. Also, the ability to take calculated risk in the case of professionally managed organizations is more than purely family oriented business houses. The relationship between the shareholders, board of directors and senior executives is an important factor which has an effect on the company's internal working environment. Even though, traditionally speaking, profit motive is the sole objective of all business houses; an important factor which clearly stands out is that all companies do not pursue a common objective. There are major differences in the vision of different companies' which in turn result not only into different internal environment but also business policies, priority and the direction to control. The internal environment of a company is not a thing which can be observed from outside. It becomes visible only with inside participation, nevertheless, rapid technological changes which also includes automation is gradually reducing the importance of tangible assets versus human assets.

Technological changes on one hand has reduced importance of skills of a manpower specific to a job, however, it has also elevated the importance of human resource management in the industries to contain the outflow of trained manpower particularly belonging to the technical stream. The level of technology an industry utilizes is a decisive factor in employing quality manpower. However, more the intelligence level of an employee more is the requirement for attention. Over the period of time industries have spread in outskirts of the city and also in the industrial estates primarily due to regulatory controls of pollution and duty concessions (e.g. Export Processing Zones or EPZ). The commuting time has increased, nuclear family concept has almost elapsed the erstwhile joint family concept. Nowadays, even family with virtual contact and transitory families are becoming the norm in highly industrialized countries. As the human nature is changing in response to the rapid industrialization so is the internal environment of the company. With increasing manpower mobility, individuals carry their own convictions and try to influence the internal environment of the company. The earlier concept of long service and integrity is giving way to short term contractual assignments. Hence, the internal environments of the companies are becoming less stable and are being replaced by a faceless professional environment.

As we have seen that the internal environment of the company influences the internal working of the company, similarly, there are various external agencies such as other organization, institutions, customer, media, competitors, and suppliers etc., which also exert tremendous influence on the organization. Their cumulative effect forms an external environment of the company. This can be classified into two types – *micro* 'and *macro*' environment. Broadly speaking, micro environment consists of elements which have a direct bearing on the operations of a company whereas, macro environment has an indirect bearing, albeit more effective in most of the times from the point of long – term sustainability.

An interesting thing is that the effect of these external and internal environments is not homogenous and differs depending on the size of the company itself. As the company grows or reduces, the influences of the key players shaping these environments also undergo changes. The following illustration would provide some clarity on the keys player of micro environment that we are discussing:-

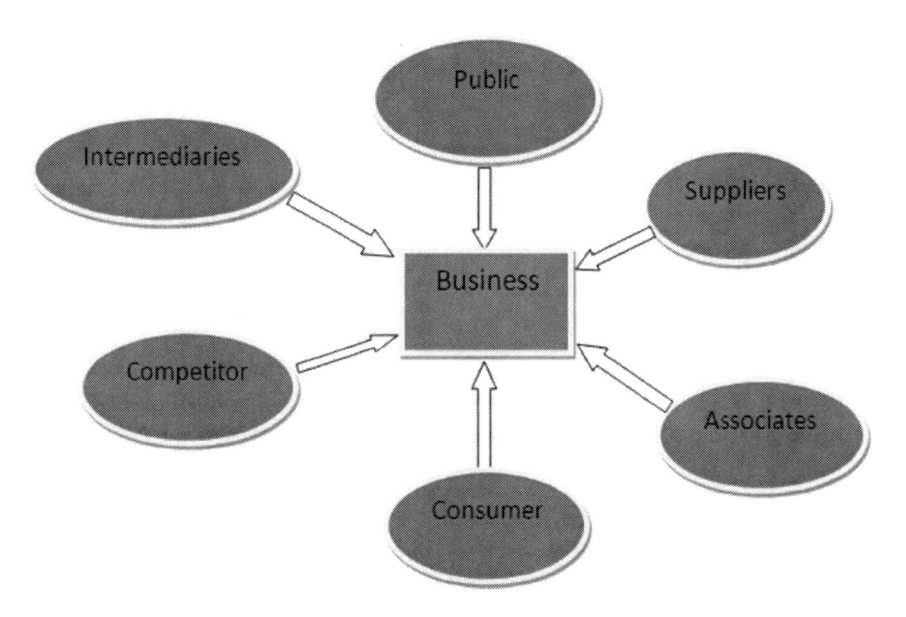

The suppliers form an important part of the total framework of business. The reason is simple. The input material to the final product is the parts or items supplied by respective suppliers. Any price increase is likely to affect the price sensitive market segment. Broadly speaking, there are two concepts which are followed while determining the number of suppliers. More than one supplier for a single item is to create a competition. But this can work out only if the volumes are substantial to realize economies of scale for two or more suppliers and the management as well as the process is equipped to deliver the standardized quality levels as desired by the application. However, the investment in terms of resources required to develop several suppliers also increases with increasing quantities of external suppliers. Normally, unless there is a capacity constraint, the Japanese companies try to develop only one supplier for one item or for a type of items to give advantage of volumes to the supplier in order to spread the cost over large quantity and thereby get cost reduction. Also, development of single supplier helps in development of gradual trust which is harnessed in number of ways such as reliability of supplies and process optimization. Also, the capability of the suppliers to undertake research and development to further improvise their parts is also an important factor as the buyer company is normally engaged in a complete product development and homologation related exercise and hence the detailed modification of the parts is largely expected from the external supplier. Therefore, external suppliers exert a lot of influence on the company and also a lot of pressure on company's exchequer as the raw input material i.e. the parts constitute a bulk of the cost percentage. However, the number of suppliers is a strategic decision based on the volume, technological competence and capacity etc., but having more than one supplier definitely provides a safer option for smaller parts which are manufactured by small or medium scale suppliers.

The associates form an integral and important part of the industry. The value of human as an asset is recognized more than the machines. After all the quality and quantity of the produce to a large extent depends on the efforts of the human asset which also operates the capital asset like machines. The associates may be organized or not organized – depends on the size of the company and initiative taken by the associates. From management point of view, a weak associate union is preferred as this takes away the bargaining power and puts the management in a favorable position. With increasing automation and awareness among management to control extreme unionization at the onset, incidences concerning labour strike have gone down considerably. The reason could be that the associates have also understood the harm which strike does to the organization and lack of easy job opportunity also makes them more moderate than yesteryears. Extreme unionization had caused much damage to the manufacturing units; hence, the labor laws are more liberal towards management from the point of exit policy or retrenchment. However, there has been an increasing understanding on both management and associates part that a confrontationist attitude and constant conflict may ultimately transform the company into a sick unit which would be a worst situation, hence, a consensus to maintain peace is most preferred by negotiations.

Companies exist for consumers – this is the bottom line. For any company to be sustainable it is bare minimum fact that there exists a customer segment either due to the long operational period or market penetration or product differentiation vis-à-vis competitors. Considering the difficulty and efforts required to create a consumer segment or even to penetrate the market in the face of stiff competition, the companies are also putting lot of efforts in trying to preserve band loyalty. This also acts as an indicator towards customer satisfaction which can easily give an insight of the market trend in the fast changing dynamic market scenario. Generally, there are different segments of consumers; hence, the product portfolio of the company should be such so as to tap buying potential of different customer segments in order to protect from fluctuations or recessions in the market; parallel to always remain active in penetrating new markets to counter dual issues – increase market share & to compensate the reduction in market share due to shift in brand loyalty.

Competition and competitor is the part and parcel of any activity especially when the activity generates revenue. In growing economies, where every company wants to foray, in order to, tap a part of market segment the competition becomes more intense. With maturity in the market the price wars become less intense but advertising to differentiate the product intensifies. The brand wars become quite visual and it ultimately benefits the customers in terms of quality and features which results from innovation. There is an increasingly tendency on part of companies to venture into unexplored markets to get foothold before the competitors arrive, many time they also take risk of the un-reliable banking systems for payments for initial orders. The government regulations do protect absolute monopoly; however, companies try to take over rival firms in order to wipe out competition to a certain degree at least for the direct product line consumers and also to harness the ready-made loyal customer segment. In order to facilitate smooth and un-interrupted transition the brand names are often not changed and the local brand is continued to avoid any confusion which might arise. This is in particular applicable to the products which are brand generic i.e. products known by their brands and not by their actual product name. As the markets stagnates, the companies plan strategies to cultivate desires for the new products in order to keep moving the new products at the expense of already sold products. Many times this is coupled with exchange offers to retain the brand loyalty as well as to boost sales.

Most of the companies do not retail the product directly to the consumers. In order to access the large and varied consumer base, they have to rely on the network of intermediaries such as wholesalers, distributors, local agencies and retails. Hence, this network is an important part of the cash flow system and its effective working is essential for success of the company. To a very large extent the brand loyalty often depends on this network which also includes after sales service. Decision to buy a particular product is greatly influenced by the consideration of the network and the quality of services provided by the network. Nowadays, companies with strong brand often run a parallel distribution retail outlets and service centers supplementing to the external intermediaries to prevent any shortcomings and have some control on the otherwise independent network of intermediaries whose brand loyalty is often questionable. There are some companies who also rely on multi – level – marketing system wherein the network consists of individuals who are also users and they share the profit. This provides dual benefit of forced brand loyalty and market penetration without much expense as the consumers drive the market penetration among their peers. Similar to product differentiation, nowadays, the companies are also designing brand specific showrooms i.e. same design to create an image of the brand which creates a degree of authenticity for the customers dealing through such outlets. Such outlets can be easily seen in the case of BMW, TATA, Mercedes Benz, Reliance Petroleum, PTT (Thailand), Lexus (Toyota), SONY etc.

Public in general are group of people or individuals such as – environmentalists, media, consumer protection groups, local lobbyists etc., which have assumed important role in democratic societies and are normally a threat to the businesses or companies. These groups are very sensitive to pollution and other health hazards and often come up with public interest litigation. Even issues like sale of alcohol in the neighborhoods of schools etc., have been severely dealt by these groups. Nowadays, media has taken a big role in issues such as consumer protectionism and are capable of putting tremendous pressure both on the companies as well as on the government to take speedy action. There have been many occasions in which lot of industries were shifted from the cities to the new industrial estate as they were polluting the residential areas. Price increase is also watched carefully by these public or pressure groups. One may recall the prolonged agitation by the these pressure groups or public to prevent industries flowing out their sewage into the Ganges in India and also in Thailand wherein, numerous public groups comprising of even NGOs put pressure on the government to curtail flights at the new airport *Suvanbhumi, Bangkok* as it was generating a lot of sound pollution for the neighborhoods. With the extremely active media and public awareness, the companies have also realized the importance of the requirements of consumers at large and this has benefitted both the companies to exist for the society and also for the consumers that they are able to exercise control on issues which are sometimes ignored by the government as well as by the companies.

Macro environment of a business corresponds to an umbrella of all economic and non-economic factors which have an influence and impact on the company with respect to business strategy in a macro perspective way. These are not necessarily positive and hence, the company has to formulate its business strategy keeping the upcoming influence the macro environment might have. Broadly speaking the macro environment of business can be categorized into economic environment and non-economic environment as under:

- Economic Environment

1. Global

2. National

- Non-Economic Environment

1. Technological

2. Socio-Cultural

3. Political

4. Demographic

5. Natural

Business activity with a particular country is determined by the economic system of the country and the growth or recession provides the probability of sustainability. Several economic indicators such as fiscal and monetary policy balance of payment, investment strategy, savings rate, rate of inflation and gross domestic product growth rate determines the overall macroeconomic scenario of the country in which the business is operational. Economic policies of the government concerning industry and trade and the stability of these policies influence the foreign direct investment. Due to liberalization and multi-national operations, it is the global economic environment which is gaining upper hand than the national one. Nevertheless, the domestic stability does have a tremendous impact at times of recession. This was very well see during 2008 / 2009 global economic recession that could not have much impact on Asia, particularly China and India, but left the American, European and Japanese economy to a low ebb.

Besides, the economic environment, non-economic environment also has significant impact in countries where the political and economic stability is still a question. It may be recalled that in 1972, Idi Amin of Uganda ordered all Asian business houses to close down and professional to be deported. Similarly the natural environment such earthquakes etc., do have their own impact.

A.3 ECONOMIC ENVIRONMENT

Single thing which differentiates between a business and a non-business activity is the profit motive. In other words, a business enterprise is an economic institution which functions for the purpose to maximize profit but within the framework of market system. Hence, the decisions within the organization engaged in business activity largely depend on the demand and supply conditions which in turn significantly influenced by both macro and micro economic environment. Even though, micro economic factors have their own influence, however, generally speaking, in broad sense it is the macro economic factors which are referred while discussing the business and the prevailing environment.

As the objective of any business is profit maximization, therefore, numerous push & pull factors makes this activity highly complex as the prevailing market situation may be interpreted in different ways which may not necessarily have a positive effect each time. The financial indicators are monitored on a regular basis to assess the health of the organization. The situation can be somewhat compared with investing in various stock options with objective of faster growth. One of the most recent examples in the automobile field is the investment to develop hybrid technology. Some companies invested heavily on hydrogen cell technology which was developed but could not be commercialized due to lack to regional infrastructure. Some companies continued to invest in the chargeable battery concept even though it was considered to be a bulky option with low transport feasibility from the point of total distance covered per charge, as compared to the hydrogen cell. However, it was the latter which started to get acceptance while the former could not take off successfully. Similarly, in 2010 we saw the world's largest scooter manufacturer *'Bajaj'* closing down its scooter manufacturing facility due to dwindling sales, although, heavy investment was made a few years back to further expand the facility. However, the management took decision to divert the resources to motorcycle manufacturing to offset the losses. So we see that in business, the decisions are taken based on a single motive – profit maximization.

The decisions are often influenced by the quantum of business volume. For example, a small entrepreneur may hold a part of their supplies during inflation expecting a higher return; however, a larger enterprise has to act uniformly to secure the image as a long term strategy which would be workable within that economic sector. Considering the type of consumerism, any economy can be broadly divided into the following sectors:

1. Business Sector
2. Capital Market Sector
3. Government Sector
4. Household Sector
5. External Sector

The business sector is closely associated with other sectors and is influenced significantly as well. Parallel, these sectors create a network which acts both independently as a separate entity and also a part of the whole – creating an environment which ultimately results in an umbrella economic environment under which the business entities function. In nutshell, the interaction creating an economic environment is not simply an outcome of a positive reaction between supply and demand but, a complex interaction between several forces which shape the overall consumption scenario.

Analogous to the difference between an individual effort and collective effort, a company may not be able to influence the economic environment. However, collectively, the business houses exert significant impact on the economic environment in order to make it conducive to their existence. At the same time, pressures from the government sector and other pressure groups persuade the law makers to float populist policies. With globalization and collective efforts of the companies gradually, the organizations are able to exert to significant clout and are able to mould the policies to a more win-win situation. Normally, the associations which are formed by various industries try to negotiate tax policies and concessions, influence fiscal and trade policies. With the population growth, it is necessary to maintain a minimum threshold GDP growth in order to sustain the employment percentage and at the same time keep the policies sufficiently attractive for foreign direct investment. Therefore, in a capitalist market environment it is the companies which normally have an upper hand and this is natural for their survival otherwise examples of communist governed countries do not portray a progressive picture. During the last three decades labour laws across the globe have been amended considerably to give an upper hand to the industries at the cost of associates. This was done primarily to secure investor's interest which otherwise would divert and to boost the foreign direct investment.

Each country has its own set of systems which is considered to be well suited to the requirement – be it political, demographic, security, per capita income etc. Hence, the interplay between the various domains of economic sectors creates an economic environment. A textbook definition could be *"Economic System is the sum total of the devices by which the preference among alternative purposes of economic activity is determined and by which the individual activities are coordinated for the achievement of these purposes. The central problem of an economic system is the allocation of resources."* Therefore, the economic systems varies from country to country and is the outcome of various historical facts, customs, institutions that have undergone changes with the passage of time and under the influence of the dominant sector of the economic as well. Existence of different currency is the single biggest factor which demarcates the economic sphere of influence. However, broadly speaking in modern world the economic system may be conveniently classified into capitalist economy and socialist economy. Capitalism is sustainable as this system allows the freedom of private property, freedom of contract and freedom of competition. Government interference is minimal and is basically to maintain the stability of the system by controlling monopoly and environmental issues etc. On the other hand, socialism does not recognize private profits. It is like a collective production system wherein the individual source of revenue may still differ based on his / her skills or amount of work done. However, socialism allows extensive government control which may not be conducive to the development of adequate motivation required for entrepreneurship. The basic reason behind the failure of socialism is it limits the scope of the fulfillment of human desire which is the force behind entrepreneurship. Therefore, it is clear that the economic system of a particular country is instrumental in shaping its economic environment. Hence, the businesses in the country have to adapt to these situations for successful growth. It is similar to the human body wherein, the individual has to adapt to the body structure to utilize the potential to the fullest. Another important difference between a capitalist economy and socialist economy is the freedom of choice for production i.e. what, how, whom. In a capitalist economy, this is freely decided by the framework of market mechanism whereas; in socialist economy this freedom is cut short by the fact that central planning gets prominence.

A capitalist economy does offer the freedom of competition, but it would be wrong to interpret that in totality, because it is neither perfect competition nor a *laissez faire*. Presence of giant conglomerates does take away a large element of competition and put the smaller competitors in the background. Although, these giant companies exert a great clout and influence the economic policy and environment, nevertheless, the government through its fiscal and monetary policies tries to keep the activities of private sector in control. This is applicable to both the largest capitalist country i.e. United States of America and also in the developing economy like India wherein both private as well as public sector operate parallel. However, gradually the government operational control from various public sector enterprises is reducing owing to the stiff competition generated by the multi-nationals and the government may like to focus on areas which are more policy oriented and related to the overall masses, defense, law and order, nuclear energy etc., which due to reasons of confidentiality and security concerns remains tightly in the domain of government portfolio.

Capitalism can best be defined as a mixed economy where both private and public enterprise co-exist and the presence of giant conglomerates have reduced the degree of competition of level of a monopolistic set-up. From the point of social welfare, sometimes the government interferes indirectly. For example, there have been several cases in India, when the government has to interfere with establishment of retailing network of conglomerates for the advantage of small retailer under pressure of losing a majority vote bank. Hence, the expansion of retailing network in India has been a very cautious approach due to low per capita income and issues related to migration from the rural areas to urban areas.

In contrast, the socialist economy is governed by a centralized planning structure because, besides labour, all other means of production are primarily owned by the government and the planning is guided by the objective of social welfare. This may also include the methodology of production and the distribution pattern which consists of private retailers as well. However, as the decision making process is largely supplemented by the government to the extent of control that private enterprises have not much scope to operate competitively due to restrictive freedom of decision. Unlike in a capitalist economy wherein business decisions are primarily taken by the business enterprises under the basic framework of fiscal and monetary policies as laid down by the government; in the socialist economy the decision making is not that decentralized and it is more or less centralized with the central planning commission of the state. Although, the economic situations are more controlled in socialist economy, nevertheless, the growth potential is somewhat restricted on account that the driving force is not bottom to top but, top to bottom which takes away the entrepreneur motivation.

Broadly speaking, starting of any business or sustainability with growth depends on the general macroeconomic environment of the country. If the economy is experiencing growth, low inflation, high savings and investment, positive balance of payment, financial stability, then generally speaking the business is likely to grow however, it is not applicable as a blanket cover to all because the economic pressures created by different segments generate variable supply and demand scenario as exceptions. Presently, in spite of recessionary trend across the globe, the BRIC countries did not went into recession and in some cases such as India and Brazil, the increase in salaries increased the demand of various commodities. For example, on one hand where in USA the automobile companies were on the verge of bankruptcy, the Indian market witnessed an unparalleled growth exceeding 27 %. According to Bloomberg, in 2009 India surpassed China as Asia's fourth largest exporter of cars. This indicates the solid fundamentals on which the market dynamics are based upon which includes the fiscal and monetary policies of the central banking system.

In view of the above, it can be understood that the macro-economic scenario does have an impact on the overall market situation in a country. It is observed that during periods of high growth such as the situation in BRIC countries and also in smaller countries such as Vietnam, the demand for consumer white luxury goods such as air – conditioner, automobiles, motorcycles, televisions, refrigerators, modern music systems, feature – rich mobiles, modular kitchen system etc., increase whereas the general commodities maintain a stable demand. In case of India, till 2003, items which were considered as luxury items suddenly experienced a surge in demand coinciding with the increase in gross domestic product (GDP) which just fell short of double digit growth rate. In 2008 / 2009, when the world was struggling with economic recession CHINDIA economy was standing firm. Companies like Land Rover, Jaguar were sold to TATA; Volvo was sold to Chinese firm Geely. Thailand which earns its majority of revenue from tourism was able to get the chunk of tourism from India and so on. It is quite clear that economic slowdown has a direct effect on the production of consumer goods as the environment becomes unfavorable to the business. With the reduction in aggregate take-off there is a slow down on all aspects of business – be it production, expansion, investment. It may be recalled that out several ECO car projects had to be shelved or indefinitely postponed due to economic slowdown which also had an impact on Thailand which is a hub of automobile market in the South – East Asia.

Fluctuation in economic environment is closely associated with inflation. A simple and layman definition for inflation could be "an increase in the price one pays for goods". Or in other words, a decline in purchasing power of the money. But there two terms which are equally important – 'Price Inflation' and Monetary Inflation'. Technically speaking, price inflation is when the prices get higher or it takes more money to buy the same item, whereas, monetary inflation is an increase in the money supply which generally results in price inflation. This acts as a "hidden tax" on the consumers. Monetary inflation is commonly referred to as the government "printing money", although, the actual process is a bit more complex than actual printing, but the effect is essentially the same. As the money supply increases the currency loses its purchasing power and the prices of goods and services increases. This process usually takes 1.5 to 2 years so that the government is able to spend the new money at the old value before consumers realize that they have accepted something that will purchase less than they originally thought it would.

The overall general upward price movement of goods and services in an economy is usually measured by the Consumer Price Index and the Producer Price Index. Over the period of time, as the cost of goods and services increase, the value of money is going to fall because an individual would not be able to purchase as much with the same money as he / she previously could have. While the annual rate of inflation has fluctuated greatly over the last half century, ranging from zero inflation to over 20 %, the regulatory agencies actively try to maintain a specific rate of inflation, which is normally 2-3 % but can vary depending on circumstances.

In the context of India, wherein, the vast population still lives close to or below poverty line in spite of breathtaking GDP growth over the past few years; inflation acts as a *'Poor Man's Tax'*. This effect gets amplified when food prices rise, since food represents more than half of the expenditure of this group. The dramatic increase in inflation will have both economic and political implications for the government, especially when the price rise plays an important part in the political elections. Economic growth in emerging markets has slowed but is far from over. With the BRIC countries (Brazil, Russia, India and China) alone accounting for more than 3 billion people, and with these people consuming more resources every year, it is likely that higher inflation rate will prevail for some time. On the contrary, another school of thought is if the economy is performing below its potential, then the fluctuation in inflation may have a net positive effect on the average output, which means that inflation within a limited range helps in increasing the overall demand which may open new avenues for business.

Interestingly, inflation does not have a uniform effect on price hike. During such periods, entrepreneurs may take wrong decisions particularly from the point of allocation of resources. Situations such as high rate of inflation is derogatory for business houses as the consumers tend to differ their purchases in speculation that the prices may stabilize and in order to match the overall market demand, the producers have to optimize their output accordingly. This may even lead to manpower adjustments in labour intensive industries. Hence, the government needs to have a check on the inflation rate as this may not provide a conducive environment for a broad spectrum of business activities.

Two major vehicles of growth could be industries and agriculture. Both of them require massive investment. In a populous country like India a major portion of the agricultural output is consumed by the producers and not much is left for exports. However, industry growth rate has been impressive in the last few years. The growth rate of the industry in India GDP has grown due to sustained manufacturing activity for the past few years. The investment in infrastructure development has given a major boost to the developmental activity. In fact, shortage of power, communication system, and inadequate transport infrastructure can pose a major obstacle in the country's growth. Some of the South – East Asian countries such as Thailand, Malaysia, Indonesia and other like South Korea and even China had invested heavily on infrastructure and this enabled them to register a spectacular growth. With liberalization and increased investment in infrastructure such as roads, energy, power etc., India is able to sustain the growth rate required to offset the unemployment generated due to ever increasing population to a large extent.

In the BRIC economies, Indian economy is considered to be the most robust one in terms of sustainability considering a long span of time. Presently, Indian economy is the twelfth largest in the world and is ranked 3 rd on purchasing power parity (PPP). The quantum of GDP was US $ 1.09 trillion in 2009. Gross Domestic Product (GDP) means the market value of all the services and goods that are manufactured within the territory of the nation during the specified period of time. The country was having the second fastest growing economy in the whole world with GDP growth rate of 9.4 % in 2006-2007. However, the global economic recession has slowed down the growth but still the economy was nowhere near recession like other European countries. The industrial sector is one of the main sectors that contribute to the gross domestic product. In terms of total output, India ranks 14 th in the world which is not that impressive considering the overall population. Taking the example of India among the BRIC countries the industrial sector accounts for approximately 27 % of the GDP and employs around 17 % of the total workforce in the country. The growth rate of the industrial sector in India GDP was 5.2 % in 2002 – 2003. In this year, within the India GDP, the mining and quarrying sector contributed 4.4 %, the electricity, water supply and gas sector contributed 2.8 % and the manufacturing sector contributed around 5.7 %. The growth rate of the industry sector in India GDP came to around 6.6 % in 2003 – 2004 and in this year, the electricity, water supply and gas sector contributed 5.3 % while the manufacturing sector contributed 7.1 % in India GDP. Industrial growth in India GDP came to 7.4 % in 2004 – 2005, with the manufacturing sector contributing 8.1 % and the mining and quarrying sector contributing 5.8 %, and the water supply, electricity and the gas sector contributing 4.3 % in India GDP. Industrial growth in India GDP came to 7.6 % in 2005 – 2006. In this year, the mining and quarrying sector contributed 0.9 %, the manufacturing sector share increased to 9.0 % and the water supply, gas and electricity sector contributed 4.3 %. The growth rate of the industrial sector finally came to 9.8 % in 2006 – 2007. This shows that the industrial growth in India GDP has been on the rise over the last few years. However, India's economic growth of 9.2 % in 2007-08 was the highest since 2004 – 2005. This reduced to a mere 6.7 % in the year 2008 – 2009, whereas it is expected to get back to at least 8.4 to 8.5 % during the financial year 2010-11. If the trend continues without any major setbacks, the double digit growth is expected to be within reach by 2012.

The reasons for the increase of industry growth rate in India GDP is due to the huge amounts of investments made in manufacturing sector and significant influx of foreign direct investment (FDI) that helped the industries to grow. Further the reasons for the rise of the growth rate of the industrial sector in India are that the consumption of the industrial goods has increased a great deal in the country, which in turn has boosted the industrial sector. Generally speaking, high investment rates in manufacturing sector and other infrastructure is sustained by an equally high domestic savings rate. As mentioned above, foreign capital obtained in large amounts help in boosting the rate of investment and accelerates both economic growth and business activity. As long as these borrowings and investment are being used to fuel production and output of commodities for use, it is ok as it prevents from falling in the debt trap. However, if it is used for unplanned expenditure like defense or non-revenue generating activities this may prove to be disastrous. As a thumb rule, economies having domestic saving as high as 30 % or higher are capable of generating self – sustained growth necessary for business expansion and growth.

> Less developed countries practice deficit financing in order to achieve a high rate of investment. Deficit financing is an approach to money management that involves spending more money than is collected during the same period. Sometimes referred to as a budget deficit, this strategy is employed by conglomerates and small businesses, governments at just about every level, and even household budgets. When used properly, deficit financing helps to launch a chain of events that ultimately enhances the financial condition rather than simply creating debt that may or may not be repaid.

One of the more common examples of government deficit financing has to do with stimulating the economy of a nation in order to bring an end to a period of recession. By establishing a specific plan of action that involves using borrowed resources to make purchases, the government can increase the demand for output from various sectors of the business community. This in turn motivates businesses to hire additional employees, reversing the usual trend of higher unemployment that takes place during a recession. At the same time, the renewed vigor in the marketplace helps to restore consumer confidence, making it more likely for consumers to buy more goods and services. When monitored closely, a carefully crafted deficit financing initiative will restore a measure of stability to the national economy over a period of months or years.

The concept of deficit spending in economics is not limited to government use. Businesses of all sizes may choose to spend more money up front in hopes of generating funds to pay off the investment at a later date. For example, a manufacturer may choose to purchase new machinery for a factory, with the understanding that the newer equipment will allow the business to produce more units of goods in less time, and possibly at a lower unit cost. Over time, the benefits derived from this strategy pay off the accumulated debt and allow the business owners to enjoy a budget surplus rather than a budget deficit.

Household budgets also engage in this form of money management, although the role of deficit financing on an individual level takes a slightly different form than with businesses and governments. An individual may choose to purchase items now with an eye to improving the home in some manner that ultimately increases the value of the property. The accumulated debt is eventually paid in full, leaving the homeowner with an asset that has a higher fair market value than it would without the enhancements. While the ultimate reward from the deficit financing is realized when the property is sold at a higher profit, homeowners and their families do get to enjoy the enhanced amenities of the home in the interim.

The idea of deficit financing in economic development is not new. Economists from John Maynard Keynes up to the present day have recognized this strategy, its benefits, and its possible liabilities if not applied properly. While not automatically the best option to correct an undesirable financial situation, the responsible use of deficit financing can ultimately improve the quality of life and the financial status of everyone concerned.

Simply stated, the government should not balance its budget. The probable reason could be that balancing the budget would lead to more frequent and severe recessions and a less productive economy. Taking the example of 2008/ 2009 recession, if a nation undergoes recession, then the basic outcome is that more and more people lose their job. At the same time, as the people are laid off or making less money during the recessionary phase they are required to pay less taxes. This decrease in revenue from taxes causes a debt increase and leads to widening of the deficit further. In order to offset the reduction in revenue, the government may have to increase taxes. This increase in taxes would further worsen the recession making it difficult for the people to spend their money and invest in the economy. The combination of higher taxes and less investment would only lead to a crippled economy. This would cause recessions to be much deeper than if the government was not required to balance its budget. Today, many countries nearing recessions avoid this situation; however, this would not have been the case if the budget would have been balanced. It is surprising to note that the government's budget deficit actually helps to improve the economic productivity and output. The amount of money that is normally made available for investment by the government would be much less if the budget is balanced. The conclusion could be drawn that a balanced budget would harm the economy in both short and long run. It would lead to more frequent and severe recessions, a far less productive economy and a loss of government funded programs. Balancing the budget would harm the nation as a whole, starving the economy of much needed funds and crippling it with high taxes. Therefore, deliberate unbalancing of the budget in such a way that government expenditure exceeded its revenue was put forth as a measure to overcome depression and necessary for economic recovery.

In a developing economy, deficit financing may lead to an increase in the purchasing power while the production does not increase simultaneously. This may result in an inflationary situation. The increase of the level of prices, at a given level of individuals and organization's nominal income, will cause the reduction of their real income, in other words a decrease in the purchasing power of these people. The conclusion could be that an important part of money issuance for financing the budgetary deficit is that it redistributes a part of the purchasing power of the income holders, both individual and legal entities, at the government's disposal, which makes use of the additional stock of the money in order to buy goods and services or to make payments for public consumption. According to Fischer and Dornbusch "this way, the government can spend more resources and the population less, exactly as if the government would increase taxes in order to finance further spending".

Regardless of the real conditions of its employment, the monetary financing of the budgetary deficit has as first effect an increase of prices. However, under certain particular conditions, this can determine an inflationary, long term increase, depending on the strategic investment of the resources collected by the government. If the resources resulting from the additional money issued in order to cover the budgetary deficit are employed to finance investment project that induce a raise in output, the original increase in the money stock available to circulation will have as equivalent to increasing the quantity of goods and services, subject to transaction. In other words, on one hand in real market scenario, the level of price increase will not be permanent; on the other hand, if additional resources are deployed to finance consumption, this will not influence the subsequent growth in GDP and the increase in price level will be of longer term and monetary financing of budgetary deficit will be inflationary. Normally, the governments resort to issuance of new money to finance unproductive expenses, it is generally apprehended that financing budgetary deficit by infusing new money results in inflation.

The resultant inflation which arises due to the effect of financing budgetary deficit by infusing new money has a negative impact on the volume of resources or revenues collected by the government. The reason is that the real value of such revenue is already devalued due to inflation and is equivalent to the purchasing power reallocated that is lower than the nominal value as a consequence of the currency depreciation caused by the action of the government. In addition to the effect of reduced government revenues, inflation, in short term can also have a positive effect in case of highly indebted countries as inflation can diminish the burden of public debt as a real value, even if this effect occurs only for the debt pertaining to national currency because with inflation, the short term debt weighs more. Nevertheless, for the indebted countries, nominal interest rates increase with the rise of inflation rate, leading to the increase in debt expenditure reflected in the budget to increase budgetary deficit.

The consequences of price rise due to inflation which results from the issuance of new money in the system in order to keep up with its expenditures gets projected in other levels of economic and social life. The degradation of value following inflation leads to the fact that prices and salaries do not play a role of guiding indices in the market economy anymore. When the national supply of goods and supply is insufficient and uncompetitive, the depreciated national currency, which normally should encourage exports, does not support, instead it encourages import in order to make up for the deficits created by the reduced amount of national output and it leads to further degradation of the balance of payments.

As far as common people are concerned, inflation operates with an unequal effect on various income slabs in the sense that it affects those having small and fixed income (employees, pensioners, unemployed) and does not have much effect on high worth or high income group segment as their purchasing power remains more or less constant. But is does effect the corporate management in terms of investment capacity and may give rise to unemployment which would definitely have severe social consequences. Moreover, excessive inflation spreads uncertainty and anxiety among people, including the social climate and erodes the credibility of the government. Many economists have put forth the argument that inflationary conditions are conducive to investment as they provide much needed incentives to private entrepreneurs to invest. However, this is true up to a point only. This is due to the fact that if inflations prolongs then it encourages investment in speculative activities rather than productive activity. This is obviously from the basic fact that rate of return on the speculative activities is likely to shoot up much more than the latter.

A country's balance of payment in terms of current account position is important for the overall business environment. Excessive current account deficit may result in shortage of foreign exchange which may have its obvious implications on the import of goods. On one hand this may provide protection to the domestic industries against competition from foreign companies but at the same time this would also result into a protective environment inhibiting international competition and discourage domestic industries to improve upon further up to the international standards. As these domestic industries will not be exposed to the global competition, their chances of survival will gradually diminish once the market if more open. Also, with closed consumption pattern, the export potential will be on the decline which will have a long term multiplying effect of the balance of payment situation. Therefore, for a healthy business environment the current account position need to be fairly balanced which can generate a favorable environment for competition as well as exports. Several steps should be taken to attract foreign direct investment. However, this should be done with the help of various incentives and not only by overvalue exchange rate failing which this will have an adverse effect on exports.

A.4 BUSINESS DYNAMICS

Presently, the global economy is dotted by almost 60,000 plus corporations. These operate in overseas market as well. The economic clout of these global giants is that out of 100 largest economies in the world, 53 are corporations and 47 are countries. The revenues of Wal-Mart which is listed at the 12 th place in the fortune 500 corporations; are more than 161 countries including Poland, Greece, and Israel etc. Similarly Toyota which was recently in news both on account of surpassing General Motors and also for recalling few millions of cars due quality defect has revenues more than Norway, while General Motor has revenues in excess of Denmark and Ford has more than Portugal. These are multinational corporations or MNCs as they are normally called. MNCs are business entities that operate in more than one country. The typical multinational corporation or MNC normally functions with a headquarters that is based in one country, while other facilities are based in locations in other countries. In some circles, a multinational corporation is also referred to as a multinational enterprise (MNE) or a transnational corporation (TNC).

The model for a multi-national corporation may vary from one conglomerate to another. However, a common model for the multi-national corporation is the positioning of the executive headquarters in one nation, while production facilities are located in one or more other countries. This model often allows the company to take advantage of benefits of incorporating in a given locality, while also being able to produce goods and services in areas where the cost of production is lower. Another structural model for a multi-national organization is to base the parent company in one nation and operate subsidiaries in other countries around the world. With this model, just about all the functions of the parent are based in the country of origin, the subsidiaries more or less function independently outside of a few basic ties to the parent. A third approach to the setup of a multi-national corporation involves the establishment of headquarter in one country that oversees a diverse conglomeration that stretches to many countries and industries. With this model, the multi-national includes affiliates, subsidiaries and possibly even some facilities that report directly to the headquarters.

There are several ways that a multi-national corporation can come into existence. One approach is to intentionally establish a new company with headquarters in one country while producing goods and services in facilities located elsewhere. In other instances, the multi-national corporation comes about due to mergers between two or more companies based in different countries. Acquisitions and hostile takeovers also sometimes result in the creation of multi-national corporations. In a world that continues to become interconnected each day, a multinational corporation sometimes has a greater ability to adapt to economic and political shifts than those corporations that function in a single nation. Along with decreasing costs associated with producing core products, this business model also opens door for diversification, which often makes it possible for a company to remain solvent even when one division or subsidiary is posting a temporary loss.

Irrespective of the modus operandi or the model, the multi-national corporations have been dominating the World Economy and setting the trends for Business Dynamics in a more pronounced way since the last three decades. They actively perform on global scene and become the major force of the World Economy. Multi-nationals have turned into global industries and supported Research & Development (R&D) in all directions: raising the technical level, improving product quality, increased the production efficiency, and contributed to the development of management models and methodology of conducting an enterprise. The role of multi-nationals in the development of global economy has systematically grown year by year. Presently multi-national or trans-national corporations are the main actors of the international investment flows and the driving force of the international industrial development due to the following facts:

- Multi-national corporations influence the international corporate exchange by organizing international manufacture and realize the expansion process, related to the intensification of direct investment flows.

- Multi-national corporations play the main role in the enlargement and development of the international investment and innovation market and they are the most active ones in searching for areas for investing.

- Multi-national corporations assure high level of sales and growth by increasing their share on the markets of development and developing countries, thereby, making efforts for market penetration and resulting in overall mass awareness towards technology and indirectly contributing to literacy levels.

- Multi-national effectively maneuver their manufacturing resources including manpower in various countries of operation which directly and indirectly provides international exposure to the manpower and contributing to overall increase in efficiency and international operations.

The essence of multi-national corporation's global domination lies in the investment outflows and their effective distribution. In turn this becomes a driving force in the formation and development of international corporations from domestic organizations. On an average each multi-national corporations has distribution of its manufacturing activity among more than six countries. Selling of goods and services by all foreign affiliates amounted for almost 19 trillion US dollars, whereas, the total volume of world trade was about 8 trillion US dollars. This proves the fact that in the modern situation the international manufacture based on foreign direct investment flows has become far more important for promoting goods in foreign markets than international trade. Nowadays, more than 10 % of the world gross domestic product and about 1/3 of international export operations represent is the result of multi-national or more appropriate trans-national corporations.

Generally speaking, presently, 100 largest non-financial multi-nationals of the world which is less than 0.2 % of their total number controlled about 10 % of all foreign assets, approximately 16 % of all accumulated volume of foreign sales and about 13 % of the total number of employees in all multi-national corporations. Roughly, 10 most powerful corporations possess approximately 1700 billion US dollars, which account for almost 36 % of all foreign assets of the first 100 multi-national corporations. They represent huge conglomerates with the activity spreading all over the branches of the modern economy and most regions of the world. As already mentioned previously, many multi-nationals have budget exceeding some of the countries. However, present scenario still portrays that a large proportion of multi-national corporations originate from the triad – three economical centers: The United States of America, European Union and Japan.

In 2005, the trans-nationality index (TNI) of 100 most powerful multi-national corporations was almost 59.9 % which means than more than half of their assets were concentrated abroad. For 50 largest multi-national corporations it was 50.6 %. In comparison, total foreign assets of the top 100 TNCs in 1997 amounted to $1.8 trillion, while total foreign sales were $2.1 trillion, and total employment 5,980,740, an increase of 0.7% over the previous year. However, out of fortune 100 listed companies only 42 have trans-nationality index greater than 50 %. Anyway, the statistical study reveals the quantum of operations these multi-national corporations have. Also, is the fact that trans-nationalization of the multi-national corporation in smaller European countries has been faster than some of the companies in developed countries. This may be explained by the passivity of some of the large corporations which have concentrated their operations mostly in their local markets, while the small European countries have been actively promoting their image and widening their sphere of influence in the markets. Active involvement of trans-national corporations from Western Europe in the global economic processes is done due to the following facts: free foreign direct investment, goods, services and labour force movements, establishment of a single regime for all European companies, no artificial barriers for competition, and large seller's market in the integrated Europe.

By analyzing the distribution of multi-national by branches of economy one can notice significant changes. In the beginning of 90's the main branches, where multi-nationals operated were: oil, chemical, electronic and automobile industries. Ten years later the dominating branches here have become the following: tele-communications, electricity and water supply services and again automobile industry. 45 out of 100 largest multinationals operate in these branches. These changes may be considered to have occurred due to next level of scientific and technological revolution, specially related to information and electronic component. From 2006 onwards, the most powerful multi-nationals invested in the automobile, oil, electronics, pharmaceutical industries, telecommunication and even social services. These branches of economy significantly contribute to the increase in state income of the host countries, establishment and developed of contacts with local enterprises, creation of work places, increase in qualification level of local labour force and above all technology transfer.

Branch specialization of trans-national corporations from developing countries is a bit different from that of corporations from developed economies. However, this fact does not contradict general trends in the international division of labour. Corporations from developed countries concentrate their effort on manufacturing highly profitable products. Less advanced production is moved in developing countries, which are close to developed ones in economic and technical development and have comparatively high level of labour force qualification, and developed financial, transport and other infrastructure. These are new industrial countries from Asia and Latin America. Multinational corporations from such countries actively penetrate into electronics, automobile industry and telecommunications.

It is evident that the two main elements that support the development of the multi-national corporation's activity are: technological changes and the changes in national policies concerning multi-national corporations. The technological changes allow a flexible organization and low cost of production activities at mass scale. However, the changes in national policies regarding multi-national corporations are more taking place in developing countries. Although, activities of multi-national corporations support economic globalization but their impact on developing economies is not positive every time. The reason could be that multi-national corporations deal with economic efficiency and exploit the scale of economies. As a result, their branches migrate from those countries which have strict regulations about corporations to other countries with permissive legislation. In order to break this process, the developing countries are forced to reduce the restrictions for multi-national corporations connected with taxes, labour and environment protection.

There exists a contradiction between the wish of multi-national corporations to maximize their profits and national legislation from those countries in which multi-national corporations operate. Some experts are of the view that multi-national corporations prefer those countries where labour rights are not guaranteed, to facilitate ease of operation. The result of this process is the failure of national policies, which is obliged to adopt concepts imposed by international corporations in pressure of foreign direct investment and employment generation. This provides an opportunity to multi-national corporations to expand the market and at the same time for the developing countries, multinational corporations represent the least bad thing which they can select for the growth of gross domestic product. For these countries, the multi-national corporations create new jobs, develop infrastructure and stimulate the demand growth.

The migration of multinational corporations across national boundaries was initiated during industrial era and got momentum after the Second World War concomitantly with GATT's initiative for world trade promotion. Various incentive schemes were promoted by developing countries to attract multi-national corporations such as tax holidays, long term loans, and capital tax rebate for new projects to the extent that foreign direct investment became one of the yardstick to measure the potential of economical development.

The bigger multi-national corporations compete with homogeneous goods in the international market initially before expanding their product portfolio. The reason could be the acceptability of the goods and readymade customer base which could be lured to switch brand loyalty. However, the same time those multi-nationals may have heterogeneous products in their own countries because they have oligopolistic positions in their internal market. This can be very well seen in the case of automobile multi-national corporations with different product portfolios which often have launch strategies with already established or often near to phase – out products in developing countries to extend the useful revenue life of the product and related capital infrastructure which can be easily re-located at depreciated cost to minimize the cost of production. This also helps in reducing the cost of relocation.

The evolution of multi-national corporations is influenced to a great extent by intergovernmental, regional and world agreements. On the other hand, the world organizations are influenced by world powers: GATT and IMF by USA, European Union by France and Germany, OPEC by Saudi Arabia etc. These countries impose specific conditions at international level which are favourable to their national companies. On the other hand, global policy is also the result of the combination between national policies and influence of pressure groups. For example, Multi-Fiber Accord was imposed as a result of American textile's company's influence and of American textile trade union pressure.

In spite of pressure groups and nationalistic polices, all three main channels of economic globalization, trade, foreign direct investment (FDI) and the international transfer of knowledge have developed very dramatically. Amongst them, the strong rise of FDI has attracted the most attention, but the increase of international technology is as impressive. International trade continues to grow stronger than world output. The degree of openness has surpassed the pre World War II levels in many countries. The deepening of worldwide economic integration has depended increasingly on rising foreign direct investment flows.

Going back, we see that up to the mid-nineteen eighties, foreign trade was the most dynamic channel of economic integration. Exports grew much stronger than foreign direct investment in the 1950S, 60s and 70s. In the 1980s this pattern changed; 16.3 % FDI growth exceeded the 6.2 % export growth per year. World real industrial production has risen by 60 % over this 24 years period. That is an annual growth rate of 2 %. International trade increased by 210 % over the whole period or 4.8 % annually, more than twice as fast as industrial production. An even more dynamic contribution to economic integration came from FDI. From 1973 to 1997, foreign direct investment increased by 780 %. That is an impressive annual growth rate of 9.5 %, twice as large as the export growth rate. The sudden and strong increase of FDI in the second half of the 1980s has been widely discussed, but its explanation remains to be one of the challenges to economic research. Worldwide foreign direct investment stocks increased from US$ 782 billion to US$ 1,768 billion in the second half of the eighties. They were more than doubled in just six years.

Worldwide foreign direct investment continued to grow in the 1990s. In the 1998 the world FDI stock reached US $ 4,088 billion. Roughly, three quarter were invested in developed countries. Especially the foreign direct investment boom in the second half of the 1980s was an OECD countries (Organization for Economic Co-operation and Development, a group of 30 countries from EU, USA, JAPAN) phenomenon. Interestingly, 85 % of the foreign direct investment flows has developed countries as source and also as host. However, in the last decade the share of foreign direct investment (FDI) received by developing countries has been somewhat higher. This higher share resulted from foreign direct investment boom started in the two fastest growing economies – China and India. However, China received a greater share of 12 % of total FDI inflows worldwide, or one third of all inflows in the developing countries in 1996, South – East Asia another third. After the Asian crisis the strong increase of foreign direct investment was mainly driven by a cross – border merger and acquisition wave among developed countries, which increased their share of total FDI inflows to 73.5 % in 1999 (UNCTAD 2000).

The share of FDI inflows in the United States increased from 18 % in the early 1970s to 40 % in the late 40 % in the late 1980s. The US experienced the most impressive increase and became by far the largest host country. An interesting picture that emerged in the second half of the 1980S was one dominant host country with many large home countries of FDI. The share of world FDI outflows coming from the US companies dropped from more than half in the early 1970s to 15 % in the second half of the 80s. It recovered again in the 1990s, without regaining its dominant position of the 60s. In the last decade, US outward foreign direct investment share has again risen to 26 %, albeit US dominance has faded a bit due to emergence of BRIC countries especially China and India as a large recipients of FDI, 1990 onwards.

Another phenomenon which is called the cyclical behavior of FDI flows, was first noticed by Knickerbocker (1973) who described that FDI trends occurs in sectoral and temporal clusters. Flowers (1976), while testing Knickerbocker's theory of oligopolistic reaction, found country-specific temporal and sectoral FDI clusters. Investments from different countries occur at different times. The clustering of investments disappeared when various countries were examined. Investors only seem to react to activities of their national competitors.

Since, booms and droughts do not occur at the same time in different countries, the aggregated world FDI outflow series is much smoother, although booms and recessions are observable in world FDI outflows, too. So far, oligopolistic reaction is the theory used to explain the wave behavior, in spite of some shortcomings (Graham 1996). Later Kleinert (1999) gave another explanation for the wave behavior within a general equilibrium model of the emergence of multi-national corporations. According to his work, waves result from changes in the competitive conditions induced by FDI on national competition. Although this approach receives some support from the empirical results of Flowers (1976), it has not been tested empirically yet. The large share of intra-industry foreign direct investment is another striking phenomenon. Cantwell and Sanna Randaccio (1992) presented large and increasing shares of intra-industry direct investment in the European Union. Furthermore, they show that foreign direct investment often takes place in technology intensive industries. These points to imperfect competition models (Brainard 1993; Markusen and Venables 1998) as explained for FDI activity, rather than perfect competition models (Helpman 1984).

The international transfer of knowledge and technology measured here as payments for royalties and licensing fees, rose about the same rate as FDI flown in the last two decades. Technology payments increased from US $ 12 billion in 1983 to US $ 65 billion in 1999 (UNCTAD 2000). The annual growth rate of 11.1 % in the 1990s even exceeded FDI outflow growth of 9.9 %. The parallel increase could be a first hint to the dominant role of multi-national enterprises in the international transfer of knowledge and technology. The regional distribution of royalties and license fees payments is more strongly dominated by developed countries than the regional structure if inward stocks. This is not surprising, given the advantage of multi-national in the production technology intensive goods and their larger capacity to develop and absorb new technologies. A large share of all payments for the use of imported technology comes from developed countries. The regional concentration is even stronger on the receipts side of royalties and license fees. The US alone received about 58 % of all royalties and license fees in the 1990s, Japan and UK, Germany and France 10 %, 9 %, 6% and 4% respectively. These large players hold strong positions in payments as well as receipts of royalties and license fees. According to

UNCTAD data, international transfer of technology takes place almost without developing countries. Developed countries account for 98.3 % of all receipts and 88.3 % of all payments. Among the developing countries, South Korea holds the highest shares, with one – third of the payments and one – fifth of the receipts within the developing countries group.

A high share of technology flows are intra-firm flows which amounts to almost 80 % considering the multi-national corporations from US, Japan and Germany. This indicates the important role of multi-national enterprises to overcome market imperfections on markets for information goods. Further, this 80 % share amounts due to internalization advantage, which, according to the OLI paradigm (Dunning 1980), is necessary for a multi-national corporation to be superior to a licensing agreement with an independent foreign company. Nowadays, new knowledge and technology is spread almost immediately to other developed countries. This phenomenon can also be observed from the pattern of patent applications. Increasingly, patents are applied not only to the authorities of the home country but to external authorities as well. However, patent applications are expensive. Therefore, applications in foreign countries point to a reduction of other sources which used to protect knowledge as information asymmetries between companies from different countries. Furthermore, it may point to a faster penetration of foreign markets not only by exports but also by production in foreign countries.

If we consider the patent application in three economies i.e. US, Japan and Germany, then it can be noticed that the number of resident patent applications has increased in all three economies over the last two decades. This fact and the internalization of the use of this knowledge have led to a rising internalization of knowledge protection. Increasing international technology flows are protected by a rising number of patents given by foreign countries authorities. It may be noted that this does not speaks about the internalization of knowledge production but about the internalization of the use of knowledge. The internalization of knowledge production has not kept pace with the globalization of trade and production. Even large companies in most cases perform most of their R&D at home country (Pavitt and Patel 1999). Therefore, globalization includes increasing international flows of knowledge and technology but not the internationalization of knowledge production at a large scale. Knowledge production still remains a task predominantly performed in the home country. The large and rising flows of knowledge from the home country to the host countries reflect the dependence of the internationalized production on the headquarter service research and development which is provided by the parent company. On an average, the US multi-nationals receive royalties and license fees to the ratio of 10: 1 for technology procurement. Foreign research and development activities often focus on the application of production processes and goods on the conditions of foreign market. For example when major automobile companies plan to launch their products in another country, they try to develop modification suitable to various factors specific to that country and this is done prior to the launch coupled with exhaustive testing.

Since the end of World War II, international trade has pushed world economic integration. Its growth rates exceeded production growth rates by far, pointing to a deepening of integration. Merchandise exports have almost tripled in nominal terms since 1980. Like FDI flows and the transfer of knowhow and technology, trade takes place mostly among developed countries. Their merchandise export share have remained relatively stable at about two third over the last two decades. The emergence of Asian exporting countries has not changes the dominance of the developed countries. Trade in services has been a bit faster than trade in goods. Its share in total trade has risen marginally. A large share of trade especially between developed countries takes place within the same industry (Grubel and Lloyd 1971). These high intra-industry trade (IIT) shares are mainly explained by imperfect competition.

Traditionally, trade has been the most important channel of integration of the world economy. It has been only very recently, that the strong rise in foreign direct investment, challenges the role of trade in goods and services as the most important factor. If we refer to the trend of inter-industry trade vs. intra intra-industry trade for US, European Union and Japan, then it is evident that there is a gradual reduction in inter-industry trade whereas, there is a gradual increase in intra-industry trade (Heitger, Schrader and Stehn, 1999). These high intra-industry trade (IIT) shares result at least partially from trade in intermediate goods. Import of intermediate goods and raw materials; make up for approximately half of all imports of developed economies. This is in part due to differences in the endowments with commodities among the countries. Raw material processing industries as wood products and furniture, paper and paper products, petroleum and coal products, non-metallic mineral products, iron and steel and non-ferrous metals are especially import dependent. The share of imported inputs, mainly raw materials, in total imports of these industries is very high. But for manufacturing sector as non-electrical machinery, professional goods, or motor vehicles, where the production process is likely to be less raw material dependent, the share of imported input as a percentage of total input is also high.

The technology intensive industries form the most interesting group as the largest share of inputs in the production of goods usually comes from the same industry. Their production process involves many different stages, with different requirements. Reasons for the import of intermediates can be manifold. Of course, availability is the motive of trade. Differences in factor content could be a reason to import some parts from countries with comparative advantages for the production of this input. Technological leadership of a company in a foreign country can be another reason to import the intermediate input. Furthermore, established network can be the source of increasing intermediate trade when companies internationalize their production.

Generally speaking, small countries tend to rely much on the imported inputs than large countries do. Due to economies of scale, large countries can support every stage of production in many differentiated goods more easily than small countries (Hummels 1998). This could explain the low import shares of intermediate goods used in production in the United States, Japan, Germany and the upcoming economies of China and India wherein efforts to localize the goods or import substitution has gained momentum primarily with the base of economies of scale. However, Germany's low share is surprising as it is situated in an integrating area with generally high trade volumes and a distinct separation of labour. Australia suffers from its geographical 'isolation', which lowers the degree of openness. The expanding multi-national enterprises network connected through intense trade relations between parent companies and affiliates and among the sub-affiliates could be the growing trade and growing production abroad. Substitution of foreign produced goods may occur but new trade opportunities are also opened with the internationalization of production.

In nutshell, business dynamics is synonym to globalization nowadays and this converts national economies into an integrated world economy. This includes a deepening and a widening of economic integration. The widening results from the inclusion of new countries like the developing countries in Central and Eastern Europe, BRIC countries in the global economic system. The intensive use of three channels gave economic integration in the era of globalization a new quality: international trade, foreign direct investment and international technology flows.

Internationalization of economic activity is driven to a large extent by multi-national enterprises. MNEs hold an important position in international business. Approximately, a third of worldwide trade takes place within MNEs; about 80 % involve at least one multi-national enterprise (MNE) at one side of interaction. This trade is increasingly intra-industry trade and consists of half of intermediate goods trade. International trade is concentrated on the developed countries so far which intensified their trade relations as can be seen by a stronger rise of trade relative to production and is now getting focused on the developing economies such as China and India. A large share of international economic activity consists of intra-industry trade (IIT) between the developed countries. This includes a large share of trade in intermediate goods. The same holds for foreign direct investment (FDI), which is strongly concentrated amongst developed countries. Intra-industry investment is also large. FDI flows are more volatile than trade flows. FDI occurs in waves with different cycles for different countries. The concentration in developed countries is strongest concerning technology flows. Their increase driven by intra-multinational flows, account for 80 % of all flows of technology. This point to the internationalization of knowledge and technology use. However, the internationalization of knowledge production remains rather modest. Research and Development remains a headquarter service which is supplied by the parent company and applied by foreign affiliates. The dominant role of large players in the globalization process calls for an explicit modeling of MNEs in the globalization process.

A.5 ECONOMICS & FINANCE

Finance is the basic requirement of business and hence, is the necessary ingredient of economics. Therefore, the development of financial system is extremely important for economic environment and business viability as a whole. Business firms have to invest in various activities for business to sustain and expand, whereas, the households have to save in order to secure their future. That builds an equation between the household sector and the business sector and this equation is of – flow of funds. For undergoing any expansion, takeover, investment etc., the companies have to raise funds from the market and this is done through issuance of share or bonds which is subscribed by the individuals. This enables mobilization of funds from the household sector to the business. However, there could be large number of passive savers who may not like to invest in these stock purchases and look for safer options like fixed deposit in banks and mutual funds with financial institutions or even insurance companies. These banks and non-banking financial institutions in turn make investments in various private enterprises and also in other infrastructure bonds in order to secure a healthy rate of return both for their operations and to attract the customers. Similarly, banks both consumer and industrial; lend money on interest to various project based on their viability. Thus, we see that the economic environment is virtually created and driven by the financial system.

Broadly speaking, the financial system can be classified into two segments:

1. Money market
2. Capital market

The money market refers to a mechanism whereby transactions in short term claims on banks are affected. Therefore, this market corresponds to short – term monetary assets. This characteristic comes out of the fact that the market is not that integrated and hence, can be safely divided into organized and unorganized parts. The organized sector of money market corresponds to the commercial banks – both national and international, co-operative banks, financial corporations. The organized sector of the money market is fairly systematic in developed countries, however, the economic recession in 2008/ 2009 opened up a big question of their foundation because even though, the organized money market in India is not comparable to the developed countries, yet it proved that the foundations are far more solid than is perceived. On the other hand, the unorganized sector of the money market consists of money lenders, venture capitalists, indigenous bankers, un-regulated non-bank financial intermediaries etc. Normally, the corporate sector or big business houses do not seek funds from un-organized money market, however, small business houses or projects which are difficult to prove from the point of instant viability, entrepreneurs with not much solid financial backing, they try to arrange funds from these un-organized money markets.

Contrary to the money market, the capital market is related to long term funding requirements. From the point of modus operandi, it can be divided into two parts:

1. Financial Institutions
2. Securities Market

Financial institutions are government agency or privately owned entities that collect funds from the public and from other institutions and invest these funds in financial assets, such as loans, securities, bank deposits, and other income generating property. In very simple terms, financial institutions act as intermediaries between savers and borrowers and are differentiated by the way they obtain and invest their funds. Among these are also Depository financial institutions that include commercial banks, savings and loan associations, mutual savings banks and credit unions which conduct business by accepting public deposits that is insured by the government against loss and channel their depositor's money into lending activities. Also, we have Non-depository financial institutions such as brokerage firms, life insurance companies, pension funds and investment companies. These fund their investment activities directly from the financial market by selling securities to the public or by selling insurance policies, in case of insurance companies. Gradually, the boundaries between depository and non-depository institutions have become less distinct. Brokerage firms can invest their customer's money in the bank, whereas banks and savings institutions have started offering brokerage and mutual funds.

Securities are bought and sold in the securities market. These have the facilities and people engaged in such transactions, the demand for and availability of securities to be traded, and the willingness of buyers and sellers to reach agreement on sales. Securities markets include over – the – counter markets, the New York Stock Exchange, the Chicago Board of Trade and the American Stock Exchange, National Stock Exchange (Mumbai) etc. Basically, securities are any form of ownership that can be easily traded on a secondary market, such as stocks and bonds. It also includes their derivatives, such as stock options, mutual funds etc. Securities are traded on a secondary market. This includes the stock market, bond market, and U.S. Treasuries market. Traders must be licensed to buy and sell securities to assure they are trained to follow the laws set by the Securities and Exchange regulatory bodies. Securities traders are always trying to find ways to make a higher return with less risk. Therefore, innovative derivatives of basic stocks and bonds are often developed. These include futures contracts and calls and put options. Even mortgages have been packaged to sell on the secondary market and these are known as mortgage – backed securities. Securities help the economy by making it easier for those with money to find those who need investment capital. By making trading easy and available to many investors, securities make market more efficient. It is easy for investors to see which companies are doing well, and which ones are not. Money can swiftly go to those companies that are growing, thus rewarding performance and providing an incentive for further growth.

In nutshell, the securities market consists of – the new issue market or the primary market & the stock exchange or the secondary market. Basically, capital markets originate as new issue markets. As large numbers of corporations become operational, secondary market develops for outstanding issues. The stock exchanges provide a channel through which the savings of the people, who wish to invest for a short term period, becomes available to companies for long term utilization. The fact is that the business enterprises retain the capital almost permanently, while the shares keep on changing hands and thereby the investor's portfolio changes but the net investment towards the company remains same. However, the value of the individual's share undergoes changes based on the performance of the company's and their dividend values.

In simple words, in every economic system some units which may be individual or institutions are surplus-generating while others are deficit-generating. Surplus-generating units are called savers and deficit-generating units are called spenders. Households are surplus generating and corporate and government are deficit-generators. By placing the surplus funds in financial securities the spending community gets funds at a cost and the saving community gets various benefits like interest, dividend, capital appreciation, bonus etc. Thus, the surplus generating units (savers) are investors and deficit generating units (spenders) are issuers. These investors and issuers of financial securities constitute two important elements of the securities market. The third critical element of markets is the intermediaries who act as conduits between investors and issuers. Regulatory bodies, which regulate the functioning of the securities market, constitute the last but very significant element of securities markets. Thus the four important elements of the securities market are:

1. Investors

2. Issuers

3. Intermediaries

4. Regulators

Also, securities can be – (i) Government or Industrial (ii) Long term or Short term (iii) Primary market or Secondary market. Primary market is the segment in which new issues are made whereas secondary market is the segment in which outstanding issues are traded. It is for this reason that the Primary market is called the new issues market and the secondary market is called the Stock market and the activities are carried out in stock exchanges.

A stock exchange fulfills a vital function in the economic development of a nation. Its main function is to *'liquefy'* capital by enabling a person who has invested money in, say a factory or railway, to convert into cash by disposing off his shares in the enterprise to someone else. Investment in joint stock companies is attractive to the public, because the value of the shares is announced day after day in the stock exchanges, and the shares quoted on the exchanges are capable of almost immediate conversion into money. In modern times, a company stands little chance of inducing the public to subscribe to its capital, unless its shares are quoted in an approved stock exchange. All public companies are anxious to obtain permission from reputed exchanges for securing quotations of their shares and the management of a company is anxious to inform the investing public that the shares of the company will be quoted on the stock exchange.

Therefore, the stock exchange is really an essential pillar of private sector corporate economy. It discharges three essential functions:

- First, the stock exchange provides a market place for purchase and sale of securities viz; shares, bonds, debentures etc. It therefore, ensures the free transferability of securities which is the essential basis for the joint stock enterprise system.

- Secondly, the stock exchange provides the linkage between the savings in the household sector and the investment in the corporate economy. It mobilizes savings, channelizes them as securities into these enterprises which are favoured by the investors on the basis of such criteria as future growth prospects, good returns and appreciation of capital.

- Thirdly, by providing a market quotation of the prices of shares and bonds – a sort of collective judgment simultaneously reached by many buyers and sellers in the market – the stock exchange serves as the role of a barometer, not only of the state of health of the individual companies, but also of the nation's economy as a whole.

Since, the savings of the investing community namely, public, needs to be protected from various kinds of malpractices, frauds, defaults etc., it was obligatory on part of the governing system to establish regulatory bodies. USA and UK had long back created separate boards for the securities market. U.K. has the Securities and Investment Board (SIB) while USA has the Securities and Exchange Commission (SEC). In India, by a notification issues on 12 th April 1988, Securities and Exchange Board of India (SEBI) was constituted as an interim administrative body to function under the overall control of the Ministry of Finance of the Central Government. The SEBI was given statutory status on 30 th January, 1992 by an ordinance to provide for the establishment of SEBI. A bill to replace the ordinance was introduced in the parliament on 3 rd March, 1992 and was passed by both the houses of parliament on 1 st April, 1992. The bill became an act on 4 th April, 1992 the date on which it received President's assent. However, this act was deemed to have come into force on 30 th January, 1992, i.e. the date on which SEBI ordinance was promulgated.

The interplay between economics and finance is significantly affected by economic policies of a government which can be broadly categorized into four types:

i. Industrial policy

ii. Trade policy

iii. Monetary policy

iv. Fiscal policy

The industrial policy of a country is directly related to business. It denotes a nation's declared, official, total strategic effort to influence sectoral development and thus, national industrial portfolio. For example, in the United States, economists favor increased involvement of the government in the allocation of capital to industries. Similarly, in Japan, the Ministry of Trade and Industry prioritized automobile industry as their priority. This indicates that industrial policies do have the peculiarity of being sector-specific, unlike broader economic policies. An industrial policy is also viewed as interventionist policy for example industrialization by substitution of imports, where trade barriers are imposed on some key sectors of manufacture. These privileged industrial sectors are expected to take advantage of these artificial protections and expand at faster rates which otherwise would not have been possible. The reason is that manufacturing has been considered as engine of growth in economic theory. Even in the United States, which is known to favor 'free-trade' has laws to protect itself from dumping by way of tax, tariff and trade barriers. In India, the industrial policy was de-regulated in a substantial manner in 1991. A number of industrial licensing was abolished except certain industries of strategic importance. The role of public sector industries has gradually witnessed withdrawal in favor of private sector enterprises. Import of foreign capital and technology was highly liberalized.

Trade policy in general plays an important role in growth and protection of industries in view of competition. This can be categorized into closed or open types. For example, India's trade policy for almost four decades after independence was primarily closed type and was helpful in protecting the domestic industries by somewhat blocking external competition. With this the domestic industries thrived without much external competition but they did not do much to bring themselves up to the international levels. In contrast, the open policy does not discriminate between production for domestic market or exports and it is also non-discriminatory concerning procurement between domestic or foreign goods. This provides somewhat liberalized economic environment wherein the industries have to become internationally competitive to survive irrespective of the fact whether they produce for domestic market or are export oriented.

Monetary policy has influence on cost and availability of credit and money and therefore is of significant importance to economic environment and business. When the economy opens up i.e. becomes more liberal, there is a need to service external debt and it is necessary to improve country's export to maintain a healthy balance of payment and to survive in the internationally competitive market. At the same time, it is also necessary to maintain the stability of the prices of various commodities. Price stability, however, does not mean absolutely static price level. According to reputed economist, C. Rangarajan, "Monetary policy is an arm of macro-economic policy and its role and importance are determined in any economy by the overall policy framework and the various instruments available for implementing policy." In simple terms, monetary policy rests on the relationship between the rates of interest in an economy, that is the price at which money can be borrowed, and the total supply of money. Monetary policy uses a variety of tools to control one or both of these, to influence outcomes like economic growth, inflation, exchange rates with other currencies and unemployment. The primary tool of monetary policy is open market operations. This entails managing the quantity of money in circulation through the buying and selling of various financial instruments, such as treasury bills, company bonds, or foreign currencies. All of these purchases or sales result in more or less base currency entering or leaving market circulation.

Within almost all modern nations, special institutions such as the Reserve Bank of India, Bank of England, Federal Reserve System in the United States, the Bank of Japan, the Bank of Canada, Reserve Bank of Australia exist which have the task of executing the monetary policy and often independent. In general, these institutions are called central banks and often have other responsibilities such as supervising the smooth operation of the financial system. Generally speaking, these central banks influence interest rates by expanding or contracting the monetary base, which consists of currency in circulation and bank's reserves on deposit at the central bank. As mentioned above, the primary way, the primary way these central banks can affect monetary base is by open market operations or sales and purchases of second hand government debt, or by changing the reserve requirements. In the central bank wishes to lower interest rates, it purchases government debt, thereby increasing the amount of cash in circulation or crediting bank's reserve accounts. Alternatively, it can lower the interest rate on discounts or overdrafts which are loans to banks secured by suitable collateral. If the interest rate on such transaction is low, commercial banks can borrow from the central bank to meet reserve requirements and use the additional liquidity to expand their balance sheets, increasing the credit available to the economy. Lowering reserve requirements has a similar effect, freeing up funds for banks to increase loans or buy other profitable assets. In Indian context, the monetary authorities have designed an array of instruments to regulate credit flow in a planned manner. This has led to a monolithic decision making process in regard to monetary policy formulation and its implementation and primacy for direct rather than indirect methods of control in monetary management.

The term fiscal policy refers to the expenditure a government undertakes to provide goods and services and to the way in which the government finances these expenditures. In other words, it formulates the taxation and public expenditure in order to flatten the fluctuations of the economic environment and business cycle so as to result in economic growth with stable prices and reasonable employment. Basically, there are two methods of financing: taxation and borrowing. Taxation takes many forms in the developed countries including taxation of personal and corporate income, so called value added taxation and the collection of royalties or taxes on specific sets of goods. The debt burden assumed by the government is itself an important policy variable and one that has implications for the conduct of monetary policy. Governments in democratic societies act on many different, occasionally conflicting objectives. They may want to smooth out the nation's income in order to minimize the pejorative effects of the business cycle or they may want to take steps designed to increase the national income. They may also want to take steps intended to achieve specific social objectives deemed to be appropriate by the political or legal process.

Coming to expenditure, it can be either money spent on the delivery of goods and services and the transfer of funds to other levels of government. The money spent by the government has a stimulative effect on the economy. The government is large enough that it can spend during periods of economic contraction thereby helping to boost up the economy and consumer confidence. This school of thought in which the government plays an activist role in stimulating the economy in times of recession and in easing their spending in times of success is called Keynesian School, after the economist John Keynes, who was a legendary speculator, formulated his theories during the Great Depression as governments in Europe and North America struggled to revive economies troubled by a pullback in the provision of private credit and the negative effects of beggar-thy-neighbour competitive currency devaluations. The problem with this school of thought is that when it is applied, it is politically very appealing to be spending money during a downturn and helping people when they need help. It is also politically very attractive to be spending money and helping people during a boom time.

It is also very appealing to try and redistribute goods to one group from other groups in the society. This is a very common objective of fiscal policy. Politicians in Western democracies often try to redistribute resources to people living in poverty from people living in comparative wealth. In Canada, one of the most controversial fiscal policy decisions of the post-war era was the Trudeau government's move during the oil crisis of 1978 to force Alberta to sell its oil and gas to Central Canadians at prices that were far below the price that Alberta could have received by selling those resources on the open international market. This constituted a real transfer of money from the people of Alberta to the people of Ontario and Quebec. People are still bitter about that policy thirty years after the fact.

Considering a situation in which a government wants to provide a great deal of goods and services to its people while not having immediate tax revenue to fund that expenditure. Then the government can turn to the capital markets to borrow the necessary money. They do this primarily by issuing securities, either Treasury Bills or Treasury Bonds. All levels of government will borrow money at the some point. These securities are obligations compelling the government to repay the borrowed amount at maturity and also pay interest at specific points of time. Borrowing has number of effects. If a country borrows too much money, it has to pay a great deal of interest every year in order to service that debt. This represents money that could have been used to pay for program spending instead. By borrowing money, the government has placed a greater emphasis on spending in the present than in the future. It has discounted the value of future expenditure. Depending on how much money the citizens of that country or that province save out of their own incomes, the borrowing government must sell its obligations to foreigners. By doing so, the government makes itself vulnerable to the shifting and often volatile sentiment of the international capital markets. If they have a sufficiently large external debt in relation to their gross domestic product (GDP), which is as an indicator of their current and future capacity to repay, speculators might attack their currency or the country's bond markets forcing higher interest rates and would cause degradation of the economy in international terms.

Thus, an excessive debt policy can lead to a vicious cycle of speculative attacks, followed by higher interest rates and higher interest payments that can cause an economic slowdown. Just when a stimulative policy is required to help the economy struggle back to its normal growth trajectory, the government finds itself crippled by high interest rates and poor liquidity. In such situations, arranging loans from other countries in order to stimulate economy; also becomes very difficult and may result a state in which loan from International Monetary Fund (IMF) per stringent conditions becomes necessary to avert a balance of payment crisis. On the other hand, it may be prudent to borrow during economic downturns in order to stimulate the economy with the intention of repaying those funds, and thereby dampening the economy, in times of economic growth. The conduct of fiscal policy is very complicated and its effect on the economy, its reliance on external factors and other value-driven objectives that characterize much of the redistribution of resources and other choices concerning fiscal policy. Therefore, fiscal corrections are necessary for providing a stable background for the economy and offsetting major disturbances in the economic system arising from different sources.

PART B

FRAMEWORK OF ECONOMY

B.1 ECONOMIC SYSTEM

Economic environment of any country is largely influenced by the prevailing economic system of the country. Although, economic systems existed since pre-historic times and progressed from barter system to modern economic system through various other intermittent systems such as gift, mutualism, mercantilism, Nordic, feudalism etc., but instead on focusing on small economic systems which were more of transient in nature, we will confine the discussions on the two main contemporary systems – capitalism and socialism. The basic difference between the two is that capitalism is market driven whereas socialism follows a central planning with major production activities carried out in public sector enterprises. However, in between these two types of economies there also exists a *'mixed economy'* which is characterized by the co-existence of public and private sectors having restrictions on private enterprises related to defense, public, nuclear energy etc.

Capitalism being self driven market situation has been obviously more successful in terms of sustainability and that is why a lion's share of economic development has been observed mostly in the countries with capitalist infrastructure. This capitalist system developed only after the disintegration of feudal system and did not exist from the beginning.

Capital evolved from *Capitale*, a Latin word based on Proto-Indo-European *kaput*, meaning "head"—also the origin of cattle in the sense of movable property. The term capitalism appeared in 1753 in the Encyclopedia, with the narrow meaning of "The state who is rich". However, accordingly to the Oxford English Dictionary, the term capitalism was first used by the India born novelist William Makepeace Thackeray in 1854 in *"The Newcombes"*, where he meant "having ownership of capital". In addition, the Oxford English Dictionary also mentions that Carl Adolph Douai, a German – American socialist and abolitionist, used the term private capitalism in 1863. The initial usage of the term capitalism in its modern sense has been attributed to Louis Blanc in 1850 and Pierre – Joseph Proudhon in 1861. Marx and

Engels referred to the capitalistic system (*kapitalistisches* system) in *Das Kapital* (1867). The use of the word "capitalism" in reference to an economic system appears twice in Volume I of *Das Kapital*, p. 124 (German Edition) and in Theories of Surplus Value, p. 493 (German edition). Marx did not extensively use the form capitalism, but instead those of capitalist and capitalist mode of production, which appear more than 2600 times in the trilogy *Das Kapital*.

Although, there does not exist a consensus between the experts of economy regarding a precise definition for capitalism, however, in simple terms, capitalism is a market-driven economy, characterized by private ownership and use of resources owned for profit without restrictions. Individuals and businesses have the right to own all material resources. Capitalism gives them free control in the production, allocation and consumption of resources for generating income, profit, and wealth. The hallmark of capitalism is the free market concept, which allows open competition to achieve these goals. Practitioners of capitalism believe that markets are efficient enough to make independent decisions on matters like investments, production, distribution, income, and prices. Thus capitalism discourages any direct involvement of the state in the markets. The role of the government in capitalism is to provide regulation, infrastructure, and protection, to perpetuate capitalist economy, privacy, and freedom. Adam Smith, regarded as the father of capitalism, wrote of the role of enlightened self-interest (aka the *"invisible hand"*). It would be worthwhile to mention the opinion of Cromwell and Czerwinski, (*In Defense of Capitalism, p. 5*) who proposed that only that system can be referred to as capitalistic, in which there is free and genuine competition for profit and there is for all to work continuously. However, this definition of capitalism cannot be considered as satisfactory as brings the capitalist economy based on *laissez faire*. From a rational point of view it would not be possible to accept such similarity because in the modern capitalist economy of today monopolistic elements have replaced competitive ones and State intervention through monetary and fiscal policies is an established fact. In comparison Cole's definition of capitalism appears to be more scientific and logical as he proposed capitalism as that profit oriented system which is characterized by private ownership of objects of labour, instruments of labour and means of labour. His definition clearly underlines the fact that private ownership of the means of production and that capitalist economic system provides sufficient scope for private business.

Although, capitalism per say, prevails in many countries such as USA, Japan, Spain, England, Sweden, South Korea etc., however, the nature of system have subtle differences in the way their economies operate practically. Some of the notable examples could be, for example, in Sweden various welfare measure have been taken with the help of schemes to enhance social welfare and with the help of fiscal policies there has been an attempt to reduce disparities among people concerning distribution of income. In the largest capitalist country like USA, measures have been taken to provide social security to the people, however, interestingly, Spain which is a part of European Union functions more or less similar to the capitalistic economy of Europe which prevailed during the 19 th century.

The private sector plays the dominant role in the U.S. economy. U.S. businesses enjoy greater flexibility than their counterparts in Western Europe and Japan to expand production, lay off workers and develop new products. U.S. firms are global leaders in technological advances, especially in computers, aerospace, medical equipment and machinery. The onrush of technology has expanded the gap in education and professional and technical skills between those at the bottom of the labor market and those at the top. The people at the bottom increasingly face difficulties in obtaining pay raises, health insurance and other benefits. Since 1975, most of the gains in household income have gone to the top 20 per cent of households. The economic downturn that began in 2008 drove the U.S. unemployment rate to 8 percent in early 2009, unacceptably high by U.S. standards but quite common in Western Europe. (Source: Central Intelligence Agency World Fact Book).

Sweden's tax burden remains one of the highest in the world. But the election victory of the center-right Alliance for Sweden coalition in September 2006 marked the beginning of a new era of Swedish economic policy — a shift away from the "cradle to grave" social welfare system that the defeated Social Democratic Party had implemented for much of the past century. The main economic theme of the new center-right coalition is strengthening economic incentives to work and diminishing the attractiveness of living off welfare payments. The coalition also seeks to reduce the public sector's role in the economy through privatization. (Source: Europa World Plus)

France has made substantial adjustments to its economy over the past two decades, decreasing public ownership and economic planning while giving more play to markets, especially financial markets. By 2000, the state's direct control of the economy had been reduced to core areas of public service, such as the post office. While it has the lowest poverty rate among the world's large economies at 7 percent, in large part due to a commitment to social equity, France struggles with the demands of more open European and global markets. The French economy is plagued by persistently high unemployment, typically between 8 percent and 10 percent. (Sources: Library of Congress and the U.S. Federal Reserve Bank).

The German economy, the largest in Europe, combines free enterprise and competition with a high level of social services. There is a social pact between employers, employees and workers' representatives that let them share power with executives in corporate boardrooms in a system known as co-determination (*mitbestimmung*). Germany is seeking to ease labor-market rigidities through a reform program known as Agenda 2010. The agenda includes easing regulations relating to work time, layoffs, taxes, welfare and social security payments. The agenda is intended to make it easier for businesses to hire and lay off workers as market conditions warrant. The agenda reduces business taxes to a maximum of 42 percent in the highest tax bracket and to 15 percent in the lowest bracket. (Sources: Library of Congress and the U.S. Federal Reserve Bank)

However, in spite of subtle differences, these economies are still grouped under capitalistic economy as they have similarities in basic feature which characterizes capitalism. Some of the main characteristics have been detailed below:-

- One of the most important features of capitalism is the **private ownership of the means of production** and this is in total contradiction with socialism. In simple terms anything which assists in production i.e. tools and machinery, raw material etc., is owned by the capitalist. However, since the majority of the population does not have resources to own the resources at a point of time, hence, the manpower is sold to the capitalists in order to earn a livelihood. Therefore, this skilled manpower is also means of production which are contracted by the capitalists. It does not necessarily means that all necessary resources are engaged only in mass production. In towns and rural areas craftsman and artisans still carry on with their traditional production methods even though at a much lesser volumes.

- Another major difference between the capitalist economy and other types of economies is that in capitalist economy the business houses produce with the **objective to sell the goods**. Therefore, a good which is produced in the market is termed as commodity and this is produced with the sole objective of exchange, hence, is also called a commodity economy.

- From the above discussions, it is quite obvious that in capitalism **labour power is also a commodity** and can be bought and sold just like any other commodity. Therefore, capitalism allows manpower to acquire the form of a commodity and this labour power also has a market value or commands a price which is essential for his / her maintenance and the family.

- Since, in the capitalistic economy the manpower is also converted into a commodity, hence, the laws of supply and demand apply as well in determining the value of this item. It would not be correct to assume that the manpower always gets a fair price in return for his / her labour power. The truth of the matter is, however, greatly at variance from this view. Karl Marx described the **exploitation of manpower in capitalistic market** situations and also Joan Robinson, a British economist explained how imperfect market competition determines the wage rate of workers well below the marginal productivity of their labour.

- Under capitalist environment the decisions concerning **price mechanism** of a commodity is based or influenced by the prevailing prices in the market and their relative profitability. Therefore, the prices are not concerned with social welfare but with the sole objective of profit maximization.

- Another important characteristics of the capitalistic economy is that possibility of new entrepreneurs do exist but the rich getting richer also exist, hence, the **wealth of capitalists grows** in a sustained manner or it is expected to grow in this manner. As profit maximization being the most important objective, there is an increased effort from the organization to eliminate competitors either by acquisition or merger and hence, in this process there is further concentration of wealth among the capitalists. For example in USA, the top ten corporations own about 12 % of GDP or approximately one – eighth of the wealth of the industrial sector. The concentration of wealth is the universal law ruling all capitalist economies. Obviously, a large part of this wealth comes from exploiting the manpower. How have corporations become so big? Many corporations have become conglomerates, or a company consisting of a number of subsidiary companies in unrelated industries. A subsidiary is a company owned or controlled by another company. For example, Pepsi Co, Inc. is a conglomerate with its obvious beverage division and with subsidiaries such as Frito-Lay and Tropicana Juices (acquired in July 1998) as well as other subsidiaries. Pepsi is horizontally integrated with these subsidiaries and vertically integrated in its soft drink operations by owning some bottling operations. Large corporations like Pepsi can keep prices low by reducing their costs through mass production and economies of scale. They can buy supplies in bulk at a discount and use technology to lower costs. However, the costs of advertising, transportation and distribution around the country, as well as mountains of bureaucratic work push up prices. Additionally, companies in industries with few significant competitors have the power to raise their price. Apart from price, other factors besides price to consider when evaluating the pros and cons of large corporations are the quality of products, working conditions, impact on the environment, ability to influence the government and laws, movement of operations to foreign countries and impact on culture.

- In the capitalist system where profit motive is main objective, wealth maximization is the outcome and has to be sustained for survival; **class distinction** is an automatic outcome. With the development of capitalism, the society gets further divided into two opposite classes. On one hand are capitalist with whom power and wealth is concentrated and on the other hand are skilled manpower who have been exploited or let themselves exploited for survival. Interestingly, the working class has to depend on the capitalist and at the same time the capitalist class also has to depend on the working class as the production could not take place automatically. Therefore, the labour power is indispensible for the survival of capitalist class. However, it is the capitalist who become rich. This paradoxical situation is bound to give rise to **class conflict**. It may be noted that the class of small bourgeoisie which is alternatively known as the middle – class gradually loses its identity over the period of time with some people joining the ranks of capitalists and the remaining merge with the working class. The two classes have their clash of interest. The working class in order to obtain higher wages collectively bargain through their trade unions. The other pressure methods also consists of strike, go – slow, work – to – rule etc., and these are counteracted by widely used techniques such as negotiations, voluntary retirement schemes, retrenchment, lock – out etc. Although, labour department have been established in the respective industrial estate areas, however, in order to attract foreign direct investment, normally the government rules are supportive in nature to capitalist.

The capitalist system is market driven and hence, the main issues of the economy remains – what to produce, how to produce and for whom to produce. Basically, the idea is to find items which can be consumed. Therefore, an item which can be consumed has to have an acceptable price determined by the market. Therefore, the established market mechanism is responsible for price mechanism as well. As any system, there has to be some limitations of this price mechanism. As discussed previously, in capitalist economy the most important feature is the absence of central state planning as the production process is market driven with the objective of profit maximization. However, it is worthwhile to consider that in spite of the absence of any central planning how the availability of items is ensured i.e. how this so called 'unplanned economy' functions. Adam Smith was the first economist which tried to ponder this question in his book *'An enquiry into the Nature and Causes of the Wealth of Nations'*. His idea was that in a free enterprise economy the self – interest of the individuals acts in the best interest of the society and in turn is responsible for the smooth functioning of the society that maintains the demand and supply equilibrium from the point of profit maximization. Basically, it is the price system which regulates the economy of a capitalist economy. In nutshell, the solution to the central problem is obtained with the help of price mechanism.

According to J.K. Galbraith, American Capitalism (Harmondsworth, Middlesex, 1968, p. 118), if the distribution of income and wealth in the country can be regarded as equitable and just, then in a perfectly competitive market structure the price mechanism will work efficiently and thereby arrive at an optimal solution to the central problems. But in the capitalist countries of today neither are the distribution of income is equitable nor is the situation of perfect competition prevails. It is a normal scene in capitalist countries that on one hand there is a scarcity of essential goods like food grain, milk, medicines and on the other hand hi-end motorcycles, high-tech mobiles, expensive motorcars and 3D television sets, flood the market. The situation in capitalist economy gradually tend to be irrational as the motive of profit maximization becomes bigger and bigger.

That means there has to be a role of the government to regulate the price mechanism in certain defined ways so that the motive of profit maximization does not go beyond the socially acceptance considering the fabric of the society. Some of the major roles can be summarized as under:

- Check the monopolistic growth of corporations. Here again, it is worthwhile to quote from Galbraith's book *"American Capitalism"* that large corporations have capacities to spend large amount of money on advertisements and influence the pattern of demand. Sometimes these promotion drives create an artificial demand in the market which shifts the equation of normal supply and demand of the essentials.

- If the economy and price mechanism depends solely on the free market equilibrium, then with the prevalent income and wealth inequalities in a capitalist economy there would be large scale starvation. Therefore, it is necessary to infuse some welfare measures such as price subsidies and rationing to address the entire social fabric. In *"Poverty and Famines"*, Amartya Sen revealed that in many cases of famine, food supplies were not significantly reduced. In Bengal, for example, food production, while down on the previous year, was higher than in previous non-famine years. Thus, Nobel Laureate Amartya Sen points to a number of social and economic factors, such as declining wages, unemployment, rising food prices, and poor food-distribution systems. These issues led to starvation among certain groups in society.

- Generally speaking, it is clear that individualistic orientation will never create a price mechanism suitable to all in a society specially for items which are public in nature for example medical facilities, education, water supply, electricity, transport and other social services which comes under nobody's responsibility but are very important for the sustainability of a nation as a whole. Therefore, it becomes imperative for the government to participate in the production of such items directly or indirectly with controlling stake. This is in particular applicable to the developing economies with large scale irregularities in development of such sectors which cannot be created solely on the basis of profit maximization.

Socialism, in contrast, differs from capitalism not only due to the absence of private ownership but also in its basic structure and function. Before, we go through the fundamentals of socialism, it would be worthwhile to review an article by Albert Einstein which was published in the first issue of Monthly Review (May 1949) named 'Why Socialism?' It is definitely interesting because we all know Einstein more as a scientist than an economist. Einstein writes -

"Is it advisable for one who is not an expert on economic and social issues to express views on the subject of socialism? I believe for a number of reasons that it is.

Let us first consider the question from the point of view of scientific knowledge. It might appear that there are no essential methodological differences between astronomy and economics: scientists in both fields attempt to discover laws of general acceptability for a circumscribed group of phenomena in order to make the interconnection of these phenomena as clearly understandable as possible. But in reality such methodological differences do exist. The discovery of general laws in the field of economics is made difficult by the circumstance that observed economic phenomena are often affected by many factors which are very hard to evaluate separately. In addition, the experience which has accumulated since the beginning of the so-called civilized period of human history has—as is well known—been largely influenced and limited by causes which are by no means exclusively economic in nature. For example, most of the major states of history owed their existence to conquest. The conquering peoples established themselves, legally and economically, as the privileged class of the conquered country. They seized for themselves a monopoly of the land ownership and appointed priesthood from among their own ranks. The priests, in control of education, made the class division of society into a permanent institution and created a system of values by which the people were thenceforth, to a large extent unconsciously, guided in their social behavior.

Second, socialism is directed towards a social-ethical end. Science, however, cannot create ends and, even less, instill them in human beings; science, at most, can supply the means by which to attain certain ends. But the ends themselves are conceived by personalities with lofty ethical ideals and—if these ends are not stillborn, but vital and vigorous—are adopted and carried forward by those many human beings who, half unconsciously, determine the slow evolution of society.

Man is, at one and the same time, a solitary being and a social being. As a solitary being, he attempts to protect his own existence and that of those who are closest to him, to satisfy his personal desires, and to develop his innate abilities. As a social being, he seeks to gain the recognition and affection of his fellow human beings, to share in their pleasures, to comfort them in their sorrows, and to improve their conditions of life. Only the existence of these varied, frequently conflicting, strivings accounts for the special character of a man and their specific combination determines the extent to which an individual can achieve an inner equilibrium and can contribute to the well-being of society. It is "society" which provides man with food, clothing, a home, the tools of work, language, the forms of thought, and most of the content of thought; his life is made possible through the labor and the accomplishments of the many millions past and present who are all hidden behind the small word "society."

It is evident, therefore, that the dependence of the individual upon society is a fact of nature which cannot be abolished—just as in the case of ants and bees. However, while the whole life process of ants and bees is fixed down to the smallest detail by rigid, hereditary instincts, the social pattern and interrelationships of human beings are very variable and susceptible to change. Memories, the capacity to make new combinations, the gift of oral communication have made possible developments among human being which are not dictated by biological necessities. Such developments manifest themselves in traditions, institutions, and organizations; in literature; in scientific and engineering accomplishments; in works of art. This explains how it happens that, in a certain sense, man can influence his life through his own conduct, and that in this process conscious thinking and wanting can play a part.

Man acquires at birth, through heredity, a biological constitution which we must consider fixed and unalterable, including the natural urges which are characteristic of the human species. In addition, during his lifetime, he acquires a cultural constitution which he adopts from society through communication and through many other types of influences. It is this cultural constitution which, with the passage of time, is subject to change and which determines to a very large extent the relationship between the individual and society. Modern anthropology has taught us, through comparative investigation of so-called primitive cultures that the social behavior of human beings may differ greatly, depending upon prevailing cultural patterns and the types of organization which predominate in society. It is on this that those who are striving to improve the lot of man may ground their hopes: human beings are not condemned, because of their biological constitution, to annihilate each other or to be at the mercy of a cruel, self-inflicted fate.

The economic anarchy of capitalist society as it exists today is, in my opinion, the real source of the evil. We see before us a huge community of producers the members of which are unceasingly striving to deprive each other of the fruits of their collective labor—not by force, but on the whole in faithful compliance with legally established rules. In this respect, it is important to realize that the means of production—that is to say, the entire productive capacity that is needed for producing consumer goods as well as additional capital goods—may legally be, and for the most part are, the private property of individuals.

Private capital tends to become concentrated in few hands, partly because of competition among the capitalists, and partly because technological development and the increasing division of labor encourage the formation of larger units of production at the expense of smaller ones. The result of these developments is an oligarchy of private capital the enormous power of which cannot be effectively checked even by a democratically organized political society. This is true since the members of legislative bodies are selected by political parties, largely financed or otherwise influenced by private capitalists who, for all practical purposes, separate the electorate from the legislature. The consequence is that the representatives of the people do not in fact sufficiently protect the interests of the underprivileged sections of the population. Moreover, under existing conditions, private capitalists inevitably control, directly or indirectly, the main sources of information (press, radio, education). It is thus extremely difficult, and indeed in most cases quite impossible, for the individual citizen to come to objective conclusions and to make intelligent use of his political rights.

The situation prevailing in an economy based on the private ownership of capital is thus characterized by two main principles: first, means of production (capital) are privately owned and the owners dispose of them as they see fit; second, the labor contract is free. Of course, there is no such thing as a pure capitalist society in this sense. In particular, it should be noted that the workers, through long and bitter political struggles, have succeeded in securing a somewhat improved form of the "free labor contract" for certain categories of workers. But taken as a whole, the present day economy does not differ much from "pure" capitalism.

This crippling of individuals is the worst evil of capitalism. Our whole educational system suffers from this evil. An exaggerated competitive attitude is inculcated into the student, who is trained to worship acquisitive success as a preparation for his future career. I am convinced there is only one way to eliminate these grave evils, namely through the establishment of a socialist economy, accompanied by an educational system which would be oriented toward social goals. In such an economy, the means of production are owned by society itself and are utilized in a planned fashion. A planned economy, which adjusts production to the needs of the community, would distribute the work to be done among all those able to work and would guarantee a livelihood to every man, woman, and child. The education of the individual, in addition to promoting his own innate abilities, would attempt to develop in him a sense of responsibility for his fellow men in place of the glorification of power and success in our present society. Nevertheless, it is necessary to remember that a planned economy is not yet socialism. A planned economy as such may be accompanied by the complete enslavement of the individual. The achievement of socialism requires the solution of some extremely difficult socio-political problems: how is it possible, in view of the far-reaching centralization of political and economic power, to prevent bureaucracy from becoming all-powerful."

Broadly speaking, socialism does not only mean social ownership of the means of production but also the functioning of economy in a way to maximize social benefits rather than private benefits. Unlike capitalism, the market mechanism is not that pronounced in determining the various planning activities concerning production and allocation of commodities. Such planning function is normally coordinated by the central planning authority or agency which is responsible in preparing estimates for the total requirement with an objective to maximize social welfare. Therefore, the scope for private businesses is not that dominant and is regulated to a large extent.

The socialist system was first established in Russia after the Bolshevik revolution in 1917. After three years, the First World War, at first greeted with enthusiastic patriotism, produced an upsurge of radicalism in most of Europe. In the Russian revolution of February 1917, workers' councils (in Russian, *soviets*) had been formed, and Lenin and the Bolsheviks called for "All power to the Soviets". After the October 1917 Russian revolution, led by Lenin and Trotsky, consolidated power in the Soviets, Lenin declared *"Long live the world socialist revolutions!"* Briefly in Soviet Russia socialism was not just a vision of a future society, but a description of an existing one.

> "If Socialism can only be realized when the intellectual development of all the people permits it, then we shall not see Socialism for at least five hundred years."
>
> *— Vladimir Lenin, November 1917*

The Soviet regime began to bring all the means of production (except agricultural production) under state control, and implemented a system of government through the workers' councils or soviets. In 1949, the communists came to power in China. At this point of time it appeared as if many more underdeveloped countries may follow the way of conversion to socialism. However, in 1990, the Soviet Union disintegrated and many other East European countries abandoned the path of socialism. Presently, the number of socialist countries has dwindled and roughly 40 former socialist countries have gradually transformed themselves to non-socialist countries embracing some form of capitalism. Due to this abrupt downfall of socialist states, experts started to predict the end of life for socialism, however, the paradigm shift of economic growth to China has candidly contradicted the assessment of these experts. According to World Bank, it took the United States of America almost 50 years and Japan close to 60 years to achieve a structural transformation similar to China. Despite rising urban-rural and regional inequalities in the post reform period the benefits of growth were widely shared. During 1978-1995, 20 Chinese provinces have per capita growth rates higher than any country. Over the last two decades, China's share in world trade jumped from 1 per cent to about 4 per cent (India's only 0.6 per cent) and is projected by the World Bank to touch 10 % by 2020. Foreign direct investment (FDI) flows into China rose from near zero in 1978 to more than US $ 40 billion in 2000. China's economic performance looks nothing short of a miracle.

Socialism once practiced by almost 26 countries has shown a marked drop and presently only 5 countries – China, Vietnam, Cuba, North Korea, Lao have the practical functioning of socialism. One of the largest socialist countries viz; Union of Soviet Socialist Republics (USSR) changed to Federal semi Presidential type in the year 1991 with the disintegration of the USSR to the present Russian Federation. If we see the governing model of these countries in light of the writings of Karl Marx indicating absence of private ownership of the means of production, then the following picture emerges:

- Abolishment of private ownership of the means of production is the common feature of all socialist countries. The transition initially was gradual from capitalist mode of production with absorption by respective State i.e. **social ownership of the means of production**. Off late, the socialist countries have undergone some changes and with liberalization to attract foreign direct investment some industries such as equipment, automobile etc., have been allowed to have players from private sector as well participate in production activity, thus opening up cautiously.

- In a socialist state, the working class collectively owns the means of production. Hence, the essence of **socialist ownership** is that the workers working in various sectors of economy are supposed to be the collective owners of the output due to the use of their labour power. The ultimate objective of socialism lies to bring an end to the exploitation of man by man. When a country decides to embrace socialism either due to any revolution or change of governance the ownership of the means of production has to change which in earlier scenario could have co-existed.

- In the socialist ownership system, the **character of labour and the relation** thereof undergoes a change. The reason is that with the producers becoming the owners of the means of production the possibilities of conflict which may arise out of the situation of exploitation from the owners diminishes, because, the labour does not retain the characteristics of a commodity due to change in the ownership pattern. The basic distinction of the division between the labour and the ownership of the means of means of production which is the bottom line of the capitalist system vanishes. Therefore, this necessitates all people to work as there is no accumulation of private ownership.

- Although, the private ownership does not exist in socialist system, however, it would not be correct to understand that the State has all the rights related to **wealth and property**. Most of the socialist societies have developed from systems which had allowed private ownership. Therefore, an abrupt change concerning private property or a total change may not be practical. Normally, the nationalization route for developed industries or sectors of national importance are the ones which are first to go. Similarly, important inputs to agriculture are owned the cooperatives. However, private property is still allowed with ceiling. On this private property people are allowed to carry out activities of their own use but not with the intention of sale. Therefore, in a socialist system, although the means of production would be owned by the state but the personal possessions of the people can be retained by them and this cannot be converted into capital as this could be used as a means of production and further exploitation.

It is evident that capitalist economy is free in structure and functioning wherein planning is determined by the market price mechanism. In comparison, the socialist economy necessitates existence of a central planning to plan and regulate the basic equations of – what to produce, how to produce, for whom to produce. Basically, in line with the central policy regarding the country's direction for economic growth, the Planning Commission is entrusted with the responsibility to carry out the central planning to allocate resources accordingly. This could be different from capitalist system wherein the production of goods is determined by market forces and these are significantly influenced by the segments or individuals having required purchasing power parity. In contrast, the socialist economic system planning is centered on to reduce inequality to the maximum possible extent but without jeopardizing the economic growth i.e. keeping a balance and formulating regulatory practices such as subsidies, rationing, ceiling, reservation etc., to cater to the less privileged segment of the society by bringing a somewhat forced equality.

Considering the system of planning and provision of various regulatory measures, it would not be wrong to state that in socialist economy market pricing is not the prime driving mechanism. Broadly speaking, in a socialist system the pricing mechanism follows the following strategies:-

- For consumer goods, the prices are determined based on the equilibrium i.e. the price at which supplies of a commodity matches with that of demand generated.

- For producer goods, due to absence of such differential supply and demand the accounting prices are used. This means that the prices are set on the basis of historical trend and not arbitrarily decided and views of the producer and producing conditions are taken into account.

Considering the contradictory nature of both capitalism and socialism and the fact that both systems have arisen due to the lacunas embedded in these, the notion of mixed economy is being embraced by more and more countries with varying degrees. In simple terms it may be defined as "A mixed economy is an economy containing the characteristics of both capitalism and socialism. In other words, it is an economy with a combination of both the private and the public ownership of means of production, with some measure of control by the central government." The United States is said to have a mixed economy because privately owned businesses and government both play important roles. Indeed, some of the most enduring debates of American economic history focus on the relative roles of the public and private sectors. The American free enterprise system emphasizes private ownership. Private businesses produce most goods and services, and almost two-thirds of the nation's total economic output goes to individuals for personal use (the remaining one-third is bought by government and business). The consumer role is so great, in fact, that the nation is sometimes characterized as having a 'consumer economy'. Although, according to Galbraith, American economy is basically a capitalist economy. Considering the active role played by the government during 2008/2009 economic crisis, it would not be wrong to state that US economy is not a 100 % *laissez faire* economy and is closer to the concept of mixed economy.

In *"The Language of Money"* Edna Carew defines mixed economy as "One containing features of both capitalism and socialism. Australia is a mixed economy, with major state-owned enterprises in communications, transport, banking, energy generation and health services, as well as privately owned enterprises in the same areas. In common with capitalist economies such as the UK and New Zealand, Australian governments are reducing these activities by privatizing state-operated businesses. Other examples are seen in Eastern Europe and the former Soviet Union, where newly independent states have embraced the principles of private enterprise. China, too, provides a striking illustration of the transition to a mixed economy." India is also an example of mixed economy wherein, the reference has been in the constitutions for socialism, but do not subscribe to Marxist-Leninist ideology. In Indian context, the word *"socialist"* was added to the definition of preamble in 1976 by constitutional amendment. In fact the proposal which was notified in context with this amendment states the following reason – to spell out expressly the high ideals of socialism, secularism and the integrity of the nation, to make the directive principles more comprehensive and give them precedence over those fundamental rights which have been allowed to be relied upon to frustrate socio-economic reforms for implementing the directive principles. It is also proposed to specify the fundamental duties of the citizens and make special provisions for dealing with anti-national activities, whether by individuals or associations.

According to Samuelson, a mixed economy has the characteristics of both capitalist and socialist systems which permits existence of both public and private entities and the decisions making is expedited by the market mechanism supplemented by some kind of central planning, the structure and control of which may differ from country to country based on the apex policy. The underlying fact is the developing economies have adopted comprehensive central planning while retaining the basic fabric of capitalism with an objective to maintain the competitive entrepreneur spirit in a channelized manner suited to the specific needs of the country. Therefore, we can say that a mixed economy is closer to a capitalist economy which is elaborated as under:-

- In a mixed economy the industrial sector consists of both the private owners, including limited companies and even conglomerates which may operate on multi-national level, parallel to public sector enterprises which normally confine to the core sectors. One of the best examples could be India, where, public sector enterprises had a larger role in the beginning due to lack of infrastructure than the private industrial players. However, with the growth of private players the government started to wrap up the industrial portfolio with more and more space to the private players. Nevertheless, the core sectors viz; defense, road, railways, telecommunication etc., still belongs to the government. Similarly the land is owned by the individuals and they can sell their produce either in the free market or to the government at prices decided by the government based on trend and market situations. Therefore, **private ownership of the means of production is permitted and the production of commodity is for profit**. The role of public sector is more supportive and supplementary to the private sector.

- The market mechanism in the mixed economy is not like a free economy per say, as it has regulative controls by the State. The reason is to imbibe the socialist elements necessary to moderate inequality to some extent. Hence, a blanket prohibition of the ownership of the means of production is not in practice. Besides licensing control as a tool for industrial planning, the State also introduces import controls, establishment of fair price shops and distribution of goods at control rate. However, these decisions are taken only from the point of creating equilibrium to rationalize the market mechanism so that it is not entirely driven by the capitalist way.

- In the mixed economy, private and public sector evolve parallel to each other. The presence of public sector can be explained by the fact that these evolved primarily after independence and at that time the private sector was neither strong nor had the willingness to invest in an economic scenario which still needed stabilization. For example, if we take the example of India, the public sector industries were necessity after the independence as a first push from the government. During the colonial rule, countries such as India, which were unfortunately under the rule of another country did not develop big industrial set-up suitable to provide a self sustaining structure for the future rather a framework more suited for a dependent establishment. Hence, establishment of public sector enterprises during the early years of 1950-60 was not a progression towards socialism but a necessity to build an infrastructure for which the private sector was not capable of at that time. This is substantiated by the fact that there has been a gradual reduction in **public sector enterprise** and more and more industries have been opened for private investment and some of the private sector enterprises have gradually entered the coveted list of Fortune 500 as well.

- Centralized **economic planning** started with the socialist countries. However, this is also followed in the countries following capitalist system. There is absolutely no doubt that socialist economy is based on the central planning however, it would be incorrect to understand that all economies with central planning are socialist in nature. A country is always free to adopt the planning needs and structure to shape the economy in the direction suitable to various parameters which are necessary ingredients contributing to the economy, however, this can be done by retaining the capitalist structure like in US or India. The basic difference would be in the regulatory controls and the degree to which the ownership of the means of production is allowed.

A comparison of these three economic systems would provide basic clarity:

Sl. No.	Mixed Economy	Socialism	Capitalism
1	Selective interference from the State	Significant control by the State	Nominal but regulatory interference by the State
2	Private & State ownership of the means of production	State ownership of the means of production	Private ownership of the means of production
3	Both private & public sector co-exist	Predominance of public sector enterprise	Predominance of private sector enterprise
4	Market driven & planning supplemented	Planning driven	Market driven
5	Business profit motive with subsidies on social items	Business social benefit oriented	Business profit oriented

B.2 ECONOMIC PLANNING

Economic planning is present in different forms be it a capitalist system, a socialist system or even a mixed economic system. The only thing which varies is the regulatory controls that determine the extent of government intervention and to some extent the maturity of the market mechanism. In capitalist and mixed economy, it is the market which holds the prominent role whereas; in socialist system market mechanism is supplementary to the centralized planning. Taking the example of mixed economy in India, one can say that the role of planning and market is more or less overlapping whereas the planning is equipped with provisions to intervene but the same is exercised with caution so that the basic underlying fabric of capitalist system is not thwarted.

It is difficult to understand the market mechanism due to its intangible nature and somewhat undefined characteristics which is influenced by the demand and supply. In nutshell, the activities are not directed in a defined manner. Basically, the profit motive is the bottom line. The producers want to produce items which could yield maximum profit or which consumers find it useful. Therefore, there does exist a mechanism which is termed by an eminent economist Adam Smith as an *Invisible Hand* due to its intangible character.

This term was term coined by economist Adam Smith in his 1776 book *"An Inquiry into the Nature and Causes of the Wealth of Nations"*. In his book he states: "Every individual necessarily labors to render the annual revenue of the society as great as he can. He generally neither intends to promote the public interest, nor knows how much he is promoting it... He intends only his own gain, and he is in this, as in many other cases, led by an invisible hand to promote an end which was no part of his intention. Nor is it always the worse for society that it was no part of his intention. By pursuing his own interest he frequently promotes that of the society more effectively than when he really intends to promote it. I have never known much good done by those who affected to trade for the public good."

Thus, the invisible hand is essentially a natural phenomenon that guides free markets and capitalism through competition for scarce resources. Smith assumes that individuals try to maximize their own good (and become wealthier), and by doing so, through trade and entrepreneurship, society as a whole will be better off. Furthermore, any government intervention in the economy isn't needed as the invisible hand would best guide the economy. The invisible hand remains an important foundation of economic analysis, continues to be a source of new analytical and explanatory devices, and is the conceptual basis of a whole class of scientific models throughout the sciences. Indeed, Smith's famous concept has experienced a resurgence of interest as several new interpretations of the concept have been published in the leading general-interest economic journals and those that specialize in the history of economic thought. In addition, there is an entire volume of Palgrave's' (1989) entries on the invisible hand. Most recently, what amounts to a textbook on the invisible hand has been published which places the invisible hand into the methodology of modern technical economics.

However, rather than establishing clarity or refining the specific mechanisms of the invisible hand, these new interpretations have placed the concept into an intellectual quagmire that threatens its scientific usefulness. The widespread effort to discover the "true" meaning of the invisible hand appears to have muddied the conceptual waters almost beyond recognition. There are now at least a dozen different versions of the invisible hand ranging from the more traditional interpretations to those which attach the phrase to such things as slavery and national defense. The existence of multiple, mutually exclusive interpretations of Smith's invisible hand threaten the phrase with what might be called a *multiple-conception disorder*. In addition to the problem of multiple definitions, there is also the problem of under-defining the concept, where the invisible hand remains clouded in mystery and belief rather than founded on a reliable scientific basis. Related to the problem of being ill-defined, is the normative battle under which the invisible hand has long been under siege, where proponents offer nebulous invisible hand solutions which are scoffed at by opponents of the market economy. The combination of these three problems with the invisible hand calls out for either a clear resolution to its meaning or abandonment of the concept.

The majority of the blame for the invisible hand problem surely rests with modern economists and their failure to solve the meaning of the invisible hand. Interpretation follows that route. The obvious problem here is that the concept remains at least partly mystical and normative and therefore unreliable in a scientific sense. To be fair to Smith, many scholars, such as Hirschman (1977) have recognized that he invoked this terminology as a rhetorical device meant to convince readers of the merits of the market economy. Despite this understanding of Smith's purpose, we still require a scientific understanding of the invisible hand. One plausible and logical solution to the mystery of the invisible hand is that Smith found all the workings of his invisible hand in Richard Cantillon's *Essai sur la Nature du Commerce en Général* (1755, hereafter, *Essai*). It is known that Smith was familiar with Cantillon because Smith names him in the *Wealth of Nations*. Second, we know that Cantillon heavily influenced Smith because many scholars have identified many telling similarities in their economics, such as in the case of wage rate differentials and their curious endorsements of the Navigation Acts. Here we extend the connection between Smith and Cantillon to the concept of the invisible hand through the use of textual evidence.

Smith's two economic applications of the invisible hand have long been thought of as completely different because in *The Theory of Moral Sentiments* it is invoked in the case of income distribution, while in the *Wealth of Nations* it is used in the case of production. However, the foundations for both applications of the invisible hand can be found in the three short chapters that follow Cantillon's calculations on the par value between labor and land. It was this calculation that led Smith to reference Cantillon in the *Wealth of Nations*. It is here we find Cantillon's *model of the isolated estate* where he takes the reader from the very visible hand of the feudal economy to the invisible hand of the market economy. His model demonstrates that production is maximized and follows the dictates of consumer demand as a result of entrepreneurs following the dictates of the price system and profit and loss. It also demonstrates that while the distribution of wealth on the isolated estate may be completely skewed, i.e. one person owns everything in the world, the distribution of income and consumption will be reasonably equal and the standard of living will improve over time if the estate owner simply follows his self interest. The fact that both of Smith's economic applications of the invisible hand appear together in Cantillon's model of the isolated estate and are explicitly driven by self interest makes Cantillon the most plausible source of Smith's concept of the invisible hand.

With Cantillon as the inspiration of the invisible hand, the phrase can now be shown to have a specific meaning. This resolution solves the problem of multiple meanings by eliminating all the modern interpretations that have appeared in academic journals. Likewise it solves the problem of ambiguity, eliminates the mystical remnant, and removes the normative image of the phrase. It also restores and refines the traditional interpretation of the invisible hand. Finally, this solution also reconciles the three different uses of Smith's invisible hand. Smith first used the phrase in 1749, prior to the publication of the *Essai* in 1755. This first use was not about economics, but about science in general. The two subsequent uses appeared in 1759 and 1776, after Cantillon's book was published. These applications were the economic applications concerning distribution and production.

At a time when the subject of the history of economic thought has been largely banished to the specialized journals on the subject, Smith's invisible hand has experienced a renaissance with economists searching ever deeper into its meaning and scholars from other disciplines employing the concept. However, this resurgence of interest has created problems, most notably the problem of multiple, mutually exclusive meanings and the more traditional problem of ambiguity. A veritable cottage industry has sprung up in recent years to define the true meaning of Smith's phrase and to capitalize on its widespread recognition and use. The concept is deemed important enough that articles have been published in some of the top ranked general-interest economic journals such as the *American Economic Review*, *Journal of Economic Perspectives*, and *Journal of Political Economy*. In addition, there have been numerous articles in specialized journals and book-length treatments of the subject—including an entire book of entries from the *New Palgraves* (1987) published under the title *The Invisible Hand* (1989) and most recently a textbook on the subject for modern economists by Aydinonat (2008). It would seem that Smith's invisible hand passes the market test of economists.

However, rather than clarifying the meaning of the invisible hand, this literature has only served to cause confusion and to create what can be called a multiple-conception disorder which threatens the scientific usefulness as a concept. For example, Syed Ahmad (1990) offers us four different invisible hands while William Grampp (2000) offers ten different possibilities. Spenser Pack (1996) offers an interpretation where the invisible hand leads to increased destitution among the poor while benefiting the wealthy. Emma Rothschild (1994) interprets the invisible hand as a joke Smith played on his readers because the meaning of the term is not consistent in its three uses. Joseph Persky (1989) finds the invisible hand is related to the production of public goods because it retards the export of capital and thus enhances the national defense, adding the odd tastes of both mercantilism and public goods theory to Smith's invisible hand. Similarly, Grampp (2000) makes the claim that the invisible hand is self-interest leading individuals to keep their capital at home, rather than exporting it, and this promotes the national defense. In Grampp's words, the "invisible hand then is self-interest operating in this circumstance, the circumstance in which a private transaction yields a positive externality that augments a public good." Grampp claims that this is Adam Smith's own interpretation of the invisible hand even though it is based solely on a somewhat tortured view of Smith's third use of the invisible hand.

Another long-standing interpretation is that the invisible hand represents God. Scholars have assumed some sort of religious element for the (Persky 1989, Minowitz 2004). Invisible hand because, as Hirschman (1977) notes, there was a need for a normative interpretation of the market to make it acceptable. Hill (2001), Waterman (2002) and Dennis (2005) provide us with recent interpretations of the invisible hand with a spiritual glove, while Evensky (1993) sketches its ethical dimensions. It is easy to see that collectively these recent interpretations add confusion to the meaning of the invisible hand and give it a multiple-conception disorder.

The purpose here is not to criticize these modern interpretations, but merely to present them and to note that they are very diverse and mutually exclusive. These interpretations are disconnected from the traditional interpretations of the invisible hand and are mostly unrelated to each other. They certainly seem removed from Smith's texts and in some cases thrust Smith's hand forward in time and into the toolbox of modern economists. Therefore, it is reasonable to conclude that these modern interpretations have not clarified the concept of the invisible hand, but have collectively threatened the scientific usefulness of Smith's most prominent and lasting contribution. The other major problem for the invisible hand is what Grampp (2000) labels the "Neo-Austrian" view where the invisible hand is the metaphor for how beneficial social orders emerge from the unintended consequences of individual actions. Grampp cites the entry on the invisible hand in the *New Palgraves* by Karen Vaughn as the basis of this interpretation. This prominent reference work is often the first source scholars and students consult when researching a new topic. Here they will find a proverbial black hole where the invisible hand is described, over and over again, as the emergence of social orders that were unintended. The actual *economics* of the invisible hand are absent, except for minor references to self-interest. Here the concept is said to be composed of three "logical" steps: (1) human action leads to unintended consequences, (2) the law of large numbers is invoked and combined with evolutionary time to generate what appears to be intelligent design, and (3) the end result is beneficial and desirable even though it was unintended.

The problem here is that step one is unnecessary, step three is normative, and step two is devoid of economic content. It is normally not a problem to invoke phrases like "spontaneous order" and "invisible hand," but when presenting such concepts in an encyclopedia, it should be pointed out (and well illustrated) that it refers to a step-by-step real-world process of individual actions that are generally very much intended and very much designed. Scientifically empty, hand-waving expressions of the invisible hand should probably be condemned, as Smith similarly did in his *History of Astronomy* (1749). It is important to note that even before these modern interpretations were "discovered," the invisible hand already had a major image problem. The phrase was appreciated by many, but it was also widely disparaged by many as mere apologetics for capitalism. Even the traditional interpretations of the invisible hand are somewhat vague and nebulous and not based on specific real-world processes. Coming from the philosophy of science perspective, David Hull (1997, p. S119) found that "the real problem with invisible-hand explanations is the specification of the mechanism that is supposed to bring about the result." A good example of a proper application of the invisible hand is provided by Selgin and White (1994). They describe the mechanisms of several competing visions of what the invisible hand might look like in the area of money and banking.

Demonstrating that Adam Smith's invisible hand is plausibly based on Cantillon's *Essai* relies on three key linkages. First, we know that Smith read Cantillon because Smith (1937 [1776], p. 68) famously named Cantillon in the first edition of the *Wealth of Nations* and discussed Cantillon's famous calculation that "the lowest species of common labourers must everywhere earn at least double their own maintenance." The issue of a par value between land and labor is now considered an intellectual black hole in economics, but this result must have been of great importance to Smith, the moral philosopher, because Cantillon had proven that the rich had to hire workers and pay workers *at least* twice their subsistence—even slaves—if they were to actually realize their wealth.

Second, numerous scholars have identified Cantillon's influence on a wide variety of Smith's economic concepts, such as competition and the circular-flow mechanism, which are components of the traditional interpretation of the invisible hand. Of course, Smith could have developed these concepts independently, or read them elsewhere, but the totality of the correlations between Cantillon and Smith reveal a plausible case that Cantillon was a critical influence on Smith's economics. Third and most importantly, both of Smith's economic applications of the invisible hand—which have long thought to have been disconnected from each other—can both be found in Cantillon's model of the isolated estate in the chapters that directly follow his famous estimate. Here he explained how the management of the isolated estate is transferred from the visible hand of the owner, i.e. feudalism, to the invisible hand of market economy.

Regarding the general influence of Cantillon on Smith, scholars have long compared and contrasted Smith with Cantillon on a variety of subjects and have found numerous similarities. For example, according to McNulty (1967 & 1968, p. 647), Adam Smith gave competition "an intellectual and ideological significance," but he was not the discoverer of how competition functioned: On the contrary, he incorporated into the *Wealth of Nations* a concept of competition already well developed in the economic literature of his time...the essence of which was the effort of the individual seller to undersell, or the individual buyer to outbid, his rivals in the marketplace, and had earlier been employed and developed by a number of writers including Cantillon. (McNulty, 1968, p.647) McNulty (1968, p. 646) found that the *model* of competition was invented by Cantillon and was adopted and developed by others, but that it was Smith's *presentation* of the concept that made Smith the prophet of competition—doing for economics what Newton did for physics and astronomy.

Several scholars have connected Smith with Cantillon on the distinction between market price and natural price. According to Robertson and Taylor (1957, p. 192), Smith's "natural price formula is applied only to the natural price of labour, and hardly goes beyond, if indeed it goes as far as, Cantillon." This is an important connection because Cantillon's concept of "intrinsic value" was an attempt to describe the value of a good in terms of the amount of land and labor that were entered into its production. This would certainly appear to resemble—as several scholars have suggested—Adam Smith's natural price. Cantillon then tried to determine a par value of land in terms of labor. However, he found that you could not calculate such a number, but his theoretical answer was that a worker would have to be paid roughly twice the amount of subsistence in order to maintain the size of the workforce over time. This is what Smith attributed to Cantillon when Cantillon is referred to in *Wealth of Nations*. Smith also broke down the price of goods into their component incomes of wages, rents and profits in a way similar to Cantillon. Schumpeter (1954, pp. 239-43) found that Cantillon, with "econometric help" from Quesnay, developed a circular-flow model of the economy based on class categories that were interdependent. This simplified model of the economy was seemingly adopted by Adam Smith, although Smith and others "fumbled" some aspects of the model.

Now let us look at the textual connection between Cantillon's *Essai* and Smith's invisible hand. Adam Smith was not the first person to use the phrase the invisible hand, as it was already in use to describe supernatural action. Indeed, Smith (1795, p. 49) used the phrase derisively in his *History of Astronomy* where he used the "invisible hand of Jupiter" to describe the beliefs of polytheism, savages, and the superstitious who would attribute all irregular events in nature, like thunder and lightning, to invisible gods. Smith was scorning those who concoct special explanations. In Smith's view these irregular events should be seen and studied scientifically as part of the natural order of the universe. Macfie (1971) argues that this use of the invisible hand should not be seen as completely at odds with its use in *The Theory of Moral Sentiments* and *Wealth of Nations*. It is, after all, an expression of Smith's scientific spirit and is a comment concerning the methodological foundation on which he would build his science of natural laws.

It should be clear that Smith took Cantillon's point of logic and observation to make the moral point that there is natural distribution of goods in society that is fair in some sense, despite the unfair distribution of land ownership. The third and final appearance of the invisible hand occurs in *Wealth of Nations*; here Smith invoked the phrase in his famous assault on mercantilism. Smith noted that population is limited by production and production is limited by the amount of capital; two points he could have derived from Cantillon. He further noted that individuals direct their capital according to self-interest to achieve the greatest value and there are economic reasons why capital is often employed domestically. By seeking to obtain the greatest value from his capital, the individual is part of the nation achieving its greatest level of production: By preferring the support of domestic to that of foreign industry, he intends only his own security; and by directing that industry in such a manner as its produce may be of the greatest value, he intends only his own gain, and he is in this, *as in many other cases*, led by an invisible hand to promote an end which was no part of his intention. Nor is it always the worse for the society that it was no part of it. As a way of ameliorating people's fears about free trade and foreign investment, Smith wrote that investors who faced equal profit opportunities at home and abroad will choose to invest domestically because there are fewer risks involved.

In other words, the economics of self-interest in capital markets will propel people to keep a large portion of their capital employed domestically. Smith believed that we could rely on self-interest—not some government decree—to direct and maintain the capital that we subsist on. Capital flight is just an example of the "many other cases" where we can count on the invisible hand. After explaining the distribution of income, Cantillon then explained that everyone is really an entrepreneur because their incomes and profits are at risk. Thereafter he presented his model of the isolated estate where the estate owner who directs his own estate "will necessarily use part of it for corn to feed the laborers, mechanics, and overseers who work for him." He described how the transition from the command or feudal economy to one based on the price system—where the motivation of profit and loss drive the economy—will *ceteris paribus* move the economy or "circulation" into harmony or equilibrium. The owner breaks up the estate into farms that are leased to farmers. Farmers, in turn, direct and sustain their workers. The owner uses rent payments from the farmers to buy goods from artisans and entrepreneurs so that "after this change all the people on this large estate live just as they did before…and that the farms of this great estate will be put to the same use as it formerly was." (79-80/61/28) If the farmers produced more of a good than previously, there would be a surplus, price would fall, and according to Cantillon (81/61/29) "farmers always take care to use their land for the production of those things which they think will fetch the best price at market." Next, Cantillon (84/65/30) introduced a change in taste on the part of the estate owner to show that changes in taste "bring about the variation of demand which cause the variations of market prices" and a new market equilibrium. Cantillon noted that successful and prudent entrepreneurs can become rich, while failed and profligate entrepreneurs will go bankrupt. He also demonstrated that members of a profession naturally proportion themselves based on the demand for their product.

Cantillon thereby presented a model of the transition from the feudal-command economy to the market economy and demonstrated the workings of what we now call consumer sovereignty and the circular-flow model of the economy. Cantillon's model makes clear that the self interest of entrepreneurs can be relied upon to regulate the economy according to the demands of consumers. Now we return to the invisible hand in the *Wealth of Nations*. Smith employed the phrase invisible hand within an example about a general point he was making that the market could be relied upon to regulate the economy and that government intervention was not required or desired. In leading up to the invisible hand Smith (1976 [1776], p. 453) made his general point that: Every individual is continually exerting himself to find out the most advantageous employment for whatever capital he can command. It is his own advantage, indeed, and not that of the society, which he has in view. But the study of his own advantage naturally, or rather necessarily, leads him to prefer that employment which is most advantageous to the society. Smith then presented his example of the invisible hand where people prefer to keep their capital at home, when profits are equal, and that the more capital at home means more production and a larger population—points first made by Cantillon who defined wealth as the ability to consume and Smith followed Cantillon on this important point.

It is plausible that Smith derived the general notion of the invisible hand in the *Wealth of Nations* from his reading of Cantillon, especially the model economy of the isolated estate. All the components of Adam Smith's invisible hand—as it appears in *Wealth of Nations*—can be found in Cantillon's *Essai* including entrepreneurship and self-interest (Chapter 13), the role of prices, profit and loss, and consumer sovereignty, and even the relationships between capital, production and population.

The case for Cantillon as a plausible source for the analytical foundations of Smith's invisible hand rests on the facts: (1) Smith knew Cantillon's work and referred to Cantillon in the *Wealth of Nations*, (2) numerous scholars have identified telling similarities between Cantillon's and Smith's writings, and (3) Smith's two economic applications of the invisible hand appear right next to each other in Cantillon's *Essai*, in the chapters that follow the chapter that Smith referenced in the *Wealth of Nations*. Scholars have also suggested that the key to unlocking the mystery of the invisible hand is making sense of Smith's three disparate uses of the phrase. The fact that Cantillon provides a plausible key to those three uses of the phrase strongly reinforces the textual evidence. This finding supports the following conclusions:

1. The modern interpretations are wrong and generally represent nothing more than modern economists trying to write their own approach into Smith.

2. The traditional interpretations regarding self interest and the market system were generally correct.

3. There is nothing mystical about the invisible hand.

4. The invisible hand consists of real world processes that are fundamentally well- grounded in logic and experience.

Specifically, the evidence suggests that we can find the mechanism of Smith's invisible hand in Cantillon's *well disguised hand*. Here, the invisible hand begins with property ownership. Property rights are the keystone of economic analysis for Cantillon and a key concern for Smith. From here, production decisions are made that result in a natural distribution of income based on mutual interdependence of interests between property owners, labor, and entrepreneurs, all of which takes place in Cantillon's "circulation," or what we call the circular-flow economy. Natural self interest regulates and harmonizes this circulation with the market mechanisms of prices and profits. Prices regulate the distribution of goods among consumers, while profits and losses regulate the use of labor and resources among the production of goods. The system is brought full circle because the accumulation of profits and bankruptcy determines the future of property distribution.

While self interest, entrepreneurship, and consumer sovereignty are certainly important, the *"hand"* may have been invisible for Smith because it represents both nothing and everything. It is *"nothing"* in the sense that there is no direction, no director, in the economy. It is *"everything"* because everyone is involved, or could be involved, in determining the economic results. When faced with such complexity, Smith may have simply resorted to the imagery of the invisible hand as a shorthand way of capturing the complex workings of the market economy in a simple, but highly effective phrase to convey his meaning. The evidence presented here is sufficiently strong to make Cantillon the most plausible source for the economics of the invisible hand and hopefully the interpretation based on it will prevent the invisible hand from succumbing to the multiple-conception disorder that currently threatens its future scientific use. Cantillon continues to offer us new insights and the reader is encouraged to read Cantillon's *Essai* for a deeper understanding of the invisible hand, and to see what Cantillon has to contribute to the normative debate over the invisible hand.

In a modern capitalist economy the conditions of perfect competition does not exist and the equilibrium is greatly influenced by various other activities which includes massive emphasis on advertisement capable of molding consumer's taste. Under such conditions, market alone may not be the determining factor when it comes to the invisible hand.

However, the basic discussion on economic planning which is the core for all three types of economies assumes different dimensions in these economic systems. With invisible hand playing a role in influencing the market mechanism, it is primarily the impact of economic planning which is a vital factor in propelling the economy in the desired direction. However, it is important that it is finely balanced so as to nurture the spirit of entrepreneurship. Normally economic planning is used for the following:-

1. To create or plan an economic system in which the production units utilizes the resources i.e. raw material, machines, manpower and produces good which are distributed as per the defined channels by the institution for economic planning.

2. To create or plan an economic system in which specific allocations are designed for both the players' i.e. public sector and private sector. This kind of planning is seen normally in capitalist economy wherein, economic planning is done with specific core objectives rather an overall holistic view.

3. To create or plan an economic system in which resource allocation is based on different branches of economy keeping in view the development requirement of specific branch both from the point of requirement assessment – sector specific combined with overall view. This kind of planning is seen in Indian context wherein the resource allocation is based on the 5-year plan by the planning commission and also based on the prioritization assessment from various states.

4. To create or plan an economic system in which regulations are enforced primarily keeping in view of private sector. The

general objective matches with that of socialistic system with an aim to let the private sector survive in a controlled environment. Such systems are normally prevalent in socialistic countries which have realized the importance of individualized entrepreneurship and allow developing such pockets without disturbing the base economic fabric.

In the context of China the economic planning is a bit complex; as the companies or manufacturers do not remain the sole authority and these bodies are replaced or supplemented to great extent by a inter-industrial body which takes all important decisions including pricing etc. Taking the discussion further to developing economies, most of the economic planning is done like mixed economy with gradual shrinking of the role of public sectors depending on the maturity level reached or growth levels achieved together with international competitiveness. The two principal components of economic planning can be defined as:-

- The government plays an active role in raising capital both from domestic market and also from the foreign resources for projects which are big such as infrastructure, power projects, irrigation projects which could be implemented with the help of private sectors as well. Also, for other projects which may involve setting up of big industries with long gestation period in the context of poverty alleviation.

- The government plays an active role in raising capital through various economic policies such as taxation, interest rates, licensing, trade tariffs etc., with a dual objective of providing selective stimulus to private sectors as well as having regulatory controls in accordance with the overall social objectives.

W. Arthur Lewis in his book *'The Principles of Economic Planning'* differentiates the economic planning as directed which is seen in socialist economy and planning through market which is an accepted fact in both capitalist economy and also to a large extent in mixed economy. His approach regarding market forces is clear – powerful but invisible. He states that in the free market economy production is controlled by demand. Capitalists produce what they can sell and it is determined by the demand of people. Production for profit is therefore controlled by invisible hand. The same way, distribution of income is also controlled. Producers cannot charge what they like as the forces of competition would bring down the prices. The free market is thus a powerful instrument of social control, which directs production to the level of demand stimulates progress and eliminates excessive earnings. It is obvious that the invisible hand exists, and that its influence is beneficial. For every economic system devised for human beings there must be self-interest as a driving force. This does not make an economic system anti-social. The very nature of the economic system is the mechanism through which society needs what is most profitable to the individual; it transmutes individual self-interest into public good. Even if the economic system is completely planned from the centre it would need a mechanism by which it can be executed. The dispute could be whether the state control could do better either as an alternative or as a supplement.

"Planning" does not by itself have any very specific content. It can refer to a wide range of arrangements: to a largely laissez-faire society, in which individuals plan the use of their own resources and government's role is limited to preserving law and order, enforcing private contracts, and constructing public works; to the recent French policy of mixing exhortation, prediction, and cooperative guesstimating; to centralized control by a totalitarian government of the details of economic activity. Along still different dimension, Mark Spade (Nigel Balchin), in his wonderful book on *"How to Run a Bassoon Factory"* and *"Business for Pleasure"* defined the deference between a planned and an unplanned business. "In an unplanned business", he writes, "things just happen, i.e. they crop up. Life is full of unforeseen happenings and circumstances over which you have no control. On the other hand: In a planned business things still happen and crop up and so on, but you know exactly what would have been the state of affairs if they hadn't". (Source: Michael Friedman, Indian Economic Planning, 1963, www.ccsindia.org, Balchin Family Society)

In Indian context, planning has come to have a very specific meaning, one that is patterned largely on the Russian model. It has meant a sequence of five-year plans, each attempting to specify the allocation of investment expenditures and productive capacity to different lines of activity, with great emphasis being placed on the expansion of the so-called "heavy" or "basic" industries. A Planning Commission in New Delhi is charged with drawing up the plans and supervising their implementation. There is some decentralization to the separate states but the general idea is centralized governmental control of the allocation of physical resources. Though Indian economic planning is cut to the Russian pattern, it operates in a different economic and political structure. Agricultural land is almost entirely privately owned and operated; so are most trading and industrial enterprises. However, the government does own and operate many important industrial undertakings in a wide variety of fields-from railroads and air transport to steel mills, coal mines, fertilizer factories, machine tool plants, and retail establishments; Parliament has explicitly adopted "the socialist pattern of society" as the objective of economic and social policy; a long list of industries have been explicitly reserved to the "public sector" for future development, and the successive plans have allocated to public sector investment a wholly disproportionate part of total investment - in the third five-year plan, 60 percent although the public sector accounts at present for not much more than a tenth of total income generated. In addition, the government exercises important controls over the private sector: no substantial enterprise can be established without an "industrial" license from the government, existing firms must get government allocations of foreign exchange and also of domestic products in the public sector; and so on in endless variety. The difference between India and Russia in political structure is at the moment even sharper that in economic structure. The British left parliamentary democracy and respect for civil rights as a very real heritage to India. Though this heritage is being undermined and weakened, as of the moment it is still very strong indeed. There is tolerance of wide range of opinion, free discussion, open opposition by organized political parties, and judicial protection of individual civil rights-except for recent emergency actions under the emergency act.

The kind of centralized economic planning India has adopted can enable a strong authoritarian government to extract a high fraction of the aggregate output the people for governmental purposes - Russia is a prime current example and China, though we know much less about her, may be another; Egypt under the Pharaohs is a more ancient example. This is one way, and almost the only way, in which such a system can foster economic growth-if the resources extracted are indeed used for productive capital investment rather than for arms or governments. But this advantage - if advantage it be - of centralized economic planning, India is not able to obtain precisely because of the difference between its economic and political structure and those of Russia or China.

Economic planning through market mechanism may be an appropriate instrument for sustainable development in Western developed economies, however, with the emergence of BRIC economies this does not seem to be the perfect mechanism, nevertheless, for developing economies this was never a suitable option as the productive resources lack adequate mobility. Also, the response to incentives provided by state is often lack luster. This often results into sluggish growth in the agricultural sector, induces large scale migration from rural to urban areas and in general inhibits industrial growth as well. Developing economies primarily start as agrarian economies and the savings are not substantial. In view of this, there is no much option but to have an economic planning which is centrally oriented equipped with regulatory controls to initiate savings and investment.

In spite of the centralized economic planning, in developing countries the gestation period for the economy was quite big. The reason was not that free market mechanism was suppressed one of the prominent reason could be the strategic orientation. It is obvious that any developing economy would like to transform its economy to modern industrial economy as fast as possible by giving high priority to heavy capital goods industries with the objective of import substitution. However, it may be noticed that this created a vacuum from the agrarian economy which was overstretched leaving gaps. The strategy was indeed ambitious but was not appropriate to the problems of poverty, unemployment and even development of sustainable technology suitable to the masses. This also created a disturbance in the existing fabric and a lot of resources were to be spent in order to overcome the initial inertia of the basic economic structure. In other words, a strategy based on agricultural development led growth could have been appropriate from the point of sustainable economic growth with better prospects of bridging income inequality. This could have also tackled the problem of balance of payment which had risen due to high investment in capital intensive industries; nevertheless, this created an infrastructure which gave the required push to break the momentum even though the equilibrium could not be maintained. The lack of political will was also and also one of the worst problems which also creates hindrance in the proper strategic orientation to short term populist measure. As Albert Waterson has commented "The cardinal lesson that emerges from planning experience of developing countries is that the sustained commitment of a politically stable government is the *sine qua non* for development".

B.3 ECONOMIC CONTROLS

Economic controls play a very important role in shaping the direction of economic development both from the point of channelizing the resources as well as putting restrictions on areas which may not be the priority considering sectored development. Even though it is said that capitalist countries practice free market mechanism, however, this does not mean a *laissez faire*. The basic difference with a socialistic set up is ultimately the degree of control. Capitalist countries do have comprehensive regulatory controls to give a planned direction to the economy. These are long range policy measures and are periodically modified to suit the country's economic condition and requirement, thereof. It is now widely recognized that a free market economy is not capable of ensuring equilibrium of aggregate demand and aggregate supply. Keyes had stated that a conscious policy is required to achieve this objective. In the present economic scenario of turmoil, the governments normally do not integrate these economic controls or regulatory instruments in the long term policy; however, these are introduced periodically on a temporary basis with a clear objective to realize certain economic results such as inflation, interest, savings etc.

In spite of the fact that due to most of the mixed economies have undergone a lot of liberalization in opening up the frontiers for foreign direct investment, however, these economic controls or regulations are part of either developed or developing economies and these are instrumental in influencing the consumer behavior, traders, exporters, importers. These consist of various fiscal instruments some of which are saving schemes, rationing, price control, subsidy, selective licensing, foreign exchange control, export-import regulation.

Two basic schools of thought have emerged on regulatory policy, namely, positive theories of regulation and normative theories of regulation. Positive theories of regulation include theories of market power, interest group theories that describe stakeholders' interests in regulation, and theories of government opportunism that describe why restrictions on government discretion may be necessary for the sector to provide efficient services for customers.

Normative theories of regulation generally conclude that regulators should encourage competition where feasible, minimize the costs of information asymmetries by obtaining information and providing operators with incentives to improve their performance, provide for price structures that improve economic efficiency, and establish regulatory processes that provide for regulation under the law and independence, transparency, predictability, legitimacy, and credibility for the regulatory system.

The economic controls or regulation can be categorized into two types:

1. Economic Policies
2. Physical Controls

Economic policies such as both fiscal and monetary are indirect means of control whereas price control, rationing, export-import regulations, licensing etc., directly affect the economic activities. These direct controls or physical controls operate outside the market for example in the case of rationing the market mechanism is virtually taken over by the administratively controlled distribution system. Therefore, physical controls are more restrictive for example industrial licensing. On the same hand, foreign exchange regulation is also a direct control to restrict the demand of foreign goods. Indirect controls which are implemented through economic policies are restrictive in nature as these operate through manipulation of prices. Physical controls could be discriminatory in nature as well due to the fact that there application and execution involves bureaucracy which could take decisions based on discretions, whereas indirect controls such as imposition of taxes or subsidies are not in the position to be selective which is a necessary element for direct controls.

Some economists, such as Nobel Laureate Milton Friedman, have sought substantially to limit economic regulation. They argue that government should limit its involvement in economies to protect individual rights (life, liberty, property) rather than diminishing individual autonomy and responsibility for the sake of remedying any sort of putative "market failure." They tend to regard the notion of market failure as a misguided contrivance wrongly used to justify coercive government action to further various political agendas. These economists believe that government intervention creates more problems than it is supposed to solve -- as well-meaning as some of these interventions may be -- chiefly because government officers are incapable of accurate economic planning, lacking any reliable mechanism to gather, integrate, or honestly evaluate the vast amounts of information that guide the invisible hand of the free market.

Notable economists, such as Ludwig von Mises, see regulations as problematic not only because they disrupt market processes, but also because they tend only to bring about more regulations. According to Austrian theory, every regulation has some consequences besides those originally intended when the regulation was implemented. If the un-intended consequences are undesirable to those with the power to regulate, there exist two alternative possibilities: do away with the existing regulation, or keep the existing regulation and institute a new one as well to treat the unintended consequence of the old one. In practice, regulators very seldom even consider that the problems they detect may actually be the consequence of prior regulation, so the second option is preferred far more often than the first. The new regulation, however, has unintended consequences of its own that bring about this cycle anew. If unchecked, the result over time is regulation so extensive as to amount to a state run economy.

Laissez-faire advocates do not oppose monopolies unless they maintain their existence through coercion to prevent competition, and often assert that monopolies have historically developed only *because* of government intervention rather than due to a lack of intervention. Specifically, every regulation has some associated cost of compliance. If these costs increase the total cost of operation enough to make new entry into a market prohibitive but allow existing firms to continue to generate a profit, the regulation effectively monopolizes the industry. When existing firms are able to lobby for regulation, this effectively becomes an opportunity to do away with competitive rivals.

Another argument against regulation is that laws against insider trading that reduce market efficiency and transparency. If a firm is "cooking the books," insiders, without restraint on insider trading, will take short positions and lower the share price to a level that aggregates both inside and outside knowledge. If insiders are restrained from using their knowledge to make transactions, the share price will not reflect their insider information. If outside investors buy shares, their purchase price would not reflect the inside knowledge and will be high by comparison to the price after the inside information becomes public. The result is an avoidable loss to the outside investor or buyer. If insiders were allowed to trade freely, the price would never get as high to begin with, and outsiders would lose less money.

Another problem created by economic regulations is government-enforced price ceiling that cause shortages. If the public is willing to buy Q units of some good at price P, and the sellers of that good are willing to sell Q units at P, then in the absence of regulation, the market for that good will clear. That is, everyone who wants to buy or sell at price P will be able to do so. If a regulation imposes a price ceiling below P, sellers will be willing to sell some lesser quantity, Q - a, and buyers will be willing to buy some greater quantity, Q + b, at the new price. In addition to a shortage of a + b units, there is also the matter of deciding who should get the units offered, since at the regulation price, demand will exceed supply. Such situations typically generate a variety of means of avoiding the effects of the market imbalance, in effect clearing the market, including 'black markets'.

However, the fact still remains that both developed and developing economies cannot depend solely on the public sector enterprises as an instruments of growth and base economic planning on them. Also, a large number of private sector enterprises do co-exist which try maximize profit. Therefore, in order to keep the balance, the situation necessitates a logical presence of a control system which is capable to drive the business enterprises in a predictive manner. Thomas Wilson in his book *"Planning and Growth"* remarked "Planning and physical controls have become so closely associated as to be regarded as almost inseparable".

The U.S and the world economy like everything else have its ups and downs. The government plays a crucial role in deciding how the economy will set over time. John Maynard Keynes felt that if either inflation or unemployment got out of hand, the government could adjust the business cycle to balance the economy. Keynes was more geared toward the bigger picture and focused on macroeconomics. His work led to the government and many economists believing that they had control over the economy. This led to economic regulations, which affected everyone from companies to the consumers. Through the history of our economy the government has made changes by enforcing many regulations to have full control of the growth and power of the economy and to protect the consumers. Regulations can be divided into two different categories, Economic regulations and Social regulations. An Economic regulation covers sectors of the economy such as electricity, natural gas, communications, transportation, aviation, agriculture, and banking. These regulations usually include barriers to entry and exit, licensing and tariff laws, and the control of prices and wages.

Examples of Social regulations from USA would include the food and drug administration and the Equal Opportunity Commission, which protects employers. Regulations were starting to appear around the time of the New Deal (this was a series of economic programs passed by US Congress during the first term of Roosevelt, from 1933 to his re-election in 1936. The programs were responses to the Great Depression, and was focused on the "3 Rs" i.e. relief, recovery and reform). The government's main purpose for enforcing these regulations was because competition among corporations was starting to fail. At the time regulations seemed to have been helping. The economy continued to grow and was doing better than it ever had been. The system was able to control price and entry competition in the nation's key industries. From 1930 through the sixties the economy was booming. There were low inflation rates that averaged 3.8 percent over that period of thirty years. The interest rates were also low at two percent over a period of three months. Bank failures were virtually non-existent, oil and gas supplies were readily available.

The reason for the downturn in the economy was due to the control, which the government had over these corporations by enforcing these regulations. The problem with these regulations was that it caused higher than necessary costs, distorted the patterns of supply and demand. The rate of return regulations was creating inefficient capital allocations. These problems brought on what is called as deregulation. Deregulation is when the government drops many of the regulations that were put on the corporations. The period of deregulating in the late 70's is stated by many economists to be very crucial in the affect of our economy today. Major corporations such as American Airlines, AT&T, El Paso Natural Gas, and Bank America went through a process of deregulation in the late 70's and into the 80's. Even though recent acts of deregulations have occurred and have been proven to be very successful, there are also benefits to regulations along with the disadvantages. Social regulations are most beneficial to the consumer, because it protects them from their employers. Without these regulations corporations might take short cuts to save on money, while in turn they are harming their consumers without us having any knowledge of it. It also protects the employees from our employers who might have been trying to take advantage of employees, or tries to refuse them of the benefits they deserve.

One of the major problems with the regulations is the burden that it puts on small companies. Many of the large corporations have the funds to follow these regulations, while small and medium sized companies do not. A small company creates two out of every three new jobs in America. This means that they play as important of a role in the economy as do the larger companies. According to the Small Business Administration (SBA) firms with fewer than 500 employees spend approximately $5,000 per employee on regulatory costs. While firms with more than 500 employees, spend only $3,500 per employee. The biggest hit is for firms with fifty to a hundred people, they pay seven to ten times higher than larger firms. When a business puts all of its resources to regulatory laws, it is using the resources less efficiently; it is forced to operate in a less productive, in a more costly way. Eventually this leads to the employees, which will deny them a higher standard of living. Many firms cannot afford to give their employees as much benefits, as they should receive due to the high regulatory costs.

Many expert economists are against over enforcing too many regulations. They feel that it cuts down the competition in the economy. Deregulation has been very popular among economists over the last 25 years. They feel that deregulating the four major industries in the late 70's were one of the best decisions for US economy. Robert Crandall and Jerry Ellig did research on how the airline, trucking, electricity sector, natural gas, and telecommunications were affected after they went through deregulations. They found many benefits that not only helped the company, but also the consumer. During the first two years after deregulation the average prices fell from 4 to 15 percent, and after ten years prices went down twenty five percent. In some cases prices even fell to half of what they used to be. They also found out the quality of service improved. Corporations were able to give their customers more options to choose from and better reliable service.

"More freedom equals more benefits" says Ellig about deregulation. Rates fell faster in parts of the market where regulators permit greater customer choice. Giving customers choices will allow for a more competitive market and in turn more benefits for everyone. From past experience we know that regulations can help the economy, but at the same time over regulation can cause the economy to hit a brick wall. Too many regulations can cause higher prices for consumers, corporations, and even the government. It also creates barriers to entry and exit, which will allow there to be less competition in the economy. Deregulating also has been proven to be a successful method of balancing the economy. It has worked for many of the major industries. As long as the regulations are kept to a minimum and are useful in protecting the consumer, there should be no problems.

For better understanding some of the direct or physical controls are as under:

- **Price Control and Rationing**: In this system of control the maximum price of a commodity is fixed with an objective to make the commodity available to the masses, so the prices are fixed below the market equilibrium price. Under this situation the demand quantity will increase and the supplied quantity will gradually decrease. This will eventually give rise to the shortage of commodity. The system of price control with or without rationing often gives rise to black market and as the administrative machinery is not expected to be strong enough to deal with this issue, the situation gives rise to a parallel economy.

- **Industrial Licensing Control**: In this system the government takes extensive powers to regulate industries in the private sector with the objectives to prevent monopoly, balanced regional development, and protection of small entrepreneurs. This ultimately weakens the private sector and imbibes more of a bureaucratic set-up rather than entrepreneurship set-up with sustainable growth.

- **Foreign Trade Control**: In this system the developing countries try to regulate their foreign trade to overcome balance of payment situation and also to protect their domestic industries. However, during the last few decades some international organizations such as GATT, WTO, and IMF have made serious attempts to dissuade countries using restrictive foreign trade practices and the members of WTO have to abandon quantities trade restrictions. However, as trade barriers serve in the interest of the country, these have not been dismantled completely.

- **Foreign Exchange Control:** In this system the market forces are disregarded and are replaced by the decisions of the government i.e. imports and other transactions involving payments liabilities are determined not only by the international price comparison, but also considering the needs of the country related to balance of payment. This system of exchange control could be rigorous, mild or partial depending on the economic situation. In case of rigorous control, all foreign receipts are to be submitted to the exchange control authorities. If a free market economy has to resort to exchange control system that means the economy faces certain limitations. The developing countries normally prefer deflation as this does not adversely affect their effort by forcing a decline. However, compared with deflation, devaluation is a better corrective measure as this does not affect the economy in terms of decline in income or employment levels. W. Arthur Lewis in his book *"Development Planning"* rejects this method by stating "Some countries have had exchange control for so long that they have persuaded themselves that it is inevitable accompaniment of economic development. This is not so; most countries have developed without exchange control; it is rather a sign of failure to allocate sufficient resources to maintenance of foreign balances, whether by paying more attention to exports or by investing more in import substitution. Countries which have made adequate plans for exportation and import substitution do not need exchange control."

Although, physical controls have become an essential instrument in all developing countries, nevertheless these may not be always the best possible solution. The reason could be that physical controls have their own limitations and require efficient administrative machinery which may not exist in most of the countries. Moreover, these physical controls normally benefit particular set of people which have vested interest in continuation of these controls. According to the study conducted by the United Nations Economic Commission for Asia and Far East – "The small business units are particularly hindered and discouraged by the multiplicity of controls, for their economic power is so weak that they can hardly deal effectively with the control authorities and cope with the delays and red-tape involved. On the other hand, existing large enterprises enjoy a comfortable semi-monopoly position under the protection of controls and make easy profits through access to the scarce factors made available to them cheaply. There is hardly any incentive for them to improve productivity or operating efficiency".

B.4 ECONOMIC IMBALANCE & FLUCTUATIONS

The industrial revolution was associated with and accompanied by political and cultural dominance of Western Europe, and especially Britain, over the rest of the world. This is sometimes referred to as Imperialism. Britain and other European countries and later, The United States and Japan, acquired colonies by having irresistible military technology. The economic effect tended to be the creation of an economic value which allowed manufactured goods to be exported from the developed countries and raw materials to be imported from the colonies but did not allow a reverse flow.

India, for example, was expected to export raw cotton and receive manufactured cotton goods from Britain. But the indigenous cotton cloth industry was allowed to atrophy. Statistics show that Indian industry actually declined during the 18th and 19th centuries. Although formal colonialism has mostly ended, the economic imbalance created then has intensified as the industrial world has increased its rate of technological change.

Most of the former colonized countries now have huge debts to banks and governments in industrial countries which they can never hope to repay. The interest on these debts exceeds the value of exports and reduces the standard of living of people in these countries. This means many starve and health services are inadequate. The result is a net flow of capital from the poorer countries to richer countries. Tariff laws and other trade restrictions continue to prevent the even spread of industry in every region. Economic development can only occur by the reinvestment of profits; but the poorest countries are making no profits to invest. There is the also the phenomenon of Mafia, corruption and feudalism which skim off any profits and prevent investment.

A similar imbalance exists within the so-called richer countries. The difference between rich and poor in Britain and the United States has increased in recent years. This may get worse as industrial jobs migrate to the newly industrializing countries. Some present ideologies prevent measures being taken to reduce inequality. These include the doctrine that "helping people makes them dependent", expressed in the United States by Any Rand in *"Atlas Shrugged"*. This is often used as an excuse to do nothing, but the real motivation is a fear by the moneyed of losing their wealth - radical selfishness. The same policies caused the mass deaths of the famine in Ireland in the 1840s. The economic depression only now (2008) being felt in the industrialized countries has been felt in some of the rest of the world since the 1970s.

Some political thinkers believe a happy society under good government should avoid great differences of wealth in order to produce social harmony, including street safety and lack of crime. In ancient Athens the difference between the richest citizen and the poorest was said to be two and a half times. In modern America the difference is 200 times. In the world as a whole the difference is much greater.

Some Muslims point out that the practice of Islamic Banking, which outlaws the charging of pure interest, would have the effect of preventing people growing rich through compound interest (without work). But it is not clear whether this could be applied to a modern economy. An Islamic Bank takes shares in an enterprise and is paid by the profits of the enterprise, thus receives less in bad times - it is the equivalent of a Mutual Fund; a conventional bank demands the same in bad times as in good.

Investors rather than lenders have an interest in the conduct of the business. The joint stock company raising its money from share issues may be healthier than financiers who borrow from banks or by issuing Junk Bonds or even ordinary bonds. Even better might be the company where employees own an important share of the capital. The Islamic principle of Zakat, an annual tax of 2.5% of individual wealth to be distributed to the poor, may also be a useful model. The Judeo-Christian tradition, to which western politicians sometimes pay lip service, also had limitations on interest payments and, in the case of the biblical Jews, the periodic wiping out of debts to the poor. In the present state of international and corporate indebtedness these principles may seem more sensible than the conventional arrangements. There is also the Christian principle of tithing - paying one tenth of income to charity, church or the poor. Some of the poor, of course, have put matters in their own hands by manufacturing and selling addictive substances such as cocaine and heroin which tend to cause the social collapse of the industrial countries and a large flow of funds.

There is a strong possibility that the poor will not wait for assistance which never comes but will move into the rich countries. Thus immigration from the "South" is already occurring. Immigration laws, it can be confidently assumed, will not prevent them. Nor even neo-fascist violence. It is therefore in the interest of the richer countries to bring about greater equality, as it is not possible to maintain permanently islands of great wealth in a sea of misery - the present situation.

Some economists propose a worldwide investment in new energy systems to combat the environmental crisis as the equivalent of Roosevelt's New Deal on a global scale. However, in the world as whole western countries have abandoned the policy of helping the poorer countries but instead enforce Structural Adjustment Programs through the IMF (cut social services such as health and education, repay debts at all costs) so that third world countries actually pay more to the west than they receive. If free trade equalizes world poverty as the North American Free Trade Area seems likely to be, there will be an incentive to rethink the nature of the human economy.

Like world economy is marked by imbalances, similarly any business activity in general is also marked by imbalance or fluctuations. If we are looking for periods of economic expansion (growth of real GDP) and economic declines (decrease in real GDP), then we have such a phenomenon. But if we are looking for such increases and decrease that occur at fixed intervals, and are of fixed amplitude, then there is no business cycle. Economic activity has its ups and downs, but there is no historical record that would suggest a regularly recurring cycle and no precise repeating causes.

In modern times, the economic theory has moved towards the study of economic fluctuation rather than a business cycle. Milton Friedman clearly states that the term cycle is a misnomer because the fluctuation is non-cyclical in nature. From his point of view, business declines are mostly a monetary phenomenon. For some economists, economic fluctuations can be modeled as a shock to the system.

Fluctuations in economy can occur for a number of reasons that economic analysts attribute to a number of reasons. Some analysts believe that fluctuations in the economy are caused by uneven government policies whereas others believe that these same government policies are responsible for balancing fluctuations in the economy that are caused by the inherent nature of the market. Regardless of the reason, fluctuations in the economy are now a natural part of life. Political responses to these economic fluctuations are also now a part of modern life and it is possible for consumers to take advantage of both the economic conditions and their political responses to purchase a home for a good price. The explanation of fluctuations in the economic activity is one of the primary concerns of macro-economics. The most popular framework which has been used to explain such fluctuations is Keynesian economics. From the Keynesian point of view, business cycles reflect the possibility that economy may reach short term equilibrium at levels below or above full employment. If the economy is operating with less than full employment i.e. with high unemployment, Keynesian theory states that monetary policy and fiscal policy can have a positive role to play in moderating the fluctuations of economics.

There are two main extremes to fluctuations in economy – recession and expansion. Economic recession refers to a period of time in which the public has less faith in the economy than in normal times. This is because economic recession is marked by general trends of decreases in overall output as well as employment. Economic recessions, at their worst, can result in conditions similar to the Great Depression of the 1930s.

Conversely, economic expansion refers to a period of time in which the public has great faith in the economy compared to normal times. It is a time where employment levels are high and so are overall output rates. Conversely, unemployment levels are low and prices of products will rise due to the positive economic conditions. These economic fluctuations are difficult to predict and do not lost for a specific amount of time. There can be numerous factors that cause these changes in the economic conditions, which can be purely economic, political, social, technological, and whatnot.

From a consumer's perspective, economic recession and expansion have a number of advantages and benefits. During an economic expansion, employment rates are increasingly high and consumers are increasingly willing to take chances with their finances. Consequently, times of economic expansion are usually periods where prospective consumers feel confident that the positive economic conditions will continue thus allowing them to make the considerable investment needed to fulfill the down payment and closing costs component of buying a commodity.

As economic expansion is a time marked by high levels of commodity purchases due to increased amount of potential consumers, the market conditions in times of economic expansion, has much more prospective consumers than they do normally. Consequently, asking prices for consumables will increase due to the rising market value of consumables. Additionally, interest rates tend to be higher in times of economic expansion due to reactions by lenders to changes in the nation's interest rates.

During a period of economic downturn or recession, there is a general trend of rising unemployment rates and decreasing overall output. Additionally, the labour rates are reduced and prices may continue to rise, although they do so at a much slower rate than during a period of economic expansion. Although this may seem like a poor time to purchase a commodity including real estate, it actually may be in the best financial interest to buy a commodity from the point of investment during a recession.

Taking the examples from a real estate we observe that an economic recession often changes the local real estate market conditions. Considering, the fiscal conservatism that people employ during periods of economic recession, these economic conditions produces few demands in the real estate market. Additionally, the increasing levels of unemployment levels caused by a recession means that many homeowners are now put into a position where they are forced to sell their commodities including real estate to accommodate changing job demands. Consequently, an economic recession also produces a large number of commodities on sale.

According to Keynesian economics, fluctuations in aggregate demand cause the economy to come to short run equilibrium at levels that are different from the full employment rate of output. These fluctuations express themselves as the observed business cycles. These can be described as Endogenous (Internal) Theories – Business Cycles caused by events or circumstances taking place within the economy which explains (Joseph Schumpeter in The Theory of Economic Development) that New Product Introductions begin slowly with market resistance. However, as resistance breaks down and other producers sense that economic profits are being made, they begin to enter the market with increased investment and production and employment increase.

Eventually the market becomes saturated and sales decline. Profits decline, inventories increase, production is curtailed, unemployment increases, economic downturn results. When a new innovation takes hold, the process begins again. If business is optimistic about future sales and profits, they invest, produce more, increase employment and promote an expansion of economic activity. When it is felt that that things cannot continue to get better, signs of pessimism and reduced investment can be seen with production, manpower reductions (employment) and an overall reduction in economic activity.

On the contrary, during periods of economic expansion, business owners are caught short of inventory, so they increase factory orders, thus causing factories to increase production, increase employment, and thus spending. Eventually inventories become plentiful and business owners cut back on restocking, reducing factory orders and inducing factory owners to cut production schedules, control costs (including employment). Spending declines and recession sets in until inventories are reduced to uncomfortably low levels. Under Consumption/ Over Production Theory states that an economy occasionally produces more goods and services than consumers want or can afford. A recession occurs until production and prices fall to the point that consumer demand again exceeds the available supply. At that point, recovery begins.

Exogenous (External) Theories -- Factors external to the economy are the causes of the business cycle which includes the War Theory. It states - a production surge caused by the preparation for and war itself; causes production increases, employment increases and spending increases. The decline in production at the end of the war reduces production, results in unemployment and reduced spending.

The "Sunspot Theory" by W. Stanley Jevons tries to explain that storms on the sun caused periodic crop failures. Since most of the world's economies were agriculturally dominated in the 1800's, crop failures caused declines in economic activity. Subsequent improvements in harvest caused economic expansions until sunspot activity occurred again. Robert E. Slavin stated "Perhaps no single explanation, whether endogenous or exogenous, can explain each of the cycles we have experienced. The best we can do is to treat each cycle separately, seeking causes that apply."

Although, it is evident that no business cycle could be similar to another, nevertheless these can be divided into broad phases. According to Arthur F. Burns and Wesley C. Mitchell in Measuring Business Cycles, the four distinct related phases of business cycles are as follows:

1. Revival
2. Expansion
3. Recession
4. Contraction

Although, Joseph Schumpeter does not completely agree to the concept put forth by Burns and Mitchell. According to him the peaks and trough as shown in the diagram below, cannot be treated as a critical mark-off points. His analysis differs from Burns and Mitchell in the sense that these critical mark-off points are "neighborhoods of equilibrium" -

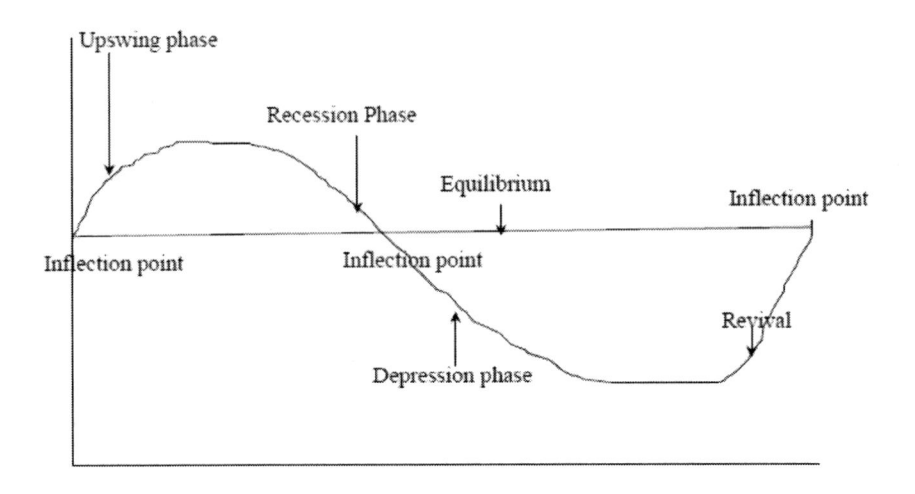

Diagram: Business cycle curve showing Upswing phase, Recession Phase, Equilibrium, Inflection points, Depression phase, and Revival.

The upswing in economy starts from an equilibrium position under the stimulus of market forces or speculation that create expectations of profits which acts as a catalyst to the entrepreneurs to either increase investment or widen the scope of activity. This results in an overall demand for raw material, employment etc. A noticeable feature in this upswing or prosperity phase is increased supply of money and consequently expansion of bank deposits. However, this has a consequential effect on the prices increase due to increase in money supply. It may be realized that in the absence of any total amount of available money, the velocity of money will increase and it would be normally proportional to the increase in the output. This means that consumer price index or inflation is most likely to see an increase under such circumstances. It is observed that prices under such situations do not increase uniformly. Per normal trend, the wholesale prices increase more that the retail prices. Changes occur not only in the relative prices of the goods but also various elements in the cost structure, however, interestingly, long term interest, salaries, taxes etc., do not follow the same trend or the pace. The prevailing situation builds up the stock prices and stock exchange securities. The share prices increase considering conducive economic conditions and banks respond by expanding their credit facilities catapulting the velocity of money. The investments increase during the prosperity phase particularly in capital goods, expansions followed by increase in wages as well. As the demand grows, the manufacturers stock their produce in the prospect of further improvement in demands. This gradually overheats the economy as this high pitch rate cannot be sustained forever. Therefore, the expansion itself gradually paves way for the beginning of recession. When the increase in cost relative to the price narrow down the margins, the expansion process gets slackened. The problem of rising prices both due to inflation and other investment related activities becomes difficult to resolve. The reason is this is met with resistance from the consumers and the diminishing elasticity of the investor's credit.

The contraction phase of business cycle is brought about by a fall in the marginal efficiency of capital relatively to the prevailing rate of interest. When all the remunerative channels for investment are fully utilized, then the scope for further investment declines. Due to excessive demand for loan able funds, the reserves of the banks get depleted. The market rate of interest goes up. The higher rate of interest induces people to save more money. The higher liquidity preference or the increasing demand for money to hold reduces the demand for consumer goods. When the business prospects appear bleak, the investors are then not prepared to renew or extend their capital equipment. Due to excess of savings over investment, the income and employment declines. It may be recalled here that J.M. Keynes has used three psychological propensities in formulating his theory of business cycle. They are: Propensity to consume, propensity to save and the marginal efficiency of capital. He also introduced the concept of multiplier in order to show the effect to increase in total income due to increase in investment. Keynes is of the view that upswing of business cycle is caused by a rise in the marginal efficiency of capital.

When the Great Depression hit worldwide, it fell on economists to explain it and devise a cure. Most economists were convinced that something as large and intractable as the Great Depression must have complicated causes. Keynes, however, came up with an explanation of economic slumps that was surprisingly simple. In fact, when he shared his theory and proposed solution with Franklin Roosevelt, the President is said to have dismissed them with the words: "Too easy." Keynes explanations of slumps ran something like this: in a normal economy, there is a high level of employment, and everyone is spending their earnings as usual. This means there is a circular flow of money in the economy, as my spending becomes part of your earnings, and your spending becomes part of my earnings. But suppose something happens to shake consumer confidence in the economy. (There are many possible reasons for this, which we'll cover in a moment.) Worried consumers may then try to weather the coming economic hardship by saving their money. But because my spending is part of your earnings, my decision to hoard money makes things worse for you. And you, responding to your own difficult times, will start hoarding money too, making things even worse for me. So there's a vicious circle at work here: people hoard money in difficult times, but times become more difficult when people hoard money.

The cure for this, Keynes said, was for the central bank to expand the money supply. By putting more bills in people's hands, consumer confidence would return, people would spend, and the circular flow of money would be re established. Keynes believed that depressions were recessions that had fallen into a "liquidity trap." A liquidity trap is when people hoard money and refuse to spend no matter how much the government tries to expand the money supply. In these dire circumstances, Keynes believed that the government should do what individuals would not, namely, spend. In his memorable phrase, Keynes called this "priming the pump" of the economy, a final government effort to reestablish the circular flow of money.

As mentioned above, Keynes' advice on ending the Great Depression was rejected. President Roosevelt tried countless other approaches, all of which failed. Almost all economists agree that World War II cured the Great Depression; Keynesians believe this was so because the U.S. finally began massive public spending on defense. This is a large part of the reason why "wars are good for the economy." Although no one knows the full secret to economic growth, wars are an economic boon in part because governments always resort to Keynesian spending during them. Of course, such spending need not be directed only towards war -- social programs are much more preferable. In seven short years, under massive Keynesian spending, the U.S. went from the greatest depression it has ever known to the greatest economic boom it has ever known. The success of Keynesian economics was so resounding that almost all capitalist governments around the world adopted its policies. And the result seems to be nothing less than the extinction of the economic depression! Before World War II, eight U.S. recessions worsened into depressions (as happened in 1807, 1837, 1873, 1882, 1893, 1920, 1933, and 1937). Since World War II, under Keynesian policies, there have been ten recessions (1945-46, 1949, 1954, 1956, 1960-61, 1970, 1973-75, 1980-83, 1990-92, 2008-09), and not one has turned into a depression. The success of Keynesian economics was such that even Richard Nixon once declared, "We are all Keynesians now."

Basically, Keynes explained the turning point from expansion to recession by a collapse in the marginal efficiency of capital. Similarly, recession ultimately merges into depression which is a phase of relatively low economic activity. Recession is often considered as a synonym to depression, in emotional terms. It is a fact that recession is decelerated phase where everything goes downhill and everything goes berserk. To reconcile, recession means decline, downturn, collapse or depression, in common understanding. In short, recession is decline in a country's GDP growth for two or more consecutive quarters of a year and is a phase where profits, employment, investment spending and household incomes experience a regular fall-down. In a more precise terminology, recession is negative growth for two consecutive quarters. It signifies a fall in real GDP, lower National Output. Recession has negative impact on economic growth and makes unconstructive impact on the nation. The impact of recession is often characterized by the following factors – impulsive rise in unemployment, rise in government borrowing, sharp decline in stock markets and share prices, lower inflation and fall in investment.

In recessionary phase, the government is always under pressure to lower tax revenues because of lower income tax and lower corporation tax revenues. Government is expected to spend higher for un-employment benefits and so it leads to higher borrowing to make both ends meet. Recession becomes a pessimistic phase for the ruling government as it is burdened up with extra weight of borrowing. Recession makes a resounding impact on share markets and so it affects share prices to great extent. It is because recession leads to lower profitability and lower dividends. It makes share market look shaky and shareholders often face disappointment. Many a time shares fall sharp as an anticipation of predictable financial disaster, arising out from fear of recession. It is not always that share prices fall as there can be any other reasons for their decline.

A recession will reduce the appropriate demand and correspondingly will enforce pressure on the prices and will rage price-war in the market. To retain consumers, the price –wars may lead to decline in rates and so it might result into lower inflation rates. Due to lower spending capacity, the lowered prices may sound impossible for many but the fact is that recession leads out cut throat competition and that sometimes affects the quality of the product. Due to recession phase, the investor always feels shaky to invest as the fear of acquiring substantial liabilities increases manifold. The investment in the market becomes more unstable and it affects the economic growth. It ultimately results to the lowering of economic growth and simultaneously other related aspects of it.

When an economy moves from recession to depression, there is a noticeable drop in production of goods and employment rates. Although, retail business is little affected, the most affected industries are those engaged in manufacturing, construction, real estate etc. During depression the general price level falls despite of reduction in output of goods and services. During the depression phase distortions also appear in cost-price relations. The reason is that costs do not fall proportionately to prices. As the contraction proceeds, the purchasing power of the people steadily falls which causes further decline in the prices. The depression phase is marked by an overall decline in economic activity. Normally, the trough of depression is short-lived; however, sometimes it may linger for a longer period such as in the case of Great Depression during the 1930's.

The economic recovery starts gradually with the restoration of normal cost – price relation. The process of initiation is not that fast or abrupt as seen in the case of recession. The turning point is when the prices stop to fall. This is triggered with the fall of inventories and the supply and demand situation starts to reach equilibrium. This is the starting point for the producers to start activities related to production. In comparison to consumables; durable goods are less in demand during recessionary or during depression. With the start of manufacturing activities, marginal efficiency of capital starts to recover. This could trigger essential investments, if necessary.

However, there has been a cost which was incurred during the recessionary phase when the goods were not moving and capital remained unutilized. With the correction of cost-price relationship, the normal price relation starts to get normalized. However, as there is a time lag between fresh investments, there is a likelihood that interests rates may fall in order to attract more takers. The stock market and securities start to show an upward trend. The increase in stock market prices provides impetus to construction and other capital intensive activities. Gradually, the cumulative process builds up supplemented with government spending and phase of recession and depression again starts to move in a positive direction with likelihood to repeat itself.

This gives rise to two simple questions to ponder – are recessions avoidable & how to survive them ? Many people look to the recession as an inevitable consequence of several years of decadent borrowing. It's like if you drink too much you 'deserve' a hangover. So the recession is often seen as a kind of a karmic punishment for our extravagance, asset bubble and irrationality. Yet, the picture is not quite as straightforward. Both Japan and Germany are in recession. Yet, they have had no extravagant boom only a mountain of personal saving, large current account surpluses and in Germany's case a government with a balanced budget. Although, the cause of this current crisis can be traced back to irresponsible lending in the US mortgage sector, it seems that high levels of saving are no protection against recessions.

Most economists argue there is a natural trade cycle, which is hard to break. Growth is not constant but comes in peaks and troughs. In this case, recessions are hard to avoid. All we can do is minimize the downturn and prevent an excessive boom. If we get an inflationary boom, a recession becomes an almost necessity. For example, the Lawson boom of the 1980s saw economic growth in the UK double our long run trend rate. But, this growth of 5% caused inflation and in reducing inflation we had a sharp slowdown. Another school of thought is that if we avoid an inflationary bubble, then we can avoid recessions. This is why Central Banks are told to target low inflation. If inflation stays low, we can avoid the boom and bust economic cycle. Up until 2006, there was a feeling that Central Banks had brought an end to the trade cycle. Up until this year, the UK avoided a recession for 17 years.

The feature of the last bubble is that it took a different form. Core inflation remained low. But, there was an asset bubble - house prices rose creating a positive wealth effect, high levels of borrowing, low savings and consumers living beyond their means. Therefore, when the asset bubble burst, it caused a strong downward movement on consumer spending. Therefore, the low inflation masked the underlying disequilibrium in the economy. Maybe if the asset bubble and mortgage defaults had been avoided and the 2008 recession would have been avoidable.

The experience of Germany, Japan, China and other countries who rely on exports is that they become reliant on the global trade cycle. As the main economies go into recession, it inevitably spreads the recession to these countries. Even if you follow prudent policies and seek to reduce debt, a global recession will push your economy into recession as well. Maybe their mistake is to put too much emphasis on relying on exports.

The main cause of this recession is the global credit crunch, which has been difficult for any country to avoid. It is sometimes argued recessions are necessary (even beneficial) to create greater efficiency and get rid of inefficient firms. This is a debatable item. Recessions are not necessary to create increased efficiency. Sometimes, recessions can cause good, efficient firms to go under due to cash flow problems. One contributing factor behind the current recession was the oil price shock in early 2008. It led to interest rate being kept high. There is little governments can do to alter the cost push shock of rising oil prices. It is hard to deal with supply side shocks of this nature.

It is said that "A recession is when other people lose their jobs. A depression is when you lose your job." With a major downturn in the US, the average consumer may be worrying how a recession might affect them and what they can do to insure against the negative effects of recession. These are some of the effects of recessions and how to deal with them. In a recession banks are less willing to lend. This is particularly a problem at the moment, because of the concurrent credit crises which is reducing the availability of loans. Therefore, unnecessary debts should be avoided. On the positive side, in a recession interest rates are likely to be lower, meaning lower interest payments for mortgage holders.

One of the most popular definitions of recessions is that they are periods when real gross national product (GNP) has declined for at least two consecutive quarters. In 1990, real GNP declined between the third and fourth quarters and again between the fourth quarter of 1990 and the first quarter of 1991. Hence, there is general agreement that a recession did occur.

Although the definition worked quite well in this instance, there are several problems with it. One is that it does not provide monthly dates of when recessions began or ended. For this purpose the National Bureau of Economic Research (NBER), whose chronology of recessions is widely accepted, uses monthly measures of production, employment, sales, and income, all expressed in real terms (after allowing for inflation). Another problem with the two-consecutive-quarters definition is that there can be serious declines in economic activity even without two consecutive quarters of negative growth. Suppose that in one period, real GNP declines 5 percent in the first quarter, rises 1 percent in the second, and declines 5 percent again in the third. In another period let's say real GNP declines 1 percent in each quarter. Obviously the first period shows a much more serious drop in GNP, but only the second period qualifies as a recession according to the definition. These and other considerations have led the NBER to use a broader definition of recessions, which takes into account three dimensions of the decline in aggregate economic activity—its depth, duration, and diffusion across industries. These are known as the three Ds.

Unemployment is the main concern over a recession. If output does fall, there is likely to be a fall in demand for labour. This problem is often concentrated in those sectors most affected by the recession. For example, in the current climate of economic downturn started in 2008, jobs related to finance and the housing market are more at risk than say the manufacturing sector. Therefore, one may think of an alternative source of revenue. Obviously, the current job is one of the options, but the avenues are never-ending. Secondly, there is no need for panic, the unemployment may not occur; there is nothing to be gained by worrying over what we have no control other. One should consider new avenues and skills that you could learn. Also recessions will be short lived; a period of temporary unemployment does not have to become permanent.

The effect of recession is more severely felt by small business owner. Lower profits could even threaten the survival of the business. Normally, the solution could be to look for ways to minimize costs without compromising the business. There are always ways to cut costs and increase inefficiency. Some economists even go so far as to say that recessions are a good thing because they force the economy to become more efficient. If any business is particularly affected by the downturn, it may be worthwhile to see whether it can be diversified to reflect the changing economic environment.

In a recession, stock markets are likely to fall as lower profits reduce dividend payments. One should diversify the investment portfolio. In a recession, commodities such as gold often do well. Even in a recession, there can be good investment opportunities. It may also be kept in mind that stock markets can often be forward looking. For example, stock markets have fallen sharply since the start of the year in anticipation of a recession. When a recession comes, stock markets often do not fall any further. Often the worst aspect of a recession is the affect on consumer confidence and people's fear about the future. The media often exaggerate the extent of a downturn in the economy. The media like to highlight sensationalist stories. However, it is often not as bad as it is made out to be. One should keep a calm and detached attitude and just make the best of the current situation. The recession does provide opportunities for borrowers as the interest rates are usually lower and as the rate of inflation is also lower one can have more savings. Sometimes difficult times can force us to reevaluate our financial situation. It can make us look for new business avenues and new ways to cut costs and spending. Although it may be temporarily unpleasant, the important thing is not to panic but try to make the best of any situation we find ourselves in.

Arthur M. Okum in *"The Political Economy of Prosperity"*, states "Recessions are generally considered to be fundamentally preventable, like airplane crashes and unlike hurricanes. But air crashes have not been banished from the land and it is not clear that we have the wisdom or the ability to eliminate recessions. The danger has not disappeared. The forces that produce recurrent recessions are still in the wings, merely waiting for their cue".

B.5 ECONOMIC DEVELOPMENT

Economic development is the development of economic wealth of countries or regions for the well-being of their inhabitants. This is the short definition of Economic Development.

Economic Growth & development are two different terms used in economics.

Generally speaking economic development refers to the problems of underdeveloped countries and economic growth to those of developed countries. By Economic Growth we simply mean increase in per capita income or increase in GNP. In recent literature, the term economic growth refers to sustained increase in a country's output of goods and services, or more precisely product per capita. Output is generally measured in terms of GNP.

The term economic development is far more comprehensive. It implies progressive changes in the socio-economic structure of a country. Viewed in this way economic development Involves a steady decline in agricultural shares in GNP and continuous increase in shares of industries, trade banking construction and services. Further whereas economic growth merely refers to rise in output; development implies change in technological and institutional organization of production as well as in distributive pattern of income.

Hence, compared to the objective of development, economic growth is easy realized. By a larger mobilization of resources and raising their productivity, output level can be raised. The process of development is far more extensive. Apart from a rise in output, it involves changes in composition of output, shift in the allocation of productive resources, and elimination or reduction of poverty, inequalities and unemployment. In the words of Amartya Sen "Development requires the removal of major sources of poverty as well as tyranny, poor economic opportunities as well as systematic social deprivation neglect of public facilities as well as intolerance or over activity of repressive states...."

Economic development is not possible without growth but growth is possible without development because growth is just increase in GNP. It does not have any other parameters to it. Development can be conceived as Multi-Dimensional process or phenomena. If there is increase in GNP more than the increase in per capita Income then we can say that Development is possible. When given conditions of population improves then we can say that this is also an indicator of economic Development.

For many people, economic development - means the analysis of the economic progress of nations - is what economics as a whole is designed to address. Indeed, what but to find the "nature and causes" of economic development was Adam Smith purpose? For modern economists, however, the status of economic development is somewhat more uncomfortable: it has always been the maverick field, lurking somewhere in the background but not really considered "real economics" but rather an amalgam of sociology, anthropology, history, politics and, all-too- often, ideology.

Nonetheless, few of the greatest economists actually ignored it outright. As already noted, Adam Smith and indeed, perhaps the entire Classical School was concerned with what might be termed "economic development". Schumpeter's first famous book was entitled a *Theory of Economic Development* (1911).

Nonetheless, "economic development", as it is now understood, really only started in the 1930s when, prompted by Colin Clark's 1939 quantitative study, economists began realizing that most of humankind did not live in an advanced capitalist economic system. However, the great early concern was still Europe: namely, postwar European reconstruction and the industrialization of its eastern fringes - as exemplified by the pioneering 1943 article of Paul Rosentein-Rodan and Kurt Mandelbaum's 1947 tome. It was only some time after the war that economists really began turning their concerns towards Asia, Africa and Latin America.

To this end, decolonization was an important catalyst. Faced with a new plethora of nations whose standards of living and institutions were so different from the European, modern development theory, by which we mean the analysis not only of growth but also of the institutions which could induce, sustain and accelerate growth, began in earnest. Early development theorists - such as Bert Hoselitz, Simon Kuznets, W. Arthur Lewis, and Hla Myint were among the first economists to begin analyzing economic development as a distinct subject.

The post-war formation of the United Nations - and its attendant agencies, such as the World Bank, the IMF, the ILO and the various regional commissions - proved to be another important impetus. The commissioning of numerous studies by these institutions led to the emergence of a non-academic strand of development theory.

Early economic development theory was but merely an extension of conventional economic theory which equated "development" with growth and industrialization. As a result, Latin American, Asian and African countries were seen mostly as "underdeveloped" countries, i.e. "primitive" versions of European nations that could, with time, "develop" the institutions and standards of living of Europe and North America.

As a result, "stage theory" mentality of economic development dominated discussions of economic development. As later made famous by Alexander Gerschenkron (1953, 1962) and, more crudely, Walt W. Rostow (1960), the stages theories argued that all countries passed through the same historical stages of economic development and that current underdeveloped countries were merely at an earlier stage in this linear historical progress while First World (European and North American) nations were at a later stage.

More enlightened attempts to arrive at an empirical definition of the concept of "underdevelopment", as exemplified by the work of Hollis Chenery, Simon Kuznets and Irma Adelman, led to the general conclusion that while there were no explicit "linear stages", countries tended nonetheless to exhibit *similar* patterns of development, although some differences could and did persist. The task of the development economist, in this light, was to suggest "short-cuts" by which underdeveloped countries might "catch up" with the developed and leap over a few stages.

By equating development with output growth, early development theorists, prompted by Ragnar Nurske (1952), identified capital formation as the crucial component to accelerate development. The celebrated early work on the "dual economy" by Sir W. Arthur Lewis (1954, 1955) precisely stressed the role of savings in development. Early Keynesian, such as Kaldor and Robinson, attempted to call attention to the issue of income distribution as a determinant of savings and growth. Even modern Marxians such as Maurice Dobb (1951, 1960) focused on the issue of savings-formation.

Of course, savings could themselves be manipulated by government intervention - as Lewis had intimated and the Keynesians insisted. Indeed, earlier, Rosenstein-Rodan (1943) had argued that increasing returns to scale made government-directed industrialization feasible. The notion of turning "vicious circles" of low savings and low growth into "virtuous circles" of high savings and high growth by government intervention was reiterated by Hans W. Singer in his doctrine of "balanced growth" and Gunnar Myrdal in his theory of "cumulative causation". Thus, government involvement - whether by planning, socio-economic engineering or effective demand management - was regarded as a critical tool of economic development.

Other economists turned to international trade as the great catalyst to growth. Already Hla Myint, Gottfried Haberler and Jacob Viner had stressed this avenue - arguing along lines similar to the classical doctrine of Adam Smith that trade and specialization can increase the "extent of the market". However, earlier in the 1930s, D.H. Robertson had expressed his doubts on this account - and these were later reiterated by Ragnar Nurkse, H.W. Singer and Prebisch.

Although capital-formation never really left the field, the meaning of the term mutated somewhat over time. T.W. Schultz, drawing upon his famous Chicago School thesis, turned away from physical capital accumulation to emphasize the need for "human capital" formation. This led to an emphasis on education and training as pre-requisites of growth and the identification of the problem of the "brain drain" from the Third World to the First (and, as would later be stressed, from the private sector to government bureaucracies). W. Arthur Lewis and Hans W. Singer extended Schultz's thesis by arguing that social development as a whole - notably education, health, fertility, etc. - by improving human capital, were also necessary pre-requisites for growth. In this view, industrialization, if it came at the cost of social development, could never be self-sustaining.

However, it was really only in 1969 that Dudley Seers finally broke the growth fetishism of development theory. Development, he argued, was a social phenomenon that involved more than increasing per capita output. Development meant, in Seers's opinion, eliminating poverty, unemployment and inequality as well. Singer, Myrdal and Adelman were among the first old hands to acknowledge the validity of Seers's complaint and many younger economists, such as Mahbub-ul-Haq, were galvanized by Seers's call to redefine economic development. Thus, structural issues such as dualism, population growth, inequality, urbanization, agricultural transformation, education, health, unemployment, etc. all began to be reviewed on their own merits, and not merely as appendages to an underlying growth thesis.

Particularly worthy of note was the resurrection of the work of Chayanov on the unique structures of peasant economies. Also emergent, in this period, was a debate on the very desirability of growth. E.F. Schumacher, in a famously provocative popular book, *Small is Beautiful* (1973), argued against the desirability of industrialization and extolled the merits of handicrafts economies. As the world environmental crisis became clearer in the 1980s, this debate took a new twist as the very sustainability of economic development was questioned. It became clear that the very desirability of development needed to be reconsidered.

The University of Iowa's Center for International Finance and Development states that:

"Economic development is a term that economists, politicians, and others have used frequently in the 20th century. The concept, however, has been in existence in the West for centuries. Modernization, Westernization, and especially Industrialization are other terms people have used when discussing economic development. Although no one is sure when the concept originated, most people agree that development is closely bound up with the evolution of capitalism and the demise of feudalism."

According to Anand S. & Ravallion M., article on Human Development in Poor Countries (The Journal of Economic Perspective, 1993), we can view the relationship between human development and economic development in three different explanations. First, increase in average income leading to improved in health and nutrition (known as Capability Expansion through Economic Growth). Second, it is believed that social outcomes can only be improved by reducing income poverty (known as Capability Expansion through Poverty Reduction). Thirdly, (known as Capability Expansion through Social Services), defines the improvement of social outcomes with essential services such as education, health care, and clean drinking water.

Broadly speaking, policies of economic development encompass three major areas:

- Governments undertaking to meet broad economic objectives such as price stability, high employment, and sustainable growth. Such efforts include monetary and fiscal policies, regulation of financial institutions, trade, and tax policies.

- Programs that provide infrastructure and services such as highways, parks, affordable housing, crime prevention, and K–12 education.

- Job creation and retention through specific efforts in business finance, marketing, neighborhood development, small business development, business retention and expansion, technology transfer, and real estate development. This third category is a primary focus of economic development professionals.

R. Sutcliffe in the Industry and Underdevelopment (Addison-Wesley, 1971) has aptly described "It is understandable that vague memories of the working class in the 19 th century Britain, the contemporary horrors of American machine-age society, and the Stalinist attack on the Russian peasantry, should arouse feelings which are hostile to industrialization. Yet to oppose machines altogether, like Gandhi, or to argue that a long run rise in the standard of living is possible without industrialization, are no more than forms of sentimentalism, especially when the conditions of most of the population of the non-industrialized world is now both terrible and worsening. It is not sentimentalism to demand that the process of industrialization should be made humane and as painless as possible and the long term aims of equality at a higher standard of living should be constantly borne in mind as the process goes on." Probably both China and India took clue from the above statement. Rarely has the economic ascent of two still relatively poor nations been watched with such a mixture of awe, opportunism, and trepidation. The postwar era witnessed economic miracles in Japan and South Korea. But neither was populous enough to power worldwide growth or change the game in a complete spectrum of industries. China and India, by contrast, possess the weight and dynamism to transform the 21st-century global economy. The closest parallel to their emergence is the saga of 19th-century America, a huge continental economy with a young, driven workforce that grabbed the lead in agriculture, apparel, and the high technologies of the era, such as steam engines, the telegraph, and electric lights.

But in a way, even America's rise falls short in comparison to what's happening now. Never has the world seen the simultaneous, sustained takeoffs of two nations that together account for one-third of the planet's population. For the past two decades, China has been growing at an astounding 9.5% a year, and India by 6%. Given their young populations, high savings, and the sheer amount of catching up they still have to do, most economists figure China and India possess the fundamentals to keep growing in the 7%-to-8% range for decades. Within three decades India should have vaulted over Germany as the world's third-biggest economy. By mid-century, China should have overtaken the U.S. as No. 1. By then, China and India could account for half of global output. Indeed, the troika of China, India, and the U.S. -- the only industrialized nation with significant population growth -- by most projections will dwarf every other economy.

What makes the two giants especially powerful is that they complement each other's strengths. An accelerating trend is that technical and managerial skills in both China and India are becoming more important than cheap assembly labor. China will stay dominant in mass manufacturing, and is one of the few nations building multibillion-dollar electronics and heavy industrial plants. India is a rising power in software, design, services, and precision industry. This raises a provocative question: What if the two nations merge into one giant "Chindia?" Rival political and economic ambitions make that unlikely. But if their industries truly collaborate, "they would take over the world tech industry," predicts Forrester Research Inc. analyst, Navi Radjou.

In a practical sense, the yin and yang of these immense workforces already are converging. True, annual trade between the two economies is just $14 billion. But thanks to the Internet and plunging telecom costs, multinationals are having their goods built in China with software and circuitry designed in India. As interactive design technology makes it easier to perfect virtual 3-D prototypes of everything from telecom routers to turbine generators on PCs, the distance between India's low-cost laboratories and China's low-cost factories shrinks by the month. Managers in the vanguard of globalization's new wave say the impact will be nothing less than explosive. "In a few years you'll see most companies unleashing this massive productivity surge," predicts Infosys Technologies CEO Nandan M. Nilekani.

To globalization's skeptics, however, what's good for Corporate America translates into layoffs and lower pay for workers. Little wonder the West is suffering from future shock. Each new Chinese corporate takeover bid or revelation of a major Indian outsourcing deal elicits howls of protest by U.S. politicians. Washington think tanks are publishing thick white papers charting China's rapid progress in microelectronics, nanotech, and aerospace -- and painting dark scenarios about what it means for America's global leadership. Such alarmism is understandable. But the U.S. and other established powers will have to learn to make room for China and India. For in almost every dimension -- as consumer markets, investors, producers, and users of energy and commodities -- they will be 21st-century heavyweights. The growing economic might will carry into geopolitics as well. China and India are more assertively pressing their interests in the Middle East and Africa, and China's military will likely challenge U.S. dominance in the Pacific.

One implication is that the balance of power in many technologies will likely move from West to East. An obvious reason is that China and India graduate a combined half a million engineers and scientists a year, vs. 60,000 in the U.S. In life sciences, projects the McKinsey Global Institute, the total number of young researchers in both nations will rise by 35%, to 1.6 million by 2008. The U.S. supply will drop by 11%, to 760,000. As most Western scientists will tell you, China and India already are making important contributions in medicine and materials that will help everyone. Because these nations can throw more brains at technical problems at a fraction of the cost, their contributions to innovation will grow.

American business isn't just shifting research work because Indian and Chinese brains are young, cheap, and plentiful. In many cases, these engineers combine skills -- mastery of the latest software tools, a knack for complex mathematical algorithms, and fluency in new multimedia technologies -- that often surpass those of their American counterparts. As Cisco's Scheinman puts it: "We came to India for the costs, we stayed for the quality, and we're now investing for the innovation."

A rising consumer class also will drive innovation. This year, China's passenger car market is expected to reach 3 million, No. 3 in the world. China already has the world's biggest base of cell-phone subscribers -- 350 million -- and that is expected to near 600 million by 2009. In two years, China should overtake the U.S. in homes connected to broadband. Less noticed is that India's consumer market is on the same explosive trajectory as China five years ago. Since 2000, the number of cellular subscribers has rocketed from 5.6 million to 55 million.

What's more, Chinese and Indian consumers and companies now demand the latest technologies and features. Studies show the attitudes and aspirations of today's young Chinese and Indians resemble those of Americans a few decades ago. Surveys of thousands of young adults in both nations by marketing firm Grey Global Group found they are overwhelmingly optimistic about the future, believe success is in their hands, and view products as status symbols. In China, it's fashionable for the upwardly mobile to switch high-end cell phones every three months, says Josh Li, managing director of Grey's Beijing office, because an old model suggests "you are not getting ahead and updated." That means these nations will be huge proving grounds for next-generation multimedia gizmos, networking equipment, and wireless Web services, and will play a greater role in setting global standards. In consumer electronics, "we will see China in a few years going from being a follower to a leader in defining consumer-electronics trends," predicts Philips Semiconductors Executive Vice-President Leon Husson.

For all the huge advantages they now enjoy, India and China cannot assume that their role as new superpowers is assured. Today, China and India account for a mere 6% of global gross domestic product -- half that of Japan. They must keep growing rapidly just to provide jobs for tens of millions entering the workforce annually, and to keep many millions more from crashing back into poverty. Both nations must confront ecological degradation that's as obvious as the smog shrouding Shanghai and Bombay, and face real risks of social strife, war, and financial crisis. Increasingly, such problems will be the world's problems. Also, with wages rising fast, especially in many skilled areas, the cheap labor edge won't last forever. Both nations will go through many boom and harrowing bust cycles. And neither country is yet producing companies like Samsung, Nokia, or Toyota that put it all together, developing, making, and marketing world-beating products. Both countries, however, have survived earlier crises and possess immense untapped potential. In China, serious development only now is reaching the 800 million people in rural areas, where per capita annual income is just $354. In areas outside major cities, wages are as little as 45 cents an hour. "This is why China can have another 20 years of high-speed growth," contends Beijing University economist Hai Wen.

But India's long-term potential may be even higher. Due to its one-child policy, China's working-age population will peak at 1 billion in 2015 and then shrink steadily. China then will have to provide for a greying population that has limited retirement benefits. India has nearly 500 million people under age 19 and higher fertility rates. By mid-century, India is expected to have 1.6 billion people -- and 220 million more workers than China. That could be a source for instability, but a great advantage for growth if the government can provide education and opportunity for India's masses. New Delhi just now is pushing to open its power, telecom, commercial real estate and retail sectors to foreigners. These industries could lure big capital inflows. "The pace of institutional changes and industries being liberalized is phenomenal," says Chief Economist William T. Wilson of consultancy Keystone Business Intelligence India. "I believe India has a better model than China, and over time will surpass it in growth."

For its part, China has yet to prove it can go beyond forced-march industrialization. China directs massive investment into public works and factories, a wildly successful formula for rapid growth and job creation. But considering its massive manufacturing output, China is surprisingly weak in innovation. A full 57% of exports are from foreign-invested factories, and China underachieves in software, even with 35 software colleges and plans to graduate 200,000 software engineers a year. It's not for lack of genius. Microsoft Corp.'s 180-engineer R&D lab in Beijing, for example, is one of the world's most productive sources of innovation in computer graphics and language simulation. While China's big state-run R&D institutes are close to the cutting edge at the theoretical level, they have yet to yield many commercial breakthroughs. "China has a lot of capability," says Microsoft Chief Technology Officer Craig Mundie. "But when you look under the covers, there is not a lot of collaboration with industry." The lack of intellectual property protection, and Beijing's heavy role in building up its own tech companies, make many other multinationals leery of doing serious R&D in China.

China also is hugely wasteful. Its 9.5% growth rate in 2004 is less impressive when you consider that $850 billion -- half of GDP -- was plowed into already-glutted sectors like crude steel, vehicles, and office buildings. Its factories burn fuel five times less efficiently than in the West, and more than 20% of bank loans are bad. Two-thirds of China's 1,300 listed companies don't earn back their true cost of capital, estimates Beijing National Accounting Institute President Chen Xiaoyue. "We build the roads and industrial parks, but we sacrifice a lot, "Chen says. India, by contrast, has had to develop with scarcity. It gets scant foreign investment, and has no room to waste fuel and materials like China. India also has Western legal institutions, a modern stock market, and private banks and corporations. As a result, it is far more capital-efficient. A *Business Week* analysis of Standard & Poor's data on 346 top listed companies in both nations' shows Indian corporations have achieved higher returns on equity and invested capital in the past five years in industries from autos to food products. The average Indian company posted a 16.7% return on capital in 2004, vs.12.8% in China. The burning question is whether India can replicate China's mass manufacturing achievement. India's info-tech services industry, successful as it is, employs fewer than 1 million people. But 200 million

Indians subsist on $1 a day or less. Export manufacturing is one of India's best hopes of generating millions of new jobs.

India has sophisticated manufacturing knowhow. Tata Steel is among the world's most-efficient producers. The country boasts several top precision auto parts companies, such as Bharat Forge Ltd. The world's biggest supplier of chassis parts to major auto makers, it employs 1,200 engineers at its heavily automated Pune plant. India's forte is small-batch production of high-value goods requiring lots of engineering, such as power generators for Cummins Inc. and core components for General Electric Co. What holds India back is bureaucratic red tape, rigid labor laws, and its inability to build infrastructure fast enough. There are hopeful signs. Nokia Corp. is building a major campus to make cell phones in Chennai, and South Korea's Pasco Iron & Steel Co. plans a $12 billion complex by 2016 in Orissa state. But it will take India many years to build the highways, power plants, and airports needed to rival China in mass manufacturing. With Beijing now pushing software and pledging intellectual property rights protection, some Indians fret design work will shift to China to be closer to factories. "The question is whether China can move from manufacturing to services faster than we can solve our infrastructure bottlenecks," says President Arvind Melligeri of Bangalore-based QUEST, whose 700 engineers design gas turbines, aircraft engines, and medical gear for GE and other clients.

However the race plays out, Corporate America has little choice but to be engaged -- heavily. Motorola illustrates the value of leveraging both nations to lower costs and speed up development. Most of its hardware is assembled and partly designed in China. Its R&D center in Bangalore devises about 40% of the software in its new phones. The Bangalore team developed the multimedia software and user interfaces in the hot Motorola RAZR cell phone. Now, they are working on phones that display and send live video, stream movies from the Web, or route incoming calls to voicemail when you are shifting gears in a car. "This is a very, very critical, state-of-the-art resource for Motorola," says Motorola South Asia President Amit Sharma and Dr. Sanjay Jha (Co-CEO Motorola) agrees to it.

Companies like Motorola realize they must succeed in China and India at many levels simultaneously to stay competitive. That requires strategies for winning consumers, recruiting and managing R&D and professional talent, and skillfully sourcing from factories. "Over the next few years, you will see a dramatic gap opening between companies," predicts Jim Hemerling, who runs Boston Consulting Group's Shanghai practice. "It will be between those who get it and are fully mobilized in China and India, and those that are still pondering." In the coming decades, China and India will disrupt workforces, industries, companies, and markets in ways that we can barely begin to imagine. The upheaval will test America's commitment to the global trade system, and shake its confidence. In the 19th century, Europe went through a similar trauma when it realized a new giant -- the U.S. -- had arrived. "It is up to America to manage its own expectation of China and India as either a threat or opportunity," says corporate strategist Kenichi Ohmae. "America should be as open-minded as Europe was 100 years ago." How these Asian giants integrate with the rest of the world will largely shape the 21st-century global economy.

B.6 ECONOMIC GROWTH

Most of the underdeveloped and developing countries have a colonial past and their economic growth is somewhat similar in many respects. The reason is the co-existence of developed and underdeveloped sectors in the country's economy in a parallel manner. In such countries the existence of economic islands are not capable to drag the entire economy. Due to the absence of connectivity between the growing sectors of economy and those which are dormant such economies have suffered a long periods of stagnation. Political colonialism which was blamed for the slow growth of such isolated economies have long been disappeared, but still a large segments of the population remains untouched by the developments. According to Robert McNamara almost 40 % of the populations of such countries have not been benefitted from the economic strides made by these countries. Therefore, it was felt that a new approach such as basic needs should be implemented to ensure proper and equitable distribution of supply of goods.

Economic growth is a complex process as it is not only influenced by economic factors but also by non-economic factors. The most important economic factors which are considered as vital tools in determining a country's growth are the available capital stock, its accumulation, capital output ratio, agricultural surplus and foreign trade situation i.e. balance of payment in general. Moreover, the availability of skilled manpower, education, population growth and sectorial development all contribute in shaping the growth pattern of a country.

The role of economic factors in determining the growth is vital. The stock of capital and the rate of capital accumulation answer the question whether the country is poised to grow or is likely to remain stagnant. The strategic role of capital in raising the level of production has been acknowledged as the vital factor. Various statistical models proposed to substantiate economic growth also acknowledge the importance of capital as a crucial factor for economic growth. Exclusive reliance on foreign aid is highly risky and not sustainable. Experts assert that lack of capital could be the basic obstacle to economic growth and no development plan could succeed until adequate supply of capital is ensured. Any country cannot hope to achieve spectacular economic growth without raising the capital formation. Japan did this during the late seventies by stepping up the savings rate by 37 % of the GDP. Even up to 1999, the saving rate was as high as 30 %. In countries such as China, South Korea, Thailand, Malaysia, Singapore and Hong Kong, the saving rate was as high as 30 % during the major part of 80s and 90s. This high rate of capital formation explains their high rates of growth during the 80s and 90s. In comparison, the rate of capital formation in India in the mid-80s had fluctuated around 19 % of the GDP which has touched almost 35 % in 2009 catapulting it out of global economic recession and even witnessing a growth.

From 1950 to 2000, growth in income per capita in the United States lay between these two extremes, averaging 2.3% per year. From 1950 to 1975, India, which started at a level of income per capita that was less than 7% of that in the United States, was falling even farther behind. Between 1975 and 2000, China, which started at an even lower level, was catching up. China grew so quickly partly because it started from so far behind. Rapid growth could be achieved in large part by letting firms bring in ideas about how to create value that were already in use in the rest of the world. The interesting question is why India couldn't manage the same trick, at least between 1950 and 1975.

Economic growth occurs whenever people take resources and rearrange them in ways that are more valuable. A useful metaphor for production in an economy comes from the kitchen. To create valuable final products, we mix inexpensive ingredients together according to a recipe. The cooking one can do is limited by the supply of ingredients, and most cooking in the economy produces undesirable side effects. If economic growth could be achieved only by doing more and more of the same kind of cooking, we would eventually run out of raw materials and suffer from unacceptable levels of pollution and nuisance. Human history teaches us, however, that economic growth springs from better recipes, not just from more cooking. New recipes generally produce fewer unpleasant side effects and generate more economic value per unit of raw material. Take one small example. In most coffee shops, you can now use the same size lid for small, medium, and large cups of coffee. That wasn't true as recently as 1995. That small change in the geometry of the cups means that a coffee shop can serve customers at lower cost. Store owners need to manage the inventory for only one type of lid. Employees can replenish supplies more quickly throughout the day. Customers can get their coffee just a bit faster. Such big discoveries as the transistor, antibiotics, and the electric motor attract most of the attention, but it takes millions of little discoveries like the new design for the cup and lid to double average income in a nation.

Every generation has perceived the limits to growth that finite resources and undesirable side effects would pose if no new recipes or ideas were discovered. And every generation has underestimated the potential for finding new recipes and ideas. We consistently fail to grasp how many ideas remain to be discovered. The difficulty is the same one we have with compounding: possibilities do not merely add up; they multiply. In a branch of physical chemistry known as exploratory synthesis, chemists try mixing selected elements together at different temperatures and pressures to see what comes out. About a decade ago, one of the hundreds of compounds discovered this way—a mixture of copper, yttrium, barium, and oxygen—was found to be a superconductor at temperatures far higher than anyone had previously thought possible. This discovery may ultimately have far-reaching implications for the storage and transmission of electrical energy.

Thinking about ideas and recipes changes how one thinks about economic policy. A traditional explanation for the persistent poverty of many less developed countries is that they lack objects such as natural resources or capital goods. But Taiwan stared with little of either and still grew rapidly. Something else must be involved. Increasingly, emphasis is shifting to the notion that it is ideas, not objects that poor countries lack. The knowledge needed to provide citizens of the poorest countries with a vastly improved standard of living already exists in the advanced countries. If a poor nation invests in education and does not destroy the incentives for its citizens to acquire ideas from the rest of the world, it can rapidly take advantage of the publicly available part of the worldwide stock of knowledge. If, in addition, it offers incentives for privately held ideas to be put to use within its borders—for example, by protecting foreign patents, copyrights, and licenses, by permitting direct investment by foreign firms, by protecting property rights, and by avoiding heavy regulation and high marginal tax rates—its citizens can soon work in state-of-the-art productive activities.

Some ideas such as insights about public health are rapidly adopted by less developed countries. As a result, life expectancy in poor countries is catching up with the leaders faster than income per capita. Yet governments in poor countries continue to impede the flow of many other kinds of ideas, especially those with commercial value. Automobile producers in North America clearly recognize that they can learn from ideas developed in the rest of the world.

India operated in a government-created protective time warp. The Hillman and Austin cars produced in England in the 1950s continued to roll off production lines in India through the 1980s. After independence, India's commitment to closing itself off and striving for self-sufficiency was as strong as Taiwan's commitment to acquiring foreign ideas and participating fully in world markets. The outcomes—grinding poverty in India and opulence in Taiwan—could hardly be more disparate. For a poor country like India, enormous increases in standards of living can be achieved merely by letting in the ideas held by companies from industrialized nations. With a series of economic reforms that started in the early 1990s, India has begun to open itself up to these opportunities. For some of its citizens such as the software developers who now work for firms located in the rest of the world, these improvements in standards of living have become a reality. This same type of opening up is causing a spectacular transformation of life in China. Its growth in the last 25 years of the twentieth century was driven to a very large extent by foreign investment by multinational firms. Leading countries like the United States, Canada, and the members of the European Union cannot stay ahead merely by adopting ideas developed elsewhere. They must offer strong incentives for discovering new ideas at home, and this is not easy to do.

The same characteristic that makes an idea so valuable—everybody can use it at the same time—also means that it is hard to earn an appropriate rate of return on investments in ideas. The many people who benefit from a new idea can too easily free-ride on the efforts of others. After the transistor was invented at Bell Labs, many applied ideas had to be developed before this basic science discovery yielded any commercial value. By now, private firms have developed improved recipes that have brought the cost of a transistor down to less than a millionth of its former level. Yet most of the benefits from those discoveries have been reaped not by the innovating firms, but by the users of the transistors. If the government confiscated most of the oil from major discoveries and gave it to consumers, oil companies would do much less exploration. Some oil would still be found serendipitously, but many promising opportunities for exploration would be bypassed. Both oil companies and consumers would be worse off. The leakage of benefits such as those from improvements in the transistor acts just like this kind of confiscatory tax and has the same effect on incentives for exploration. For this reason, most economists support government funding for basic scientific research. They also recognize, however, that basic research grants by themselves will not provide the incentives to discover the many small applied ideas needed to transform basic ideas such as the transistor or web search into valuable products and services.

It takes more than scientists in universities to generate progress and growth. Such seemingly mundane forms of discovery as product and process engineering or the development of new business models can have huge benefits for society as a whole. There are, to be sure, some benefits for the firms that make these discoveries, but not enough to generate innovation at the ideal rate. Giving firms tighter patents and copyrights over new ideas would increase the incentives to make a new discovery, but might also make it much more expensive to build on previous discoveries. Tighter intellectual property rights could therefore be counter-productive and slow growth down. The one safe measure that governments have used to great advantage has been to use subsidies for education to increase the supply of talented young scientists and engineers. They are the basic input into the discovery process, the fuel that fires the innovation engine. No one can know where newly trained young people will end up working, but nations that are willing to educate more of them and let them follow their instincts can be confident that they will accomplish amazing things.

Perhaps the most important ideas of all are meta-ideas. These are ideas about how to support the production and transmission of other ideas. The British invented patents and copyrights in the seventeenth century. North Americans invented the modern research university and the agricultural extension service in the nineteenth century. The challenge now facing all of the industrialized countries is to invent new institutions that encourage a higher level of applied, commercially relevant research and development in the private sector. As national markets for talent and education merge into unified global markets, opportunities for important policy innovation will surely emerge. In basic research, the United States is still the undisputed leader, but in key areas of education, other countries are surging ahead. Many of them have already discovered how to train a larger fraction of their young people as scientists and engineers.

The country that takes the lead in the twenty-first century will be the one that implements an innovation that more effectively supports the production of new ideas in the private sector. Moreover, new meta-ideas of this kind will be found. Only a failure of imagination—the same one that leads the man on the street to suppose that everything has already been invented—leads us to believe that all of the relevant institutions have been designed and that all of the policy levers have been found. For social scientists, every bit as much as for physical scientists, there are vast regions to explore and wonderful surprises to discover.

Lets try to consolidate some of the interesting facts of economic growth supplemented with analytical approach for a conceptual understanding on the complex topic. Going to the past, throughout most of the history, GDP per person has remained mostly constant and the real GDP and population grew at the same rate. However, since 200-300 years, the GDP growth per person has seen an incremental increase.

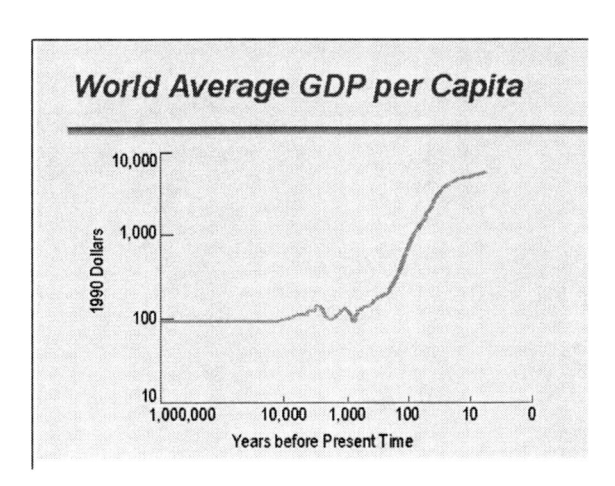

Economic growth is the rise in real GDP per capita. Rate of economic growth from 1900-2000 can be shown as under:

[(Real GDP per person in 2000 − Real GDP per person in 1900)/(Real GDP per person in 1900)] * 1/100

The rule of 72 states that if the growth rate of a variable is X percent per year, then the variable doubles after every 72/X years. It may be observed that the world's real GDP is almost four times greater than 1900. But the economic growth has slowed down since 1973. US economic growth rate has fallen to an almost 1.3 % per year to the present. In 1860, Japan's GDP per capita was one-third of that of US. However, Japan's GDP per capita is roughly equal to the US.

Economists use models of economic growth to isolate the factors that cause some nations to grow faster than others. The level of real GDP depends on technology and available inputs of labour and capital. Mathematically, this can be shown as under:

Real GDP = A fn (I, K)

Wherein,   I = economy's labour input

K = economy's capital input

A = economy's technology level

The economy's production in per person terms: Real GDP per Person = Y / I = A fn (K / I)

GDP per Worker Depends on Capital per Worker

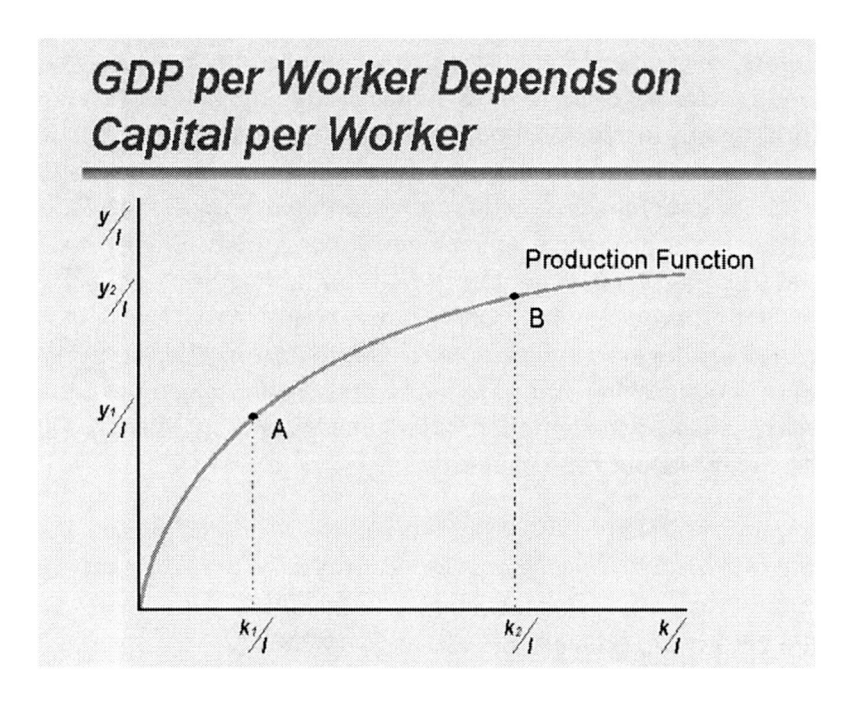

An increase in technology changes real GDP per person. On the other hand, an increase in capital per worker moves the economy along the production function.

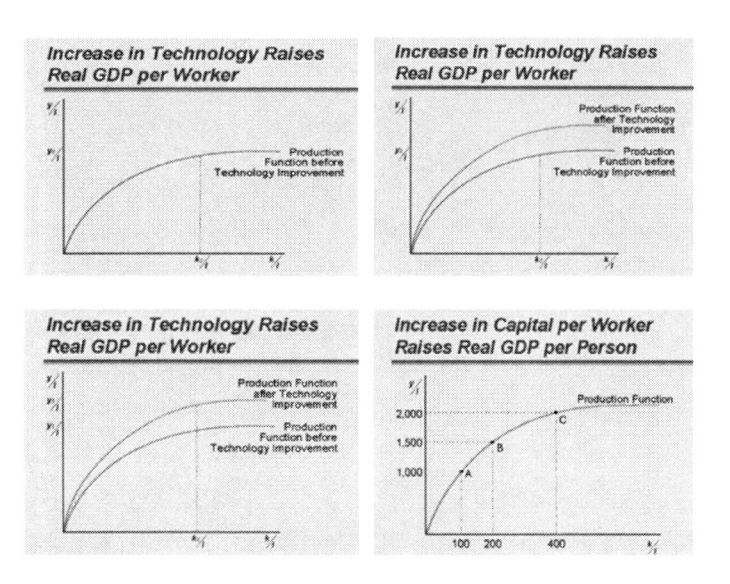

By investing, an economy can grow without technical progress. Therefore, excessive foreign direct investment may not necessarily creates a sustainable economy as in the case of China. But an economy can progress by increasing inputs of both physical and human capital. Equilibrium savings and investment determines how fast the economy adds to its capital, and equilibrium economic growth. Increase in investment has a positive impact on higher growth. Investment in capital stock results in economic growth but at long term equilibrium it does not propel economic growth. It may be noted that the economic growth slows down as the economy closes to its long term equilibrium because of diminishing returns to the capital. Diminishing returns to the capital means that the benefit of additional investment falls over-time as the capital-labour ratio increases.

With more capital equipment per worker, the economy gets a smaller benefit of investing in even more capital. Gradually, the economy inches towards steady state which is long run equilibrium during which the capital per person remains more or less constant.

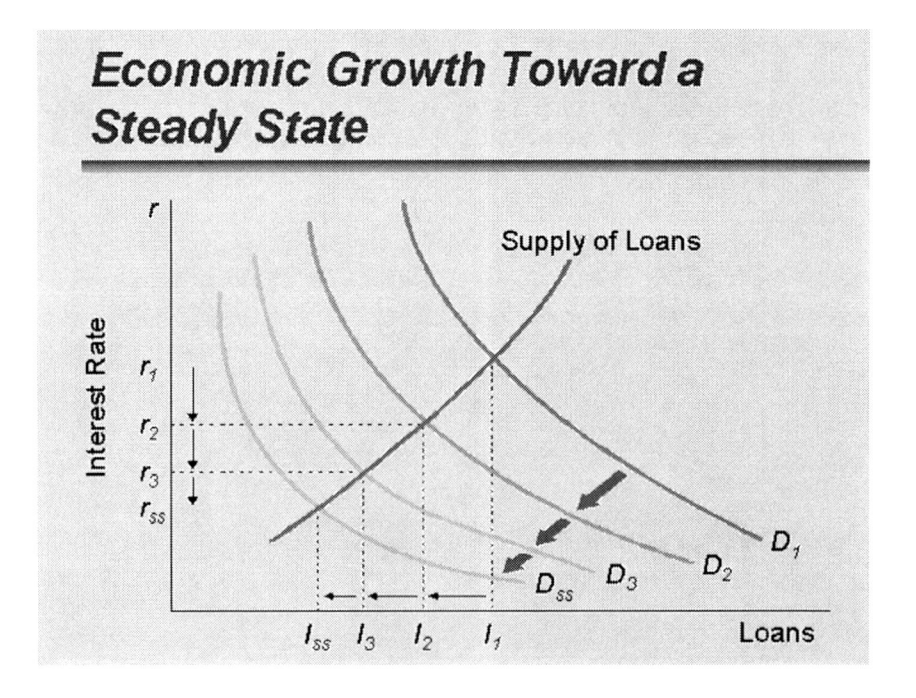

Economic Growth Toward a Steady State

Let's assume that the real GDP per person depends on the capital per person in the following way:

If K / L is less than or equal to 20 then Y / L = 2 (K/l)

If K/L exceeds 20 then Y/L = 30 + (K/L) / 2 and suppose people save 5 % of real GDP:

Numerical Example of Growth that Stops at Steady State

Capital per Person	Real GDP per person	Savings per person	Depreciation per person
0	0	0	0
20	40	4	2
40	50	5	4
60	60	6	6
80	70	7	8
100	80	8	10

Numerical Example of Growth that Stops at Steady State

Capital per Person	Real GDP per person	Savings per person	Depreciation per person
0	0	0	0
20	40	4	2
40	50	5	4
60	60	6	6
80	70	7	8
100	80	8	10

Production Function in the Numerical Example

Steady State Capital per Worker and GDP per Worker

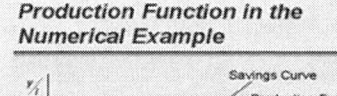

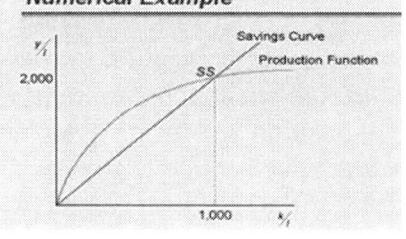

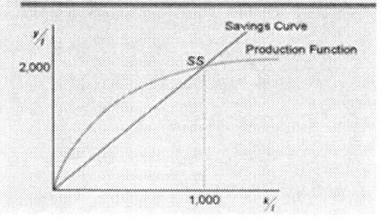

Therefore, from the above model, it may be observed that the economic growth slows and eventually stops. Real interest rates fall over-time as economy reaches its steady state. However, in reality, the long term economic growth has not slowed and the interest has not fallen overtime. Hence, the economy stops growing when its capital per worker reaches the steady state. But, continual technical progress can still push continuous growth.

Technical changes appear as increase in the variable A, in the per-person production function. Therefore, Real GDP per person = A fn (K/l, N/l). This indicates that technical changes raises production per person without any change in capital per person. In view of this, technical progress and long term growth can be achieved through investments in research and development and in education and skills. Technical changes and economic growth would slow down and eventually stop if there were diminishing returns to technical change. Therefore, economic growth could continue indefinitely if knowledge does not have diminishing returns.

An economy's effective labour input is its labour adjusted for knowledge and skills. Economic growth can continue indefinitely if the economy continually adds to its effective labour input through education and training. On the same lines, renewable resources are natural resources that can be replenished, whereas, fixed resources are natural resources that cannot be replenished but are not depleted in production such as land. Exhaustible resources cannot be physically replenished and are depleted in production such as coal.

The existence of fixed resources means that economy will reach the steady state because of diminishing returns. The existence of exhaustible resources means that world real GDP may fall in the future. But, according to Malthus, a rising population means more people working with a fixed amount of land. This would result diminished food production until starvation eliminates the population increase. That would mean that population could stabilize at subsistence level. Some people argue that increases in population and falling quantities of exhaustible resources will result in negative economic growth. On the other hand, there are suggestions that as the resources will become scarce people respond with innovation.

The situation arises that prices of exhaustible resources have fallen because technical progress has increased their supply. On the other hand, the demand for these resources has also reduced by creating substitutes. Therefore, the private benefit of producing a good or investing in research is the benefit to the people who produce it or invest. The social benefit is the benefit to everyone in the society of the production or investment. A positive externality occurs when the social benefit of producing a good or investing in research exceeds the private benefit.

As it is observed that economic disparity between countries are increasing. Sometimes the term, economic development is also referred to economic growth in under-developed countries. The growth pattern depicts the story of economic growth witnessed by these countries –

Real GDP per Capita Around the World, 1750-1998

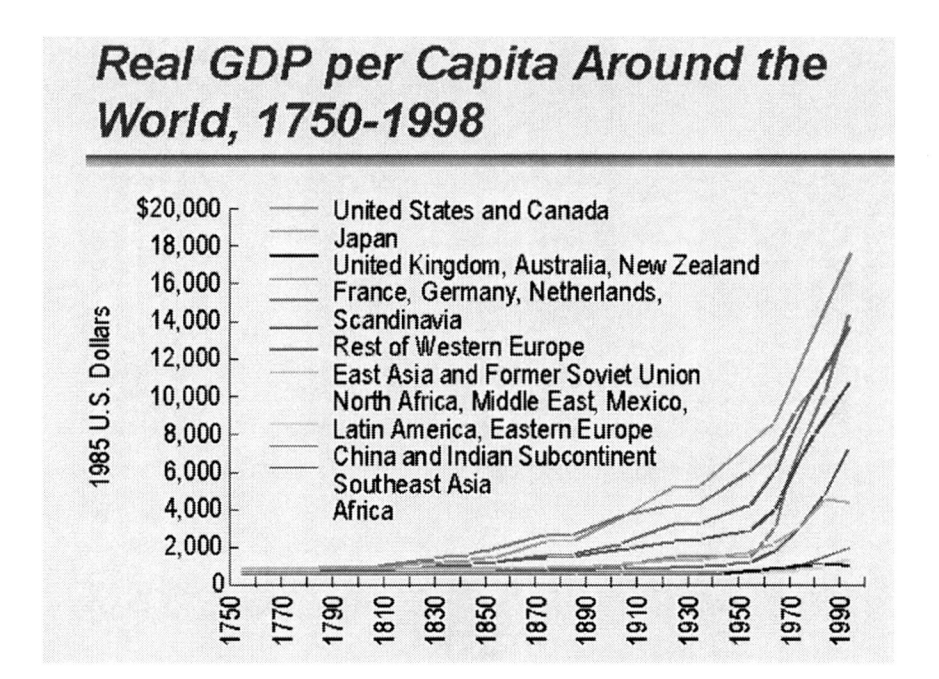

——	United States and Canada
——	Japan
——	United Kingdom, Australia, New Zealand
——	France, Germany, Netherlands,
——	Scandinavia
——	Rest of Western Europe
——	East Asia and Former Soviet Union
——	North Africa, Middle East, Mexico,
——	Latin America, Eastern Europe
——	China and Indian Subcontinent
——	Southeast Asia
——	Africa

(Y-axis: 1985 U.S. Dollars, 0 to $20,000; X-axis: 1750 to 1990)

All the developed countries initiated economic growth by limiting restrictions on foreign investment, improving the skill level of manpower and stimulate high levels of investment. Under-developed countries on the other hand attract less foreign investment as they lack skilled manpower and good banking infrastructure. Moreover, the population due to low education levels is seen as not equipped to adapt high technology levels. In addition, instable political conditions often complicate the problems as the multi-nationals do not feel secure enough to initiate investment in these countries. The government taxation policy and significant levels of regulations and restrictions make doing business difficult. Taking the example of Asian tigers viz; South Korea, Taiwan, Hong Kong, Singapore and now the BRIC countries it is clear that the path for 'economic growth' is to become more competitive by opening up the markets so that they are prepared to sustain not succumb to international players.

PART C

FUNCTIONING OF ECONOMICS

C.1 ECONOMICS OF MONEY

Money is a good that acts as a medium of exchange in transactions. Classically it is said that money acts as a unit of account, a store of value, and a medium of exchange. Most authors find that the first two are nonessential properties that follow from the third. In fact, other goods are often better than money at being intertemporal store of value, since most monies degrade in value over time through inflation or the overthrow of governments. So money is not just pieces of paper. It is a medium of exchange that facilitates trade.

The double coincidence is the situation where the supplier of good A wants good B and the supplier of good B wants good A. The point is that the institution of money gives us a more flexible approach to trade than barter, as dual coincidence of wants.

Since money is a recognized medium of exchange, there is no need to find someone who has a pair of new shoes and is looking for a Wayne Gretzky hockey card. The individual just needs to find someone who is looking for a Gretzky card who is willing to pay enough money. This is a far easier problem, and thus our lives are a lot easier, and our economy more efficient, with the existence of money.

Money doesn't have any inherent value. It is simply pieces of paper or numbers in a ledger. A car has value because it can help a person to get where he/sheou need to go. Water has a value because it has a use; if you don't drink enough of it you will die. Unless you enjoy looking at pictures of deceased national heroes, money has no more use than any other piece of paper.

It didn't always work this way. In the past money was in the form of coins, generally composed of precious metals such as gold and silver. The value of the coins was roughly based on the value of the metals they contained, because you could always melt the coins down and use the metal for other purposes. Until a few decades ago paper money in different countries was based on the *gold standard* or *silver standard* or some combination of the two. This meant that one could take some paper money to the government, who would exchange it for some gold or some silver based on an exchange rate set by the government. The gold standard lasted until 1971 when President Nixon announced that the United States would no longer exchange dollars for gold. This ended the Bretton Woods system, which will be the focus of a future article. Now the United States is on a system of fiat money, which is not tied to any other commodity. So these pieces of paper in their pocket are nothing but pieces of paper.

So why does a five-dollar bill have value and some other pieces of paper do not? It's simple: Money is a good with a limited supply and there is a demand for it because people want it. Goods and services are what ultimately matter in the economy, and money is a way that allows people to give up goods and services which are less desirable to them, and get ones that are more so. People sell their labor (work) to acquire money now to purchase goods and services in the future.

The system of money operates on a mutual set of beliefs; so long as enough of us believe in the future value of money the system will work. What could cause us to lose that belief? It is unlikely that money will be replaced in the near future, because the inefficiencies of a dual coincidence of wants system are well known. If one currency is to be replaced by another, there will be a period in which one can switch the old currency for new currency. This is what happened in Europe when countries switched over to the Euro. So our currencies are not going to disappear.

Then why else might we think that our money might not be of value to others in the future? Well, what if we believed our money wouldn't be nearly as valuable in the future as it is today? This inflation of the currency causes people to want to get rid of their money as quickly as possible. Inflation and the rational way citizens react to it, causes great misery for an economy. People will not sign into profitable deals which involve future payments because they'll be unsure what the value of money will be when they get paid. Business activity sharply declines because of this. Inflation causes all sorts of other inefficiencies, from the café changing its prices every few minutes, to the homemaker taking a wheelbarrow full of money to the bakery in order to buy a loaf of bread. The belief in money and the steady value of the currency are not innocuous things. If citizens lose faith in the money supply and believe that money will be worth less in the future, economic activity can grind to a halt.

Money is essentially a good, so as such is ruled by the axioms of supply and demand. The value of any good is determined by its supply and demand and the supply and demand for other goods in the economy. A price for any good is the amount of money it takes to get that good. Inflation occurs when the price of goods increases; in other words when money becomes less valuable relative to those other goods. This can occur when:

- The supply of money goes up.
- The supply of other goods goes down.
- Demand for money goes down.
- Demand for other goods goes up.

The key cause of inflation is increases in the supply of money. Inflation can occur for other reasons. If a natural disaster destroyed stores but left banks intact, we'd expect to see an immediate rise in prices, as goods are now scarce relative to money. These kinds of situations are rare. For the most part inflation is caused when the money supply rises faster than the supply of other goods and services.

Money has value because people believe that they will be able to exchange their money for goods and services in the future. This belief will persist so long as people do not fear future inflation. To avoid inflation, the government must ensure that the money supply does not increase too quickly.

Economic activity can take place without money. All transactions can be barter transactions in which people obtain a good or service that they want by trading away some other good or service that they value less. Because barter is inconvenient, barter systems exist only when exchange is uncommon. Suppose we have the mini-economy in the table below. If Crusoe visits Friday to buy coconuts, a trade may not take place. Crusoe wants coconuts, but Friday does not want fish. Exchange will take place only when one of the two realizes that they will have to accept something they do not want but which they can trade later. With only two people and two commodities, this realization may take place. However, if there are a hundred people with a hundred different commodities, the pattern of barter transactions necessary for everyone to end up with what he or she wants may be so complex that trade may not occur. As trading patterns become more complex, groups need to find a way to reduce the cost of making transactions. They spontaneously begin to use one commodity as an intermediary: they invent money.

The invention of money makes trading easier. With money, all prices can be expressed in the same way, in terms of how much money is needed to buy the product. The unit of money becomes the measuring stick of value, or what economists call the standard of value. With a standard of value, computing the costs and benefits of various options, that is, making choices becomes easier.

A standard of value is most useful when it does not change over time. If the measuring stick changes with time, comparing costs and benefits of some options may be more difficult. Inflation or deflations change the measuring stick, and a reason people dislike inflation is that it makes comparing options over time more difficult.

In addition to its function as a medium of exchange, money also serves as a store of value. Though this function is not what makes money important in macroeconomics, it is vital in explaining how much money people want to hold. Any item that people consider as a way of holding wealth is a store of value. Land, stocks and bonds, old paintings, factories, and jewelry are just some of the other ways people can hold wealth. When money is a good way to hold wealth compared to these alternatives, people will want to hold a lot of it. On the other hand, when money is a poor way to hold wealth, people try to keep little of it. For example, in the German hyperinflation people tried to spend money as soon as they got it because it lost value so quickly. This idea, that people are willing to hold large amounts of money when it is a good store of value, but try to hold small amounts when it is a poor way to hold wealth, is a key idea for those who believe that changes in the amount of money have been

The velocity of money is the one of the factors that determines GDP.

The well-known formula is GDP = M x V; that is, Gross Domestic Product equals the quantity of Money times its Velocity. Velocity refers to how many times a given quantity of money is spent during the period under consideration, usually one year. Less understood is how changes to money's velocity come about. The formula makes clear that a decrease in velocity can adversely affect GDP and vice versa. But, that just begs the question, what causes changes in monetary velocity?

The primary determinant of how often a given quantity of money is spent is the desire of the public to hold money; that is, the public's demand for money. When demand for money is high, meaning that the public wishes to hold more money in the form of cash balances, the velocity of money decreases. Likewise, when the public's demand for money is low, velocity accelerates. Therefore, we have entered the realm of perception, which is not an exact science in the sense that one can establish a formula of the magnitude and time frame for changes in perception. Nevertheless, it is possible to establish the factors that eventually will change perception and, therefore, will cause the demand for money to increase or decrease.

The demand for money is influenced primarily by the quantity of money. This simple statement reveals something very important—that if the quantity of money changes very little, then the demand for money will change very little and the economy will experience stable conditions. Commodity money—that is, gold and silver—experiences very small changes in its quantity; therefore, one would expect that commodity money velocity would change very little. But even in the days of the gold standard, the demand for money varied. The reason was that the money supply was not backed one hundred percent by gold but, rather, only a fraction of the money supply was backed by gold. The rest of the money supply was anchored in bank loans instead. As banks increased lending during temporary boom times, the quantity of the fiduciary media, as Ludwig von Mises called this money not backed by gold, increased, which caused the demand for money to decrease and money's velocity to rise. This is the very definition of a boom. However, eventually this increase in the money supply causes prices to rise, among other evils, revealing that the boom is unsustainable. There exists no new, real capital to fund it.

When bank loans become uncollectable, the quantity of fiduciary media decreases. Now the demand for money increases dramatically, as the public scrambles to convert their fiduciary media—bank checking accounts now of questionable value—into currency. This increase in the demand for money causes a decrease in money's velocity, exacerbating the bust. The only way out of this predicament is for prices to fall, so that the remaining, smaller supply of money will be sufficient to allow the market of goods and services to clear.

In today's fiat money, central bank monetary system the bust phase can be papered over for quite some time with increases in fiduciary media. But the demand for money detects subtle changes, thusly precipitating changes in money's velocity. For instance, rising prices are a signal to money holders to reduce their demand for money. A reduction in money demand causes its velocity to increase, putting further upward pressure on prices. If there are other assets in which the public can easily invest, then one would expect to see upward price movements. Stock market and commodity price increases are symptoms of such movements out of money, reflecting reduced demand for money, furthering an increase in money's velocity.

It is typical of such boom periods that credit is readily available. Businesses, then, are more prone to reduce cash holdings in the certainty that bank loans can be used as a substitute for ready cash to meet business needs. This drop in business demand for holding money is a further spur to an increase in money's velocity. Furthermore, since central bank manipulation of the interest rate in a downward direction was the precipitous cause of the temporary boom, business has even less incentive to moderate its borrowing in lieu of holding cash. Better to invest in inventories that may rise in value than hold cash, especially when loans not only are easy to obtain but are cheap, too. Therefore, what economists see as an increase in money's velocity is actually a rational decision by market participants to reduce their demand for money following central bank intervention to lower the interest rate and ignite a temporary boom. But, when the boom turns to bust, the reverse happens. Now the market demands more cash at a time when fiduciary media is being wiped out by bank loan losses. Prices fall, making it wise to hold cash in the expectation of even further price reductions. Businesses begin to hoard cash when bank lending dries up in the face of falling bank capital ratios due to loan losses. And they stop investing in inventories that become less valuable each day. Finally, the public bails out of a falling stock and commodity market in favor of the comfort of cash holdings. Money velocity drops even more.

In a free market, capitalist economy marked by little government intervention and the existence of sound—that is, commodity—money, the demand for money and its inverse, the velocity of money, are of little interest to economists let alone the public. The demand for money reflects real choices based upon market forces rather than opportunistic or defensive choices based upon wild, temporary swings in economic fortunes based upon government and central bank intervention. Prices change very slowly. Banks are institutions of probity and practice good asset-liability management; that is, they match loan maturities to deposit maturities. This may sound dull to some, but it beats the wild boom/bust cycles that create millionaires one day and paupers the next.

Money supply is the total supply of money in circulation in a given country's economy at a given time. There are several measures for the money supply, such as M1, M2, and M3. The money supply is considered an important instrument for controlling inflation by those economists who say that growth in money supply will only lead to inflation if money demand is stable. In order to control the money supply, regulators have to decide which particular measure of the money supply to target. The broader the targeted measure, the more difficult it will be to control that particular target. However, targeting an unsuitable narrow money supply measure may lead to a situation where the total money supply in the country is not adequately controlled.

The different types of money are typically classified as **Ms'**. The numbers of Ms' usually range from M0 (narrowest) to M3 (broadest) but which Ms' are actually used depends on the system. The typical layout for each of the Ms' is as follows:

- **M0**: In some countries, such as the United Kingdom, M0 includes bank reserves, so M0 is referred to as the monetary base, or narrow money.

- **MB**: is referred to as the total currency. This is the base from which other forms of money (like checking deposits) are created and is traditionally the most liquid measure of the money supply.

- **M1**: Bank reserves are not included in M1.

- **M2**: represents money and "close substitutes" for money. M2 is a broader classification of money than M1. Economists use M2 when looking to quantify the amount of money in circulation and trying to explain different economic monetary conditions. M2 is a key economic indicator used to forecast inflation.

- **M3**: Since 2006, M3 is no longer published or revealed to the public by the US central bank. However, there are still estimates produced by various private institutions.

- **MZM**: Money with zero maturity. It measures the supply of financial assets redeemable at par on demand.

In the money supply statistics, **central bank money** is **MB** while the **commercial bank money** is divided up into the **M1-M3** components. Generally, the types of commercial bank money that tend to be valued at lower amounts are classified in the narrow category of **M1** while the types of commercial bank money that tend to exist in larger amounts are categorized in **M2** and **M3**, with **M3** having the largest. Some examples of Money supply as calculated around the world per respective country's defined system are:

United States {The Federal Reserve Bank}

M0: The total of all physical currency, plus accounts at the central bank that can be exchanged for physical currency.

M1: The total of all physical currency part of bank reserves + the amount in demand accounts.

M2: M1 + most savings accounts, money market accounts, retail money market mutual funds, and small denomination time deposits.

M3: M2 + all other CDs (large time deposits, institutional money market mutual fund balances), deposits of Eurodollars and repurchase agreements.

United Kingdom {Bank of England}

M0: Cash outside Bank of England + Banks' operational deposits with Bank of England.

M4: Cash outside banks (i.e. in circulation with the public and non-bank firms) + private-sector retail bank and building society deposits + Private-sector wholesale bank and building society deposits and Certificate of Deposit.

European Union {European Central Bank}

M1: Currency in circulation + overnight deposits

M2: M1 + Deposits with an agreed maturity up to 2 years + Deposits redeemable at a period of notice up to 3 months

M3: M2 + Repurchase agreements + Money market fund (MMF) shares/units + Debt securities up to 2 years

India {Reserve Bank of India}

Reserve Money (M0): Currency in circulation + Bankers' deposits with the RBI + 'Other' deposits with the RBI = Net RBI credit to the Government + RBI credit to the commercial sector + RBI's claims on banks + RBI's net foreign assets + Government's currency liabilities to the public − RBI's net non-monetary liabilities.

M1: Currency with the public + Deposit money of the public (Demand deposits with the banking system + 'Other' deposits with the RBI).

M2: M1 + Savings deposits with Post office savings banks.

M3: M1+ Time deposits with the banking system = Net bank credit to the Government + Bank credit to the commercial sector + Net foreign exchange assets of the banking sector + Government's currency liabilities to the public − Net non-monetary liabilities of the banking sector (Other than Time Deposits).

M4: M3 + All deposits with post office savings banks (excluding National Savings Certificates)

Money supply is important because it is linked to inflation by the equation of exchange: MV = PQ, wherein; M is the total money in the nation's money supply, V is the number of times per year each monetary unit is spent P is the average price of all the goods and services sold during the year, Q is the quantity of assets, goods and services sold during the year. Money supply may be less than or greater than the demand of money in the economy. If the money supply grows faster than its use, inflation in a class of goods or assets is likely to follow (according to Milton Friedman, "inflation is always and everywhere a monetary phenomenon").

C.2 ECONOMIC INDICATORS

An economic indicator is simply any economic statistic, such as the unemployment rate, GDP, or the inflation rate, which indicate how well the economy is doing and how well the economy is going to do in the future. The investors use all the information at their disposal to make decisions. If a set of economic indicators suggest that the economy is going to do better or worse in the future than they had previously expected, they may decide to change their investing strategy.

The gross domestic product (GDP) is the godfather of the indicator world. As an aggregate measure of total economic production for a country, GDP represents the market value of all goods and services produced by the economy during the period measured, including personal consumption, government purchases, private inventories, paid-in construction costs and the foreign trade balance.

The gross domestic product (GDP) is one the primary indicators used to gauge the health of a country's economy. It represents the total dollar value of all goods and services produced over a specific time period - one can think of it as the size of the economy. Usually, GDP is expressed as a comparison to the previous quarter or year. For example, if the year-to-year GDP is up 3%, this is thought to mean that the economy has grown by 3% over the last year. Measuring GDP is complicated, but at its most basic, the calculation can be done in one of two ways: either by adding up what everyone earned in a year (income approach), or by adding up what everyone spent (expenditure method). Logically, both measures should arrive at roughly the same total.

The GDP is a measure of all currently produced goods and services valued at market prices. One should notice several features of the GDP measure. First, only currently produced goods (produced during the relevant year) are included. This means that if someone buys a 150-year old classic Heritage house, it does not count towards the GDP, but the service rendered by the real estate agent in the process of buying the house does. Secondly, only final goods and services are counted. In order to avoid double counting, intermediate goods used in the production of other goods and services do not enter the GDP. For example, steel used in the production of automobiles is not valued separately. Finally, all goods and services included in the GDP are evaluated at market prices. Thus, these prices reflect the prices consumers pay at the retail level, including indirect taxes such as local sales taxes.

A measure similar to GDP is the gross national product (GNP). The difference between GNP and GDP is rather small. The GDP excludes incomes earned abroad and includes earnings of foreign firms and residents in the country. Several other measures of output and income are derived from the GNP. These include the net national product (NNP), which subtracts from the GNP an allowance for wear and tear on plants and equipment, known as depreciation; the national income, which mainly subtracts indirect taxes from the NNP; the personal income (measures the income received by persons from all sources, and is arrived at by subtracting from the national income such items as corporate profit tax payments and social security contributions that individuals do not receive, and adding such items as transfer payments that individuals do receive but are not part of the national income); and the personal disposable income (which subtracts personal tax payments such as income taxes from the personal income measure). While all these measures move up and down in a related manner, it is personal disposable income that is intimately tied to consumer demand for goods and services, the most dominant component of aggregate demand.

It should be noted that the aggregate income/output measures discussed above are usually quoted both in current prices (in "nominal" terms) and in constant monetary unit such as, dollars (in "real" terms). The latter are adjusted for inflation and are thus most widely used since they are not subject to distortions introduced by changes in prices.

The income approach, which is sometimes referred to as GDP (I), is calculated by adding up total compensation to employees, gross profits for incorporated and non incorporated firms, and taxes, less any subsidies. The expenditure method is the more common approach and is calculated by adding total consumption, investment, government spending and net exports. As one can imagine, economic production and growth, what GDP represents, has a large impact on nearly everyone within that economy. For example, when the economy is healthy, one would typically see low unemployment and wage increases as businesses demand labor to meet the growing economy. A significant change in GDP, whether up or down, usually has a significant effect on the stock market. It's not hard to understand why: a bad economy usually means lower profits for companies, which in turn means lower stock prices. Investors really worry about negative GDP growth, which is one of the factors economists use to determine whether an economy is in a recession.

In simple terms, the gross domestic product is an estimate of the final value of goods and services sold in the economy at a given point of time at market prices and with the value of imports subtracted. Since, each person's income is also another person's income. Therefore, the gross domestic product can be calculated by adding all the incomes in the economy such as from employment, trading profits, self employment, and capital consumption with stock appreciation deducted. Moreover, if the gross domestic product is the final value of the goods and services sold as mentioned earlier, then it should be possible to calculate by adding the contributions made by respective industries as well. However, as every output is not the final product, hence, it requires adjustment for double counting to calculate the sector contribution. Even then, the gross domestic product as calculated does not provide a clear economic scenario of an economy. For example, the activities which are done which transaction of money are not a part of calculation. Hence, GDP figures are understatement to some extent of that is actually produced and consumed. Nevertheless, this provides a good indication of the performance and trend of each sector and the yearly comparison can tell the shift in the structure of economy. As the gross domestic product is calculated at current prices, therefore, it is likely to give a higher projection due to price rise of the goods and not because of the volume of the goods sold. This means that the price figures need to be adjusted for inflation. This adjustment utilizes relevant price indices such as retail price index, wholesale price index etc., and the component series of GDP is adjusted and summarized with the total divided into gross domestic product at current prices; resulting a GDP deflator which is a measure of inflation in GDP. Therefore, GDP deflator is GDP at current price divided by GDP at constant price.

The wholesale price index as mentioned above is calculated from the movement of basket of separate items that are produced and manufactured in that country. It is a base weighted index and gives an indication of the core inflation. On the other hand, the retail price index measures the overall change in the prices of things people buy, including services as well as goods from the shop. However, the savings and income tax are not included. The retail price index is not a cost of living index although it may appear like that. Basically, it measures the price changes and therefore provides an indication of what people would need to spend every month so as to repurchase the things they bought initially. Therefore, it could be best regarded as a close approximation to the change in the cost of living. It can also be used to check whether the take – home pay has kept pace with the prices. In nutshell, retail price index reflects the experience of an average household and is a broad indicator of inflation for majority of people.

The important thing is that gross domestic product is estimates in local currency and international comparison of GDP would be misleading, due to reasons of different exchange rates and difference in economic development. Therefore, gross domestic product is also calculated using Purchasing Power Parity. Basically, in this method the currencies are somewhat equalized in the sense to determine what a basket of items would cost irrespective of the currency so as to arrive at an international dollar concept.

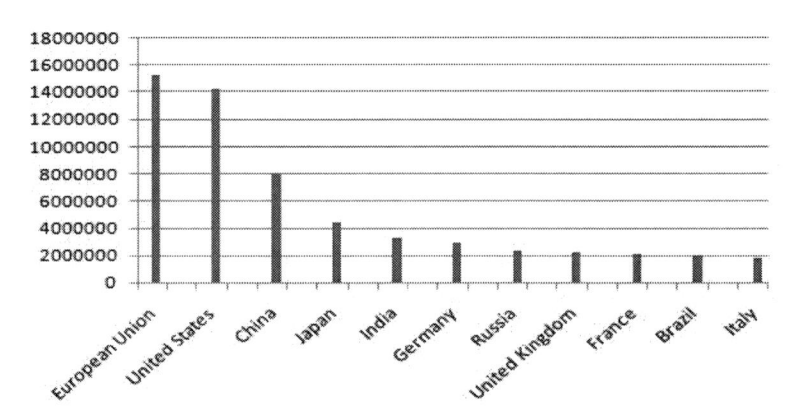

The ten largest economies in the world and the European Union in 2008, measured in GDP PPP (millions of USD), according to the International Monetary Fund are compared in the graph.

Gross Domestic Product is valued in money terms. Therefore, as discussed earlier, with inflation the value will undergo change. However, in case there is no inflation, then the value of money does not change and the real GDP is same as that of nominal GDP. **Nominal GDP** is GDP evaluated at current market prices. Therefore, nominal GDP will include all of the changes in market prices that have occurred during the current year due to **inflation** or **deflation**. Inflation is defined as a rise in the overall price level, and deflation is defined as a fall in the overall price level. In order to abstract from changes in the overall price level, another measure of GDP called **real GDP** is often used. Real GDP is GDP evaluated at the *market prices of some base year*. For example, if 2005 were chosen as the **base year**, then real GDP for 2010 is calculated by taking the quantities of all goods and services purchased in 2010 and multiplying them by their 2005 prices. Nominal GDP indicates the present-time prices of the types of services available, and the goods produced, whereas, real GDP indicates costs according to various base years. Gross Domestic Product is the rate of services and final goods; therefore, if there is a growth in the GDP, it does not necessarily mean that there is also a growth in the services and goods provided.

The equation to calculate Real GDP is: Nominal GDP / GDP Deflator X 100. In nutshell, real GDP calculation for the year is the same as the amount determined for nominal GDP that is stated in the price level for the base year. This indicates the growth of nominal GDP as a percentage which has been accommodated for inflation. Real GDP focuses on price changes and the inflation rate that takes places within the entire year. The population can also have an effect on the real GDP.

It is essential to calculate gross domestic product on annual basis for all types of major sectors, like government investments, public consumption, exports and imports etc. The basic equation to calculate Gross Domestic Product could be:

GDP = C + G + I + EIM, wherein,

- C - refers to all types of consumer spending or private consumption that occurs within a country's economy.

- G - refers to the amounts of government spending.

- I - refer to the capital expenditure of businesses.

- EIM - refers to the net exports of a country, including exports and imports.

Therefore, nominal GDP represents the current prices of all types of services and goods produced whereas; real GDP is the cost of the services rendered and goods indicated by the base year.

One should not forget that any economy is basically a set of integrated individual markets and gross domestic product is the measure of the final value of goods and services sold in each individual market. Market mechanism to a large extent depends on the people and their decisions to save or spend. But saving is basically withdrawal from the flow of gross domestic product and will result in the reduction in flow. Similarly, import indicates flow of money into another country's economy and hence, will also have the same impact as that of saving i.e. reduction of GDP flow. The same way, taxation is also a withdrawal and will have negative effect on the GDP flow. Therefore, savings, imports and taxation would result in a negative impact on the GDP flow. In order to negate the withdrawal effect to the GDP, injections are affected by spending money in the system. This increases the flow of GDP. Comparing to the withdrawal, there are three main ways to carry out injections viz; investment, export and government spending. Therefore, a GDP system has positive or negative impact based on injections and withdrawal respectively. It may be noted that the movement in GDP flow or system is determined by the amount of money in the system and the rate at which it circulates in the system i.e. velocity of money.

In simple words, in any economic system, if the amount of money increases and the velocity of money i.e. rate of transaction, remains the same then, the nominal GDP will increase. Similarly, on the other hand, if the amount of money remains constant but the rate of transaction goes up, the GDP increases correspondingly. Therefore, the effect on the increase or decrease in GDP is a combination of both the factors. The amount of money in the system is determined by the domestic banking system and its velocity by the individuals and corporate who decide on expenditure and saving depending on their own individual economic situation. Therefore, the economic system undergoes a complex interplay between various factors. One the most important factor is the multiplier. It is the effect of any change in the spending behavior of any part of the whole system which has effect on the system like a small uncritical change in the system causes whole system to change depending on its impact in terms of its multiplier effect. Since, economies are never in equilibrium due to transactions, therefore, the multiplier effect always exists.

Market mechanism consists of a complex interplay between the buyers and the sellers which results in determination of the price level. Basically, it is the demand – supply situation which could cause inflation as well if the demand is higher than the supply. Every economy at any given point of time has a specific installed capacity and the potential to stretch if necessary. This depends on various factors which not only includes the capital equipment but also the availability of skilled manpower. In a balanced economy there would be full employment and full utilization of the capacity. Also the there would be a balance on the external account i.e. balance of payment and due to demand – supply equilibrium the inflation remains constant. But any economy does not remain in equilibrium as a multiplier effect.

For example, if the imports increase as compared to exports and other factors remain stable, it would give rise to unemployment due to spare capacity. On the other hand, if the exports go up and the imports remain constant but matches with export, then the economy will again return to the equilibrium condition. Consider another situation wherein, there is a price rise in both goods and services, but the output still remains the same as there has not been any capacity enhancement or investment. The balance of payment concerning export – import remains stable and equal. In this case, there is inflation because the prices have gone up whereas the output remains the same. Real GDP remains unchanged but the nominal GDP goes up due to inflation. In simple words although, it may apparently appear that GDP has gone up but the standard of living will remain the same. Now let us go back to the original situation wherein it was assumed that the economy is in equilibrium with full employment and balance of payment. Due to reasons of either opening up of market or innovation or fall in interest rates there has been a surge in investment. Due to project start-up and the lead time associated with producing saleable items there would be un-utilized capacity for certain period of time. This time gap and the money supply would yield inflationary trend and would push the prices up and imports. Therefore, this inflationary gap would be filled by the price rise and in spite of increase in investment there would not be proportionate rise in employment and growth in GDP. Another unique situation would be if the there is price rise coupled with rise in salaries in accordance with the retail price index, but instead of spending the consumers and the manufacturers increase their saving in the same proportion as increase in prices and salaries. Due to low investment, this saving does not get offset by spending. Therefore, the prices would be up even though the output remains the same. This situation is known as stagflation. Another situation could be that the volume of gross domestic product goes down but the value can increase, if the producers raise their prices and reduce their output as well. This situation is known as slumpflation.

C.3 ECONOMICS CONDITIONS

Economic conditions can be considered the economic characteristics that describe the state of an economy. Often, people comment that the economy is in terrible shape, that the economy is doing well, or that the economy is inherently sound. All such statements are based on certain characteristics of the economy that the issuer of the statement has in mind.

There are a large number of variables or characteristics used to gauge the health of an economy, with four of them usually referred to as the key **macroeconomic** variables: aggregate output or income, the unemployment rate, the inflation rate, and the interest rate. There are, however, numerous additional measures or variables that are collected and used to understand the behavior of an economy. In the United States, for example, additional measures include: the index of leading economic indicators (which gives an idea where the economy is headed in the near future); retail sales (which indicate the strength of consumer demand in the economy); factory orders, especially for big ticket items (which indicate the future growth in output, since the orders will have to be filled); housing starts (robust increase in housing starts are usually taken as a sign of good growth in the future); the consumer confidence index (which indicates how likely consumers are to make favorable decisions to buy both durable and nondurable goods, services, and homes). Other variables tracked are more innocuous than the ones included in the preceding list, such as: aluminum production, steel production, paper and paperboard production, industrial production, hourly earnings, weekly earnings, factory shipments, orders for durable goods, new factory orders, new-home sales, existing-home sales, business inventories, initial jobless claims, help-wanted advertising, purchasing managers' survey, and the foreign trade deficit.

An economy's overall economic activity is summarized by a measure of aggregate output. Since the production or output of goods and services generates **income,** any aggregate output measure is closely associated with an aggregate income measure. Most commonly used concept is that of an aggregate output concept known as the gross domestic product (GDP).

When is the economy considered to be in good shape? Of course, zero growth in the real gross domestic product (a stagnant economy) or negative growth in the real GDP (a shrinking or a recessionary economy) is not a good reflection on the economy. Positive growth is considered desirable. Whether or not a given positive growth rate is good enough, however, depends on whether it can be sustained without generating serious inflationary pressures. Once an economy reaches full employment, a 3 percent rise in the real GDP is considered sustainable on a long-term basis—higher rates are considered inflationary. Nevertheless, when an economy is coming out of a recession, a growth rate of more than 3 percent may not generate a serious inflationary pressure due to unemployed resources. Thus, how well an economy is doing in terms of real GDP growth should be judged on the basis of the 3-percent benchmark, with appropriate upward adjustment for slack in the economy.

The level of employment is the next crucial macroeconomic variable. The employment level is often quoted in terms of the unemployment rate, defined as the fraction of labor force not working (but actively seeking employment). Contrary to what one may expect, the labor force does not consist of all able-bodied persons of working age. Instead, it is defined as consisting of those working and those not working but seeking work. Thus, the labor force as defined leaves out people who are not working but also not seeking work—termed by economists as being voluntarily unemployed. For purposes of government macroeconomic policies, only people who are involuntarily unemployed really matter when calculating the unemployment rate.

For various reasons, it is not possible to bring down the unemployment rate to zero in the best of circumstances. Realistically, economists expect a fraction of the labor force to be unemployed at all times—this fraction for the U.S. labor market has been estimated to be 6 percent. The 6-percent unemployment rate is often referred to as the bench mark unemployment rate. In effect, at 6 percent unemployment, the economy is considered to be at full employment.

Whether or not the economy is doing well in terms of the unemployment rate depends on how far this rate is above the 6-percent benchmark. If the economy has an unemployment rate around 6 percent, it is said to be doing well. Higher unemployment rates reflect worse economic conditions. During the Bush recession, the unemployment rate peaked at 7.7 percent; during the Reagan recession, it peaked at 9.7 percent; and during the Great Depression, it reached more than 25 percent.

The third key macroeconomic variable is inflation. The inflation rate is defined as the rate of change in the price level. Most economies face positive rates of inflation year after year. The price level, in turn, is measured by a price index, which measures the level of prices of goods and services at a point in time. The number of items included in a price index varies depending on the objective of the index. Government agencies periodically report three kinds of price indexes, each having their particular advantages and uses. The first index is called the consumer price index (CPI); it measures the average retail prices paid by consumers for goods and services bought by them. A couple thousand items, typically bought by average households, are included in this index.

A second price index used to measure the inflation rate is called the producer price index (PPI). It is a much broader measure than the consumer price index. The PPI measures the wholesale prices of approximately 3,000 items or as defined. The items included in this index are those that are typically used by producers (manufacturers and businesses) and thus include many raw materials and semi finished goods. The third measure of inflation is the called the implicit GDP price deflator. This index measures the prices of all goods and services included in the calculation of the current GDP. It is the broadest measure of price level.

The three measures of the inflation rate are most likely to move in the same direction, even though not to the same extent. Differences can arise due to the differing number of goods and services included in compiling the three indexes. In general, if one hears about the inflation rate in the popular media, it is most likely to be the one based on the CPI.

Zero percent inflation may appear ideal, but it is neither practical nor desirable. A moderate rate of inflation e.g. 1-2 percent is considered desirable by a vast majority of economists. An inflation rate of up to 5 percent is tolerable. Double-digit inflation rates, however, are definitely considered undesirable by most economists.

The concept of interest rates used by economists is the same as that used widely by other people. The interest rate is invariably quoted in nominal terms i.e., the rate is not adjusted for inflation. Thus, the commonly followed interest rate is actually the nominal interest rate. Nevertheless, there are literally hundreds of nominal interest rates, including: savings account rate, six-month certificate of deposit rate, 15-year mortgage rate, variable mortgage rate, 30-year Treasury bond rate, and the commercial bank prime-lending rate. One can see from these examples that the nominal interest rate has two key attributes—the duration of lending/borrowing involved and the identity of the borrower.

Fortunately, while the hundreds of interest rates that one encounters may appear baffling, they are closely linked to each other. Two characteristics that account for this linkage are the risk worthiness of the borrower and the maturity of the loan involved. So, for example, the interest rate on a 6-month Treasury bill is related to that on a 30-year Treasury bond, as bonds/loans of different maturities command different rates. Also, a 30-year General Motors bond will carry a higher interest rate than a 30-year Treasury bond, as a General Motors bond is riskier than a Treasury bond.

Finally, one should note that the nominal interest rate does not represent the real cost of borrowing or the real return on lending. To understand the real cost or return, one must consider the inflation-adjusted nominal rate, called the real interest rate. Tax and other considerations also influence the real cost/return. But the real interest rate is a very important concept in understanding the main incentives behind borrowing or lending.

The desirable level of the nominal interest rate is linked to the desirable level of the inflation rate. If we consider that an inflation rate of 1-2 percent is desirable, then the short-term nominal interest rate will lie in the 4-5 percent range (assuming a real interest rate of 3 percent).

There are a number of economic variables that are used to project or forecast future economic conditions. There exist theoretical as well as empirical reasons why economists believe that certain variables are harbingers of future economic activities. Some of the variables often used by economists and policy makers to gauge future economic conditions are briefly described below.

Changes in the number of houses being built (simply referred to as housing starts) have an important implication for the direction in which the economy is headed. Notice first that houses are bulky items involving large sums of money—in fact, in the United States, a home is considered an individual's biggest investment. Thus, potentially, housing starts can either lead to a powerful expansion in the economy (by augmenting the aggregate demand) or a serious downturn (by reducing the aggregate demand), depending on the direction and the magnitude of the change in housing starts. Housing starts project the future state of the economy for two main reasons. First, once construction on a house starts it will, most likely, be completed. Thus, work on a "started house" will continue for several months. Second, once the new house is completed, the first occupant of the newly completed house may need to buy additional items (such as a refrigerator, washer, or dryer) to make the house comfortable. This provides a secondary (and, generally, quite large) push to the aggregate demand for goods and services in the economy. Because of these reasons, housing starts are routinely used by economists and participants in financial markets to gauge the future direction of the economy.

Building permits indicate the intention of builders to start building new homes and buildings. Thus, the number of building permits issued today tells us something about the number of housing starts in the near future, with the usual implications for changes in output and employment. If the number of building permits issued is rising, it bodes well for future economic growth. A falling number of building permits issued, on the other hand, has the opposite implication.

Building permits, by nature, can project future economic conditions even further than housing starts, since a building permit must be obtained before construction on a house begins. Nevertheless, one should notice that building permits are far less potent in projecting future growth than housing starts. Although houses started are normally completed, a building permit obtained does not imply that a house will necessarily be built—a change in circumstances can force the builders to defer or scrap building plans.

New factory orders indicate new orders for goods by retail outlets or other businesses. An increase in these orders will generally lead manufacturers to increase production of the items ordered. Thus, an increase in new factory orders is a precursor to an increase in output and employment in the economy. A fall in factory orders will have the opposite effect.

While looking at new factory orders, economists particularly concentrate on big ticket items, items that involve relatively large sums of money. Big-ticket items can be consumer goods, such as automobiles, washers, or dryers, or capital goods, such as machines and equipment. An increase in orders for big-ticket items provides a big forward push to the economy not only because these items have to be produced, but also because they can generate secondary demands for raw materials. For example, an increase in automobile production would necessarily increase the demand for steel, causing steel production to go up as well.

Businesses maintain certain levels of inventories to meet unexpected product demand—economists often refer to businesses' usual inventory levels as normal levels of inventories. When firms stock up on inventories, output and employment rise. Rising or falling inventories serve to indicate the future direction of output and employment as well. This can be explained as follows. Suppose that business inventories rise far above the normal level because firms are unable to sell the current output of goods. Businesses have only one sure cure to trim the piling inventories—cut future production. Thus, a rise in inventories can often be precursor to a decline in output and employment in the next period. The opposite is true when business inventories fall far below the normal level. To replenish inventories, manufacturers must increase production in the near future, spurring economic growth and lowering the unemployment rate.

The consumer confidence index is an index that attempts to measure the level of consumer confidence. This index is based on a survey of consumers regarding their outlook. An increase in the consumer confidence index implies that consumers feel more confident about the economy and their own economic well-being. A rise in the consumer confidence index is most likely to lead to an increase in consumer spending, increasing the level of aggregate demand. This, in turn, implies that output and employment will increase in the near future. By contrast, decline in the consumer confidence index will most likely lead to a decline in output and employment.

The index of leading indicators combines several factors that are considered useful in indicating the future course of the economy. In the United States, the index of leading economic indicators (often abbreviated as the LEI) is based on about a dozen economic series that are deemed capable of forecasting future economic activities. Some of the important leading variables included in the construction of the LEI are: new orders for durable goods, average workweek, building permits, stock prices, certain wholesale prices, and claims for unemployment insurance.

If the index of leading indicators keeps increasing, then economists take this as a sign that the economy will keep expanding (if it is already growing) or that it will start expanding (if the economy is in a recession or if it is experiencing stagnation). The opposite is the case if the index starts to decline. In that case, economists take this as a warning sign that the economy will slow down or even dip into a recession (if the economy is growing) or that the downturn will become worse (if the economy is facing a recession or stagnation).

As is apparent from the preceding discussion, economists and financial observers use observations on numerous economic variables to understand the behavior of an economy. However, the four key macroeconomic variables—aggregate output measure, the unemployment rate, the inflation rate, and the interest rate—do summarize the most important characteristics of a macro economy. These four variables can be reduced to an even smaller group because they are related.

Notice that if the real gross domestic output goes up, employment will go up sooner or later. Producers may first request overtime from existing workers if they are not sure whether the increased level of output can be maintained in the future. But as soon as they feel reasonably sure that the increased output level is relatively permanent, they will hire additional permanent workers. This will raise the level of employment of the labor force in the economy and will, in general, reduce the unemployment rate. Thus, the aggregate output measure and the unemployment rate variable go hand in hand. Either will suffice to convey roughly the same information about economic conditions in the economy. Of the two, it is has been customary to use the unemployment rate because it is more readily understood than a measure of aggregate output such as GDP.

Similarly, the nominal interest rate and the inflation rate are linked. If the inflation rate goes up, so does the nominal interest rate. This is because people care about the real interest rate (the interest rate adjusted for the inflation rate). Thus, if the inflation rate goes up, the real value of a given nominal interest rate declines. As a result, savers require higher nominal interest rates in order to be compensated for the higher inflation rate. Usually, the difference between the nominal interest rate and the inflation rate is 3 percent—a level at which lenders feels comfortable lending. Thus, the nominal interest rate and the inflation rate also go hand in hand. Out of these two variables, it has been customary to use the inflation rate to describe economic conditions because the public readily understands it.

Thus, the minimum numbers of characteristics used to describe economic conditions are two: the unemployment rate and the inflation rate. They both have negative connotations—neither a higher unemployment rate nor a higher inflation rate is considered desirable. Even reporting information on these two variables gets a little complicated as it is widely believed that there is a trade-off between the unemployment rate and the inflation rate. That is, macroeconomic policy makers can follow an economic policy that may lower one rate while increasing the other. Thus, an expansionary monetary policy may reduce the unemployment rate by increasing the aggregate demand in the economy—due to a lower interest rate, consumers are able to finance additional spending through borrowing, and businesses are able to invest more as the cost of borrowing goes down. The upward pressure on aggregate demand, however, also places upward pressure on the price level, raising the inflation rate.

Because of the above mentioned trade-off, it is desirable to examine information on both the unemployment rate and the inflation rate to better understand the economic conditions in the economy. Sometimes, these two variables are combined, in an attempt to give a better picture than when unemployment and inflation rates are looked at separately. The sum of the unemployment rate and the inflation rate has been dubbed as the misery index. The adjective "misery" alludes to the negative connotations associated with the unemployment and inflation rates. Adding them together takes care of the trade-off—one rate may go up and the second may go down, but the misery index captures both. Thus, the higher the value of the misery index, the worse is the overall economic conditions. Stagflation was experienced globally by many countries during the 1970s when world oil prices rose sharply, leading to the birth of the Misery Index. The Misery Index, or the total of the inflation rate and the unemployment rate combined, functions as a rough gauge of how badly people feel during times of stagflation. The term was used often during the 1980 U.S. presidential race. One must, however, realize that the use of a single broad concept such as the misery index is probably not adequate to describe economic conditions properly. At the bare minimum, one should use the unemployment rate and the inflation rate separately to summarize the economic conditions of an economy.

Inflation has been since long as it is a part of the system design, therefore, this remains one of the crucial macroeconomic problems in most of the countries. Keynes did provide a new framework and the definition was also modified suitably. G. Crowther in his *An Outline of Money* defines inflation that reflects the shift in economic thinking. According to his definition "The simplest and most useful definition seems to be that inflation is a state in which the value of money is falling i.e. prices are rising. Inflation is usually associated with rising activity and employment."

The identification of the root cause of inflation has always been a controversial topic. For identifying the sources of inflation, aggregate demand and aggregate supply functions have been used. Thomas F. Dernburg in his book *Macroeconomics* (1985) defines aggregate demand function as follows: "The level of aggregate expenditure associated with different price levels is called aggregate demand function." Aggregate demand function can easily be derived using IS-LM model. The IS/LM model is a macroeconomic tool that demonstrates the relationship between interest rates and real output in the goods and services market and the money market. The intersection of the IS and LM curves is the "General Equilibrium" where there is simultaneous equilibrium in all the markets of the economy. IS/LM stands for Investment Saving / Liquidity preference Money supply. The IS/LM model was born at the Econometric Conference held in Oxford during September, 1936. Roy Harrod, John R. Hicks, and James Meade all presented papers describing mathematical models attempting to summarize John Maynard Keynes' General Theory of Employment, Interest, and Money.

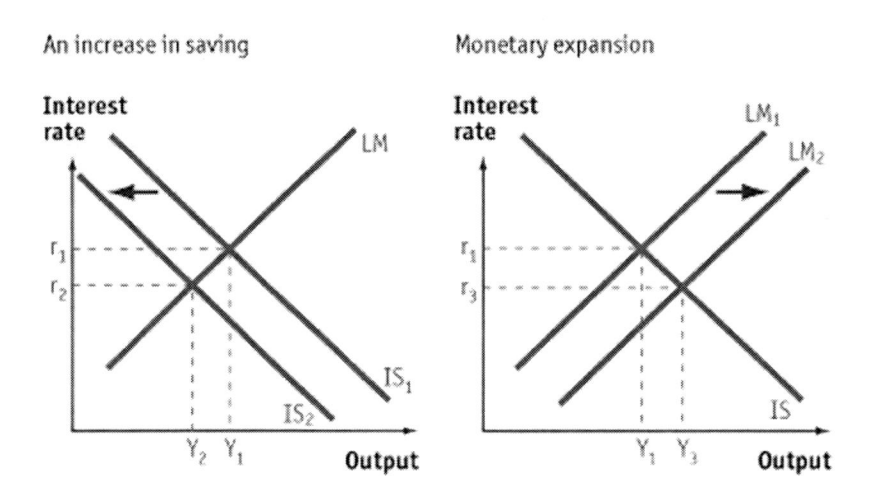

An increase in saving

Monetary expansion

The IS-relation can be said to describe the equilibrium in the goods market for a given level of the real interest rate. The IS relation is derived from the demand components:

$$C = \alpha_o + \alpha_1 (Y - T)$$

Where, C is (real) consumption, Y is output, and T is net taxes (taxes minus transfers) and we refer to Y - T as disposable income. Let us assume that $\alpha_1 < 1$.

$$I = \beta_0 - \beta_1 r$$

Where, I is fixed investment, r is the real rate of interest, and β_1 is a positive parameter. Government consumption G is usually taken to be exogenous. Define total demand as E = C + I + G and it is obtained by adding up that

$$E = \text{constant} - \beta_1 r + \alpha_1 (Y - T)$$

For fixed T and given r this can plotted as a line with slope less than one as a function of Y. The "supply function" is simply Y, which means that all demand will be satisfied - this is the 45 degree line in a Y,E plot or output is demand determined. Setting E = Y, the IS-curve can be solved for Y as a function of r (or r as a function of Y).

The LM relation is derived from the demand for money

$$M^d = P\, L(Y, r + \pi^e)$$

where P is the price level and π^e is expected inflation. Sometimes we just write the relation as

$$M^d = P\, L(Y, i)$$

where 'i' is the nominal interest rate $r + \pi^e$. The L-function is the demand for real money and if 'i' is the interest rate on bonds then it should be 'i' that enters the relation because the alternative to holding money is holding bonds (or buying goods). Given an exogenous supply or money M, setting $M = M^d$ (equilibrium in the money market) gives

$$M = P\, L(Y, i)$$

and for a fixed M and fixed price level P this is gives Y as an implicit function of r. Because L is increasing in Y and decreasing in i (and thus in r) setting L(Y; i) = constant gives Y as an increasing function of r (if Y increase, L will tend to increase, so to keep it constant r has to also increase). The intersection of the LM and the IS curves and thereby find the equilibrium in the economy. As far as the LM-curve is concerned an increase in P has the same effect as a decrease in M. This gives the AD-curve: output as a function of P.

The IS/LM model is considered out-of-date in academia because there is no modeling of behavior. However, modern forecasting models usually contain an IS/LM core. Consider the multiplier. This is really important; if the government lowers taxes or increases G how much will the economy expand. The question of the effect of government stimulus is the main question. In the model, the effect is bigger the larger the marginal propensity to consume (α). For example, that temporary tax breaks have very small effects unless many consumers are credit constrained. The main feature underlying models with Keynesian properties is that producer will satisfy supply at given prices. In most modern models with optimizing agents this is still assumed to be the case and little progress has been made on modeling price setting (modern models will typically assume prices are only fixed for one period and have a dynamic dimension, nonetheless the fix-price assumption is central.). So it is still quite fair to say that the agenda of modern macroeconomics is still the agenda set by Keynes, although the details of models look very different from the basic IS/LM model.

In nutshell, the Keynes effect arises because variation in price level changes the real amount of money. This in turn affects the rate of interest which affects investment and aggregate demand. A rise in price level results in a reduction of real balances. Wealth holders in this situation find that their wealth has been reduced and as a consequence they tend to cut down their spending at all levels of income. This is called *"Pigou effect"* or *"real balance effect."* Moreover, a rise in aggregate demand indicated by an upward shift in the aggregate demand function may result in a mild increase in the general price level so long the economy is characterized by involuntary unemployment. However, when the economy reaches full employment, any increase in aggregate demand will simply raise the general price level without any impact on real national income.

Inflation cannot continue endlessly if the money supply remains constant. A rise in the general price level is always accompanied by an increase in the transactions demand for money which is met by securing cash balances otherwise used for satisfying speculative demand. As a consequence, the rate of interest rises which in turn reduces the investment spending. In some cases, however, when the prices continue to rise for a long period and the investors do not anticipate any reduction in them, a rise in the rate of interest may turn out to be a very weak incentive. But in all other cases, a rise in interest rate by dampening the enthusiasm of investors reduces their spending, which, through the fall in income will also reduce consumption spending in subsequent periods. Hence, in course of time the inflationary pressure will be reduced and eventually the process may also come to an end. The notion of cost inflation is old. Any increase in money wage rates matched by an increase in labour productivity will not be inflationary. Edward Shapiro in his book "Macroeconomics Analysis" argues, " Wage push inflation can follow only from 'spontaneous' or 'autonomous' upward shifts in the supply function as opposed to those that are induced by excess demand for labour. Wage push inflation will not occur in an economy in which labour markets are perfectly competitive. In such situation, wage rates will vary with the marginal productivity in labour."

Regarding inflation sometimes it is wrongly believed that inflation is either demand pull or cost push. In fact, most of the inflationary processes contain some elements of both which sustain each other. As a result, inflationary forces once initiated by demand pull factors persist for a long period and the price rise continues. Once an inflationary process starts due to rise in autonomous spending and the general price level rises, the real wages of workers tend to decline. In this situation, the trade unions try to negotiate increase in wages. If the management has to agree for increase, then this situation may further increase the price. This is a situation in which money wage rates and the general price level chase each other in an upward spiral. This is called wage-price spiral.

In addition, it has been observed that under the conditions of smaller unemployment and tighter labour markets, organized labour becomes more aggressive and succeeds in getting higher wage increase, while under opposite conditions labour would be less demanding. Therefore, it is evident that there exists an inverse relationship between the rate of wage increase and the rate of employment. This relationship was first propounded by A.W. Phillips in his pioneer work "Relation between Unemployed and the Rate of Change in Money Wage Rates in the United Kingdom". This theory of inflation is considered in terms of the **"Phillips Curve"** named after A.W. Phillips. A Phillips curve shows that there is an inverse relationship between the rate of money wage increase and the rate of unemployment of the labour force. A Phillips curve can be derived from an economy's data for a period of years by plotting for each year the percentage of money wage rate increase.

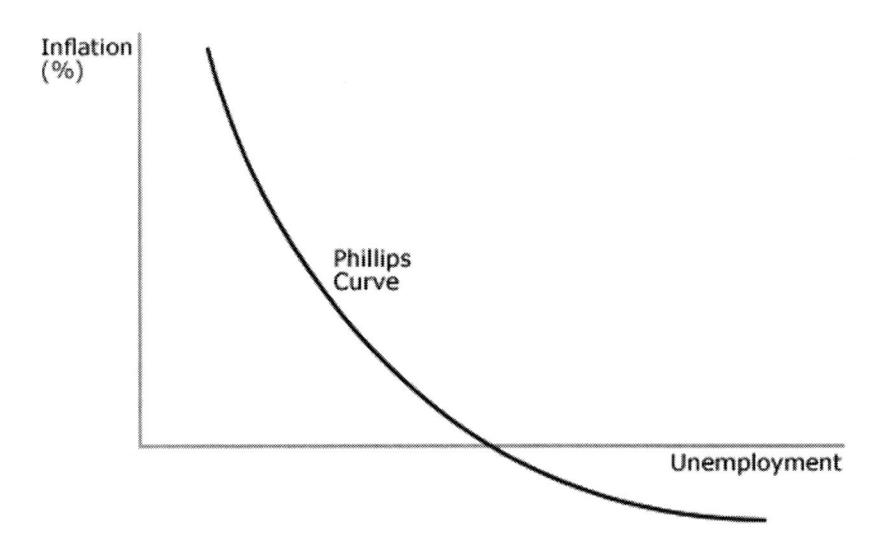

Graph: Phillips Curve showing downward-sloping relationship between Inflation (%) on the y-axis and Unemployment on the x-axis.

Since, wages constitute an important component of production costs; a rise in wage rate normally leads to a rise in prices. But every money wage increase is not inflationary. When wage rate increase is only that much that is required due to increase in the labour productivity, it does not lead to inflation. The Phillips curve relationship points out that low unemployment is associated with rapid wage increase which, in turn, leads to inflation. High employment, on the contrary implies soft labour market in which wages cannot be pushed up easily. Hence, high unemployment does allow inflationary pressures to build up. The Phillips curve thus stressed "the idea of a trade-off between unemployment and inflation. Society, it suggested, can opt for low unemployment, but only at the price of higher rate of inflation, or it can opt for price stability, but at the cost of a high unemployment rate."

Stagflation is a term used by economists to define an economy that has inflation, a slow or stagnant economic growth rate and a relatively high unemployment rate. Economic policy makers across the globe try to avoid stagflation at all costs. With stagflation, a country's citizens are affected by high rates of inflation and unemployment. High unemployment rates further contribute to the slowdown of a country's economy, causing the economic growth rate to fluctuate no more than a single percentage point above or below a zero growth rate. Now it is a commonly accepted fact that supply shock is the basic cause of stagflation. The supply shock (decrease in supply) by itself adequately explains the simultaneous existence of inflation, unemployment and stagflation. A reduction in supply implies lack of growth and increase in unemployment. It also leads to a rise in the general price level. If the aggregate demand remains unchanged, a decrease in aggregate supply due to supply shocks in commodities such as oil and food grains will raise the price level and bring down the output level. Obviously this fall in the output level will lead to unemployment which may not be necessarily proportionate to decrease in output.

It is generally agreed that although there are some common cause of stagflation, yet each case of stagflation is somewhat unique. Therefore, there are no easy cures for stagflation. According to Rendall Hinshaw in his "Stagflation", he mentioned "The combination of unemployment and inflation is a very delicate matter; if we fight recession, we stimulate inflation and if we fight inflation, we stimulate recession." The Keynesians recommend wage control to moderate price rise. A restrictive monetary policy is also suggested to tone down inflationary pressures. According to Keynesians, expansionary fiscal policy can be relied upon to increase output (real income) and employment. According to monetarists, stagflation is a monetary disorder, and can be controlled by reducing the money supply. Milton Friedman, the chief exponent of the monetarist school, has suggested that money supply should be expanded at the same rate at which the output increases. By pursuing this policy it may be possible to avert stagflation.

C.4 ECONOMICS POLICIES

Market economies have regular fluctuations in the level of economic activity which we call the business cycle. It is convenient to think of the business cycle as having three phases. The first phase is expansion when the economy is growing along its long term trends in employment, output, and income. But at some point the economy will overheat, and suffer rising prices and interest rates, until it reaches a turning point -- a *peak* -- and turn downward into a recession (the second phase). Recessions are usually brief and are marked by falling employment, output, income, prices, and interest rates. Most significantly, recessions are marked by rising unemployment. The economy will hit a bottom point -- a *trough* -- and rebound into a strong recovery (the third phase). The recovery will enjoy rising employment, output, and income while unemployment will fall. The recovery will gradually slow down as the economy once again assumes its long term growth trends, and the recovery will transform into an expansion.

The approach to the business cycle depends upon the type of economic system. Under a *communist* system, there is no business cycle since all economic activities are controlled by the central planners. Indeed, this lack of a business cycle is often cited as an advantage of a command economy. Both *socialist* and *fascist* economies have a mix of market and command sectors. Again, the command sector in these economies will not have a business cycle -- while the market sector will display a cyclical activity. In a full *market* economy -- like the United States -- the nation can suffer extreme swings in the levels of economic activity.

The economic policies used by the government to smooth out the extreme swings of the business cycle are called contra cyclical or stabilization policies, and are based on the theories of John Maynard Keynes. Writing in 1936 (the Great Depression), Keynes argued that the business cycle was due to extreme swings in the total demand for goods and services. The total demand in an economy from households, business, and government is called *aggregate demand*. Contra cyclical policy is increasing aggregate demand in recessions and decreasing aggregate demand in overheated expansions.

In a market economy (or market sector) the government has two types of economic policies to control aggregate demand -- fiscal policy and monetary policy. When these policies are used to stimulate the economy during a recession, it is said that the government is pursuing *expansionary* economic policies. And when they are used to contract the economy during an overheated expansion, it is said that the government is pursuing *contractionary* economic policies.

Monetary and fiscal policies are two powerful tools that are generally used to regulate the economy towards equilibrium. The problem is that stability in a free market economy cannot be predicted for long due to involuntary unemployment, balance of payment, inequality in distribution of income, steady economic growth. All these issues cannot be left to the market forces to resolve but the government need to take actions in order to channelize market forces in the way which could further stabilize the market economy. These actions are taken with the help of instruments which are basically – monetary and fiscal policies. Before starting detailed discussion on both the policies, let us examine some of the basic differences.

Fiscal policy and monetary policies are instruments utilized by governments to give impetus to the economy of a nation and sometimes they are used to curb the excess growth. The fiscal policy is the underlying principle through which the government controls the economy with the collection and expenditure of money. This is revealed in the government's fiscal policy of a particular period.

The government engages in manipulating the available fund within the economy. This is described in the monetary policy of the government. It deals with the issuing of currency and administration of banks for smooth operations. A good flow of money enables customers to have more cash at hand and in turn encourages spending.

The fiscal policy relates with the programs and plans of the government and creates an increasing demand for workers resulting in lowering of unemployment position. The automatic fiscal plans correct the sliding down of economy, like the unemployment insurance to give relief to persons who lose jobs. Tax cuts are brought in to give back more money to business and consumers which they can spend in turn to strengthen the economy.

The fiscal policy revolves around the economic position of the nation and the related strategy to impose taxes to make maximum use of fund. This is not a onetime affair but goes on changing every year to suit the position of the economy and its needs during the specific period.

The monetary policy differs with the fiscal policy on the ground that it is exclusively for banks and the circulation of money in an efficient way. This is also changed every year on the demand and supply of the money and makes effect on the rate of interest on loans. This monetary policy acts as the key regulator through the key bank of the nation such as the Federal Reserve System in US or Reserve Bank of India.

Fiscal policy is fundamentally an attempt of the nation to give direction to the economy through manipulation of tax structures. Whereas, the monetary policy is the procedure by which the nation or its key bank influences the supply of fund, rates of interest and so on. The main objectives of both the procedures are attainment of growth of economy and its stability.

In the monetary policy, the central bank attempts to bring in four principles to either increase or reduce money supply to make a change in the structure. The primary principle is to change the cash reserve ratio of commercial banks. This restraint compels banks to maintain a deposit at the central bank. The increase in the ratio means dearth of funds at the hands of commercial banks, which makes loans to consumers difficult. Accordingly interest rates on short-term borrowings are settled. The central banks also employ the process of buying or selling of government bonds to control the supply of money in the market. These are basic differences between fiscal policy and monetary policy of a country.

- Fiscal policy gives the direction of economy of a nation. Monetary policy controls the supply of money in the nation.

- Fiscal policy relates to the economic position of a nation. Monetary policy focuses on the strategy of banks.

- Fiscal policy administers the taxation structure of the nation. Monetary Policy helps to stabilize the economy of the country.

- Fiscal policy speaks of the government's economic program. Monetary policy sets the program of key banks of the nation.

When the economy is in a recession (when business and consumer confidence is very low and perhaps where deflationary pressures are taking hold) monetary policy may be ineffective in increasing current national spending and income. The problems experienced by the Japanese in trying to stimulate their economy through a zero-interest rate policy might be mentioned here. In this case, fiscal policy might be more effective in stimulating demand. Other economists disagree – they argue that short term changes in monetary policy do impact quite quickly and strongly on consumer and business behavior. Consider the way in which domestic demand in both the United States and the UK has responded to the interest rate cuts introduced in the wake of the terror attacks on the USA in the autumn of 2001. However, there may be factors which make fiscal policy ineffective aside from the usual 'crowding out' phenomena. Future-oriented consumption theories hold that individuals undo government fiscal policy through changes in their own behavior – for example, if government spending and borrowing rises, people may expect an increase in the tax burden in future years, and therefore increase their current savings in anticipation of this.

Monetary policy is one of the tools that a national Government uses to influence its economy. Using its monetary authority to control the supply and availability of money, a government attempts to influence the overall level of economic activity in line with its political objectives. Usually this goal is "macroeconomic stability" - low unemployment, low inflation, economic growth, and a balance of external payments. Monetary policy is usually administered by a Government appointed "Central Bank", the Bank of Canada and the Federal Reserve Bank in the United States, Reserve Bank of India etc.

Central banks have not always existed. In early economies, governments would supply currency by minting precious metals with their stamp. No matter what the creditworthiness of the government, the worth of the currency depended on the value of its underlying precious metal. A coin was worth its gold or silver content, as it could always be melted down to this. A country's worth and economic clout was largely to its holdings of gold and silver in the national treasury. Monarchs, despots and even democrats tried to skirt this inviolate law by filing down their coinage or mixing in other substances to make more coins out of the same amount of gold or silver. They were inevitably found out by the traders, money lenders and others who depended on the worth of that currency.

The advent of paper money during the industrial revolution meant that it wasn't too difficult for a country to alter its amount of money in circulation. Instead of gold, all that was needed to produce more banknotes was paper, ink and a printing press. Because of the skepticism of all concerned, paper money was backed by a "promise to pay" upon demand. A holder of a "pound sterling" note of the United Kingdom could actually demand his pound of silver! When gold became the de facto backing of the world's currency a "gold standard" was developed where nations kept sufficient gold to back their "promises to pay" in their national treasuries. The problem with this standard was that a nation's economic health depended on its holdings of gold. When the treasury was bare, the currency was worthless.

Modern central banking dates back to the aftermath of great depression of the 1930s. Governments, led by the economic thinking of the great John Maynard Keynes, realized that collapsing money supply and credit availability greatly contributed to the savagery of this depression. This realization that money supply affected economic activity led to active government attempts to influence money supply through "monetary policy". At this time, nations created central banks to establish "monetary authority". This meant that rather than accepting whatever happened to money supply, they would actively try to influence the amount of money available. This would influence credit creation and the overall level of economic activity.

Modern monetary policy does not involve gold to a great extent. In 1968, the United States rescinded its promise to pay in gold and effectively removed itself from the "gold standard". Since then, it has been the job of the Federal Reserve to control the amount of money and credit in the U.S. economy.

Economists debate the relevant measures of money supply. "Narrow" money supply or M1 is currency in circulation and the currency in easily accessed chequing and savings accounts. "Broader" money supply measures such as M2 and M3 include term deposits and even money market mutual funds. Economists debate the finer points of the implementation and effectiveness of monetary policy but one thing is obvious. At the extremes, monetary policy is a potent force. By affecting the money supply, it is theorized, that monetary policy can establish ranges for inflation, unemployment, interest rates, and economic growth. A stable financial environment is created in which savings and investment can occur, allowing for the growth of the economy as a whole.

Albert Gaillard Hart in *'Monetary Policy for Income Stabilization'* defines monetary policy as an economic policy "which influences the public's stock of money substitutes, or the public's demand for such assets, or both that is, policy which influences the public's liquidity position." Sometimes, the economists distinguish between *monetary policy* and *credit policy*. The difference between the two is that monetary policy is related with changes in the supply of money whereas, credit policy is more concerned with changes in the supply of credit. Some of the main objectives of monetary policy can be summarized as:

1. Maximum feasible output
2. High rate of growth
3. Fuller employment
4. Price stability
5. Equality in the distribution of income and wealth
6. Equilibrium in the balance of payment

It is also important to understand the *transmission process* by which a change in money supply brings about a change in aggregate demand and in the level of income and production. According to Keynesian theory, changes in money supply and changes in level of income is not closely linked whereas, the monetarists see a close and stable linkage. Two primary transmission processes may be defined as – (a) Portfolio mechanism – acts through investment multiplier and market rates of interest (b) Wealth mechanism – acts through changes in market value of capital stock.

In order to achieve the objectives of monetary policy, the monetary authorities need to decide on certain strategy to identify 'target variables' that are capable to influence the objectives in the desired manner. Traditionally, three variables have been identified as the target variables for monetary policy. These are: (1) Money supply (2) Bank credit (3) Interest rates in the securities market.

Fiduciary or paper money is issued by the Central Bank on the basis of computation of estimated demand for cash. Monetary policy guides the Central Bank's supply of money in order to achieve the objectives of price stability (or low inflation rate), full employment, and growth in aggregate income. This is necessary because money is a medium of exchange and changes in its demand relative to supply, necessitate spending adjustments. To conduct monetary policy, some monetary variables which the Central Bank controls are adjusted-a monetary aggregate, an interest rate or the exchange rate-in order to affect the goals which it does not control. The instruments of monetary policy used by the Central Bank depend on the level of development of the economy, especially its financial sector. The commonly used instruments are discussed below.

- Reserve Requirement: The Central Bank may require Deposit Money Banks to hold a fraction (or a combination) of their deposit liabilities (reserves) as vault cash and or deposits with it. Fractional reserve limits the amount of loans banks can make to the domestic economy and thus limit the supply of money. The assumption is that Deposit Money Banks generally maintain a stable relationship between their reserve holdings and the amount of credit they extend to the public. Reserve requirements are a percentage of commercial banks', and other depository institutions', demand deposit liabilities (i.e. chequing accounts) that must be kept on deposit at the Central Bank as a requirement of

Banking Regulations. Though seldom used, this percentage may be changed by the Central Bank at any time, thereby affecting the money supply and credit conditions. If the reserve requirement percentage is increased, this would reduce the money supply by requiring a larger percentage of the banks, and depository institutions, demand deposits to be held by the Central Bank, thus taking them out of supply. As a result, an increase in reserve requirements would increase interest rates, as less currency is available to borrowers. This type of action is only performed occasionally as it affects money supply in a major way. Altering reserve requirements is not merely a short-term corrective measure, but a long-term shift in the money supply.

- Open Market Operations: The Central Bank buys or sells (on behalf of the Fiscal Authorities - the Treasury) securities to the banking and non-banking public in the open market. One such security is Treasury Bills. When the Central Bank sells securities, it reduces the supply of reserves and when it buys back securities-by redeeming them-it increases the supply of reserves to the Deposit Money Banks, thus affecting the supply of money. Open market operations are just that, the buying or selling of Government bonds by the Central Bank in the open market. If the Central Bank were to buy bonds, the effect would be to expand the money supply and hence lower interest rates; the opposite is true if bonds are sold. This is the most widely used instrument in the day to day control of the money supply due to its ease of use, and the relatively smooth interaction it has with the economy as a whole.

- Lending by the Central Bank: The Central Bank sometimes provide credit to Deposit Money Banks, thus affecting the level of reserves and hence the monetary base.

- Interest Rate: The Central Bank lends to financially sound Deposit Money Banks at a most favorable rate of interest, called the minimum rediscount rate (MRR). The MRR sets the floor for the interest rate regime in the money market (the nominal anchor rate) and thereby affects the supply of credit, the supply of savings (which affects the supply of reserves and monetary aggregate) and the supply of investment (which affects full employment and GDP).

- Direct Credit Control: The Central Bank can direct Deposit Money Banks on the maximum percentage or amount of loans (credit ceilings) to different economic sectors or activities, interest rate caps, liquid asset ratio and issue credit guarantee to preferred loans. In this way the available savings is allocated and investment directed in particular directions.

- Moral Suasion: The Central Bank issues licenses or operating permit to Deposit Money Banks and also regulates the operation of the banking system. It can, from this advantage, persuade banks to follow certain paths such as credit restraint or expansion, increased savings mobilization and promotion of exports through financial support, which otherwise they may not do, on the basis of their risk/return assessment. Basically, this is a persuasion tactic used by an authority to influence and pressure, but not force, banks into adhering to policy. The word *'suasion'*, is for persuading banks and other financial institutions to keep to official guidelines. The *'moral'* aspect comes from the pressure for 'moral responsibility' to operate in a way that is consistent with furthering the good of the economy.

- Prudential Guidelines: The Central Bank may in writing require the Deposit Money Banks to exercise particular care in their operations in order that specified outcomes are realized. Key elements of prudential guidelines remove some discretion from bank management and replace it with rules in decision making.

- Exchange Rate: The balance of payments can be in deficit or in surplus and each of these affect the monetary base, and hence the money supply in one direction or the other. By selling or buying foreign exchange, the Central Bank ensures that the exchange rate is at levels that do not affect domestic money supply in undesired direction, through the balance of payments and the real exchange rate. The real exchange rate when misaligned affects the current account balance because of its impact on external competitiveness.

- <u>Discount Window:</u> is where the commercial banks, and other depository institutions, are able to borrow reserves from the Central Bank at a discount rate. This rate is usually set below short term market rates (T-bills). This enables the institutions to vary credit conditions (i.e., the amount of money to loan out), there by affecting the money supply. It may be noted that the Discount Window is the only instrument which the Central Banks do not have a total control over.

Of the above measures, moral suasion and prudential guidelines are direct supervision or qualitative instruments. The others are quantitative instruments because they have numerical benchmarks.

Implementation of monetary policy and to get the desired effect is not simple and fast. There is a substantial lag between the point of time at which the need for an expansionary or contractionary monetary policy is felt and the time at which the policy can really alter aggregate demand. Because of time lag of uncertain duration and unreliability of forecasts some of the economists have argued that the central bank should defer the practice of implementing various monetary policies and follow a different way. The chief protagonist of this theory is Milton Friedman who is not in favor of discretionary monetary policies but increase in money supply at a gradual, constant rate. However, economists as well as developing countries are skeptical about this approach as a discretionary monetary policy could outperform Friedman's theory.

The monetary policy also gets affected by the presence of various alternate banking systems other than commercial banks such as, mutual savings bank, development bank, insurance companies, pension funds etc. The financial institutions act as financial intermediaries and with increasingly participation can affect the money supply. These financial intermediaries can frustrate the attempts of the central bank to restrict money supply by increasing the velocity of money. Sometimes, the objectives of monetary policy contradict each other. This often happens when the governments try to pursue the dual of objectives of growth and stability, particularly in developing countries which often accelerates the mild inflationary trends to severe levels. The economic costs of this policy are heavy as income inequalities increase making rich richer and poor poorer. According to Michael P. Todaro in his Economic Development in the Third World, "The biggest limitation of monetary policy in the context of developing countries arises from the fact that money and capital markets and financial institutions in them are highly unorganized, often externally dependent, and spatially fragmented."

Fiscal policy should not be seen is isolation from monetary policy.

Monetary policy is seen as something of a blunt policy instrument – affecting all sectors of the economy although in different ways and with a variable impact

Fiscal policy changes can be targeted to affect certain groups (e.g. increases in means-tested benefits for low income households, reductions in the rate of corporation tax for small-medium sized enterprises, investment allowances for businesses in certain regions)

The effects of using either monetary or fiscal policy to achieve a given increase in national income because actual GDP lies below potential GDP (i.e. there is a negative output gap)

Fiscal policy is the means by which a government adjusts its levels of spending in order to monitor and influence a nation's economy. It is the sister strategy to monetary policy with which a central bank influences a nation's money supply. These two policies are used in various combinations in an effort to direct a country's economic goals. Here we take a look at how fiscal policy works, how it must be monitored and how its implementation may affect different people in an economy.

Fiscal policy is the use of government spending and taxation to influence the economy. When the government decides on the goods and services it purchases, the transfer payments it distributes, or the taxes it collects, it is engaging in fiscal policy. The primary economic impact of any change in the government budget is felt by particular groups—a tax cut for families with children, for example, raises their disposable income. Discussions of fiscal policy, however, generally focus on the effect of changes in the government budget on the overall economy. Although changes in taxes or spending that are "revenue neutral" may be construed as fiscal policy—and may affect the aggregate level of output by changing the incentives that firms or individuals face—the term "fiscal policy" is usually used to describe the effect on the aggregate economy of the overall levels of spending and taxation, and more particularly, the gap between them. Before the Great Depression in the United States, the government's approach to the economy was laissez faire. But following the Second World War, it was determined that the government had to take a proactive role in the economy to regulate unemployment, business cycles, inflation and the cost of money. By using a mixture of both monetary and fiscal policies (depending on the political orientations and the philosophies of those in power at a particular time, one policy may dominate over another), governments are able to control economic phenomena.

Fiscal policy is based on the theories of British economist John Maynard Keynes. Also known as Keynesian economics, this theory basically states that governments can influence macroeconomics productivity levels by increasing or decreasing tax levels and public spending. This influence, in turn, curbs inflation (generally considered to be healthy when at a level between 2-3%), increases employment and maintains a healthy value of money. The idea, however, is to find a balance in exercising these influences. For example, stimulating a stagnant economy runs the risk of rising inflation. This is because an increase in the supply of money followed by an increase in consumer demand can result in a decrease in the value of money - meaning that it will take more money to buy something that has not changed in value.

The most immediate effect of fiscal policy is to change the aggregate demand for goods and services. A fiscal expansion, for example, raises aggregate demand through one of two channels. First, if the government increases its purchases but keeps taxes constant, it increases demand directly. Second, if the government cuts taxes or increases transfer payments, households' disposable income rises, and they will spend more on consumption. This rise in consumption will in turn raise aggregate demand.

Fiscal policy also changes the composition of aggregate demand. When the government runs a deficit, it meets some of its expenses by issuing bonds. In doing so, it competes with private borrowers for money loaned by savers. Holding other things constant, a fiscal expansion will raise interest rates and "crowd out" some private investment, thus reducing the fraction of output composed of private investment.

Taking an example of an economy that has slowed down. Unemployment levels are up, consumer spending is down and businesses are not making any money. A government thus decides to fuel the economy's engine by decreasing taxation, giving consumers more spending money while increasing government spending in the form of buying services from the market (such as building roads or schools). By paying for such services, the government creates jobs and wages that are in turn pumped into the economy. Pumping money into the economy is also known as *"pump priming"* ". In the meantime, overall unemployment levels will fall. With more money in the economy and less taxes to pay, consumer demand for goods and services increases. This in turn rekindles businesses and turns the cycle around from stagnant to active. If, however, there are no reins on this process, the increase in economic productivity can cross over a very fine line and lead to too much money in the market. This excess in supply decreases the value of money, while pushing up prices (because of the increase in demand for consumer products). Hence, inflation occurs. For this reason, fine tuning the economy through fiscal policy alone can be a difficult, if not improbable, means to reach economic goals. If not closely monitored, the line between an economy that is productive and one that is infected by inflation can be easily blurred.

When inflation is too strong, the economy may need a slow down. In such a situation, a government can use fiscal policy to increase taxes in order to suck money out of the economy. Fiscal policy could also dictate a decrease in government spending and thereby decrease the money in circulation. Of course, the possible negative effects of such a policy in the long run could be a sluggish economy and high unemployment levels. Nonetheless, the process continues as the government uses its fiscal policy to fine tune spending and taxation levels, with the goal of evening out the business cycles.

- **Expansionary Fiscal Policy = G > T**. That means that government spending is greater than the rate of taxation, so it is a boost to the economy. The disadvantage to this is that a **budget deficit** will ultimately build up.

- **Contractionary Fiscal Policy = G < T**. This has a contractionary, deflationary effect on the economy, but it will improve the government finances over time.

Unfortunately, the effects of any fiscal policy are not the same on everyone. Depending on the political orientations and goals of the policymakers, a tax cut could affect only the middle class, which is typically the largest economic group. In times of economic decline and rising taxation, it is this same group that may have to pay more taxes than the wealthier upper class. Similarly, when a government decides to adjust its spending, its policy may affect only a specific group of people. A decision to build a new bridge, for example, will give work and more income to hundreds of construction workers. A decision to spend money on building a new space shuttle, on the other hand, benefits only a small, specialized pool of experts, which would not do much to increase aggregate employment levels.

- Fiscal policy is weak when investment is very sensitive to interest rates and when consumers pierce the veil and attempt to offset the actions of the government (e.g. saving a tax cut, or increasing their saving when higher government spending leads to expectations of higher taxes in the future)

- Monetary policy is weak when consumers are willing to hold large quantities of money rather than spend them even when interest rates are very low

One of the biggest obstacles facing policymakers is deciding how much involvement the government should have in the economy. Indeed, there have been various degrees of interference by the government over the years. But for the most part, it is accepted that a degree of government involvement is necessary to sustain a vibrant economy, on which the economic well being of the population depends.

In line with the instruments of monetary policy, the main instruments of fiscal policy are taxation, public borrowings, forced saving or deficit financing and public expenditure.

- Taxation: This is the most important source of revenue to the government for all kinds of economy - be it developed, developing or under-developing. The difference could be in quantum and the methodology. Tax revenue constitute of either direct taxes such as levied on individuals and companies or indirect taxes which are levied on commodity. Examples of direct taxes are personal income tax, corporate income tax, property and wealth tax whereas, and examples indirect taxes are sales tax, excise duty, custom duty. Developing economies depend more on the indirect taxes for revenues whereas, developed economies depend on direct taxes. This is primarily due to relative poverty of the masses in the developing countries as compared to developed countries.

- Public Borrowing: This is the second most important source of public revenue. Borrowings are meant to be paid whereas, taxes are not returned (barring excess tax return cases). The government can raise public debt either in the form of voluntary loan or in the form of compulsory loan. Examples of voluntary loan could be bills and securities in the money market whereas examples of compulsory loan could be infrastructure bonds, provident fund. Public borrowing is a common practice in most of the countries as it is much faster than taxes. The logic of borrowing and incurring such loans is that these are required for developmental process such as roads, railways, power, and irrigation. Financing such big project through taxation would place heavy burden on the masses, hence, raising resources to meet such expenditures through public loan is desirable.

- Deficit Financing: This concept of deficit financing was introduced during the period of Great Depression of the 1930 in order to get out of the depression rut. Normally, deficit financing occurs when there is an excess of expenditure over current receipts. It was used to stimulate private investment. While deficit financing is suggested to increase effective demand during periods of depression in the developed countries, mobilization of saving is recommended for developing countries. Generally, the total resources that the government can mobilize from taxation, public borrowing and assistance from foreign countries i.e. external aid or loan, is insufficient to meet the demands for investment and deficit financing is required to bridge this gap.

- <u>Public Expenditure</u>: During recession or in developing countries during the initial phases of development it is generally observed that the private sector does not have the willingness or the resources to invest in infrastructure such as roads, railways, communications, and power. The reason is that investments in such projects are heavy with long payback period. However, without these industrialization cannot be sustained. Therefore, responsibility of building up of infrastructure of the economy and large capital goods industries has to be borne by the government. This requires massive expansion in public expenditures and once these investments are undertaken, the private sector also gets benefitted. Public expenditure is the value of goods and services bought by the State and its articulations. Public expenditure plays four major roles:

1. It contributes to current effective demand.

2. It expresses a coordinated impulse on the economy that can be utilized for stabilization, business cycle inversion and growth purposes.

3. It increases the public endowment of goods for the masses.

4. It gives rise to positive externalities to economy and society, through its capital component.

A GDP component as it is, public expenditure has an immediate impact on gross domestic product. An increase of public expenditure raises

GDP by the same amount, other things equal. Moreover, since income is an important determinant of consumption, that increase of income will be followed by a rise in consumption: a positive feedback loop has been triggered between consumption and income, exactly as in the case of shocks in export, investment or autonomous consumption. The full extent of this mechanism will depend, however, by the reactions of the other economic agents. Firms have to decide whether to increase production or prices in response to demand. Moreover, if consumers interpret the increase in public expenditure as a fall in their disposable income (i.e. after-tax income), consumption may fall accordingly. Subsidies are also a form of public spending. For example, export subsidy that helps to increase export earnings by reducing the price of export goods in international market.

Fiscal Policy is the use of Government spending and taxation to influence the level of economic activity. In theory, fiscal policy can be used to prevent inflation and avoid recession. But, in practice there are many limitations of using fiscal policy.

- **Disincentives of Tax Cuts**: Increasing Taxes to reduce aggregate demand may cause disincentives to work, if this occurs there will be a fall in productivity and aggregate supply could fall. However higher taxes do not necessarily reduce incentives to work if the income effect dominates.

- **Side Effects on Public Spending**: Reduced government spending to Increase aggregate demand could adversely affect public services such as public transport and education causing market failure and social inefficiency.

- **Poor Information**: Fiscal policy will suffer if the government has poor information. For example, if the government believes there is going to be a recession, they will increase aggregate demand, However if this forecast was wrong and the economy grew too fast, and the government action would cause inflation.

- **Time Lags**: If the government plans to increase spending this can take a long time to filter into the economy and it may be too late. Spending plans are only set once a year. There is also a delay in implementing any changes to spending patterns.

- **Budget Deficit**: Expansionary fiscal policy (cutting taxes and increasing G) will cause an increase in the budget deficit which has many adverse effects. Higher budget deficit will require higher taxes in the future and may cause crowding out.

- **Aggregate Demand**: If the government uses fiscal policy its effectiveness will also depend upon the other components of aggregate demand, for example if consumer confidence is very low, reducing taxes may not lead to an increase in consumer spending.

- **Multiplier Effect**: And change in injections may be increased by the multiplier effect, therefore the size of the multiplier will be significant.

- **Crowding Out**: Increased government spending (G) to increased aggregate demand may cause *"Crowding out"* that occurs when increased government spending results in decreasing the size of the private sector. For example if the government increase spending it will have to increase taxes or sell bonds and borrow money, both method reduce private consumption or investment. If this occurs aggregate demand will not increase or increase only very slowly. Increased government borrowing can also put upward pressure on interest rates. To borrow more money the interest rate on bonds may have to rise, causing slower growth in the rest of the economy.

The growing importance of monetary policy and the diminishing role played by fiscal policy in economic stabilization efforts may reflect both political and economic realities. Generally speaking, democratically elected governments may have more trouble using fiscal policy to fight inflation than unemployment. Fighting inflation requires government to take unpopular actions like reducing spending or raising taxes, while traditional fiscal policy solutions to fighting unemployment tend to be more popular since they require increasing spending or cutting taxes.

Political realities, in short, may favor a bigger role for monetary policy during times of inflation.

One other reason suggests why fiscal policy may be more suited to fighting unemployment, while monetary policy may be more effective in fighting inflation. There is a limit to how much monetary policy can do to help the economy during a period of severe economic decline, such as the United States encountered during the 1930s. The monetary policy remedy to economic decline is to increase the amount of money in circulation, thereby cutting interest rates. But once interest rates reach zero, the Federal can do no more. The United States has not encountered this situation, which economists call the "liquidity trap," in recent years, but Japan did during the late 1990s. With its economy stagnant and interest rates near zero, many economists argued that the Japanese government had to resort to more aggressive fiscal policy, if necessary running up a sizable government deficit to spur renewed spending and economic growth.

C.5 ECONOMIC STABILIZATION

Economic stability and growth is what a country and its people desire. However, there are various factors that result in economic fluctuations, inflation, stagflation etc. These have an impact on destabilizing the economy. Economic stability with steady growth provides an opportunity for higher level of employment with enhanced quality of life. Hence, economic stability is the necessary condition for prosperity. Economists have tried to evaluate different ways and their suitability in having effect on economic stability; however, the ways are not in unison. Considering the importance accorded to monetary or fiscal policies, these can be categorized into – Keynesians and Monetarists.

According to Michael Parkin in his book "Macroeconomics" the basic difference between the two schools of thoughts is "Keynesians regard the economy as being inherently stable and as requiring active governmental intervention to achieve stability. They assign a low degree of importance to monetary policy and a high degree of importance to fiscal policy. Monetarists' macroeconomists assign a high degree of importance to variations in the quantity of money as the main determinant of aggregate demand and who regard the economy as inherently stable."

In the 1930s, with the United States reeling from the Great Depression, the government began to use fiscal policy not just to support itself or pursue social policies but to promote overall economic growth and stability as well. Policy-makers were influenced by John Maynard Keynes, an English economist who argued in The General Theory of Employment, Interest, and Money (1936) that the rampant joblessness of his time resulted from inadequate demand for goods and services. According to Keynes, people did not have enough income to buy everything the economy could produce, so prices fell and companies lost money or went bankrupt. Without government intervention, Keynes said, this could become a vicious cycle. As more companies went bankrupt, he argued, more people would lose their jobs, making income fall further and leading yet more companies to fail in a frightening downward spiral. Keynes argued that government could halt the decline by increasing spending on its own or by cutting taxes. Either way, incomes would rise, people would spend more, and the economy could start growing again. If the government had to run up a deficit to achieve this purpose, so be it, Keynes said. In his view, the alternative -- deepening economic decline -- would be worse. Keynes's ideas were only partially accepted during the 1930s, but the huge boom in military spending during World War II seemed to confirm his theories. As government spending surged, people's incomes rose, factories again operated at full capacity, and the hardships of the Depression faded into memory. After the war, the economy continued to be fueled by pent-up demand from families who had deferred buying homes and starting families.

In view of this, it is apparent that the government policy to reduce unemployment should be based on the aggregate demand. In any society, the tendency to consume remains relatively stable. Therefore, the aggregate demand can be enhanced only by increasing the level of investment. There could be two probable ways to expedite this — either by making the institutional credit cheaper by reducing interest rates or by providing or providing tax relief or concessions. However, in recessionary conditions these actions may not be enough to induce investments high enough to raise the aggregate demand. Therefore, for higher investment levels, the government may have to put resources in public projects that are of high value. In such cases, increased government investment in public projects coupled with private investment would increase the total supply of money in circulation in a given country's economy at a given time. There are several measures for the money supply, such as M1, M2 and M3. The money supply is considered an important instrument for controlling inflation by those economists who say that growth in money supply will only lead to inflation if money demand is stable. In order to control the money supply, regulators have to decide which particular measure of the money supply to target. The broader the targeted measure, the more difficult it will be to control that particular target. However, targeting an unsuitable narrow money supply measure may lead to a situation where the total money supply in the country is not adequately controlled.

In *The General Theory of Employment, Interest and Money*, Keynes had tried to explain the problems arising out of depression and its applicability was assumed to only recessionary phase. However, in *How to Pay for the War,* Keynes clarified that the issues apply to periods both with inflation and deflation. Keynes also disagreed on the effect of money on aggregate demand. Keynes theory of money and prices is of general nature and he accepts that changes in the quantity of money will in general will be associated with the changes in price level, although, the relationship between the two may not be directly proportional. However, he disagreed with the quantity theory of money that money supply has a direct, positive relationship with the price level. According to Keynes, if there is increase in the quantity of money, the first effect would be that the rate of interest would go down, in line with the supply – demand theory. From Keynes point of view, interest is a monetary phenomenon and is governed by the simple demand and supply correlation. He suggested that people in general hold money for various reasons. However, their transaction and precautionary demand of money is not elastic in nature instead it varies with the level of income. Moreover, it is the speculative demand of money which is primarily affected by the interest rate.

Let us assume that,

- M = total supply of money in a country.
- M1 = money held by people for transactions and precautionary purposes.
- M2 = money held by people for speculative purposes.

Therefore, M = M1 + M2

As the rate of interest, primarily depends on the speculative demand for money in relation to the amount of money available for that purpose. Hence, if the quantity of money increases then it will not have any effect on the transaction demand till there is a consequential change in the level of income. Therefore, the increase in money would add on to the money for speculative purposes i.e. M2 and this would result in the fall of interest unless there is a corresponding increase in the speculative demand of money at the same period. Normally, any decrease in the rate of interest would act as an impetus to the investors as investments are likely to be linked to interest or in other words are interest elastic. However, Keynes did not agree to this notion completely. His point of view was that in reality, the investment takes place primarily on other factors such as liberalization of market, growth in population, innovations and other such similar factors which are expected to enhance the profit of entrepreneurs. Although, the rate of interest is taken into consideration for any project feasibility and break even period because this accounts for the cost of borrowing, however, this would definitely be weighed with the opportunity cost. Nevertheless, it can be safely assumed that if there are no significant changes in the society then the rate of interest would normally generate interest in the prospective investors from the point of advancing their plans if the cost of borrowing makes a significant portion of the total cost.

A situation of having full employment is somewhat normally not achievable and every society has a certain degree of shortfall. This implies that any increase in investment would result in fall of unemployment and increase in output, with or without increase in the price level.

The primary aim of any government is to enable the nation to increase its living standards each year. This is nothing but economic growth. In other words, the government would like to ensure that value added per person grows year on year. Therefore, the main objective of economic policy is to produce growth. Hence, the fundamental purpose of economic activity is to reduce scarcity i.e. the gap between the desire of people and what is available. In any market economy, there is a mismatch between the rate of growth in the total spending and the ability of the system to supply goods and services, then prices in general increase. A low and stable inflation, say 2 % per annum is not a problem, but a variable rate of inflation is a problem.

In order to ensure economic stabilization, the second objective of the economic policy should be to ensure a stable price level – not necessarily zero, but a low and stable inflation is acceptable. The third aim of the economic policy should be to ensure that resources are fully employed or utilized. In a world of scarcity unemployment or underemployment is wastage. Real GDP per capita would be less than what it could be. Therefore, it is desirable to run the economy as close to possible full employment. In addition to the above objectives, the fourth aim of economic policy should be to ensure that a trading surplus or deficit with the rest of the world is not too large measured as a percentage of GDP. The world is a closed system; therefore, one country's surplus is another country's deficit. Therefore, the endeavor of governments is to maintain a rough balance on the external account so that there is no significant trade deficit.

In any market economy, relative prices are always shifting and these movements provide signals to the players in the system. The rate of interest is the price of money for investment. It is also the return to savers. The rate of interest should always move to equate savings and investment. The exchange rate is the value of one's country's currency in terms of another. The foreign-exchange rate, forex rate or FX rate between two currencies specifies how much one currency is worth in terms of the other. It is the value of a foreign nation's currency in terms of the home nation's currency. The foreign exchange market is one of the largest markets in the world. By some estimates, about 3.2 trillion USD worth of currency changes hands every day. The spot exchange rate refers to the current exchange rate. The forward exchange rate refers to an exchange rate that is quoted and traded today but for delivery and payment on a specific future date. Basically, the exchange rate is determined by market forces and should move to always equalize the demand of for currencies and supply of that currency. Changes in currency values change the relative prices of internationally traded goods, which in turn can turn can cause volume to change. In principle, the exchange rate should move to match the value of imports and the value of exports. A foreign exchange rate must be at its equilibrium level - the rate which produces a stable current account balance. A nation with a trade deficit will experience reduction in its foreign exchange reserves which ultimately lowers (depreciates) the value of its currency. The cheaper currency renders the nation's goods (exports) more affordable in the global market place while making imports more expensive. After an intermediate period, imports are forced down and exports rise, thus stabilizing the trade balance and the currency towards equilibrium.

The government can also determine the structure of taxation. The level of GDP and its rate of change will determine the yield. The government can also plan its own level of spending, but the level and rate of change in GDP will determine the amount actually spent. If the sum of withdrawals is matched by the sum of injections then the economy remains in the stable state. However, this is more or less a hypothetical situation due to multiplier effect. Economic instability is the result of an imbalance between withdrawals and injections. If withdrawals exceed injections for a period then economy will contract. Similarly, if injections exceed withdrawals the economy will expand. Economic instability is the norm, because injections are seldom, if ever matched with withdrawals. The basic reason is that the people who save within the economy are different from those who invest.

- Growth is a form of instability if, Injections > Withdrawals

- Recession is a form of instability if, Injections < Withdrawals

- Stagnation = Stable = Injection = Withdrawals

Governments of any country would like to deliver growth at a rate that can be sustained without inflation or a balance of payments deficit. The reason is that borrowing is unsustainable in the long term and countries will be burdened with high interest payments. Balance of payments (BOP) may be used as an indicator of economic and political stability. For example, if a country has a consistently positive balance of payments, this could mean that there is significant foreign investment within that country. It may also mean that the country does not export much of its currency. This is just another economic indicator of a country's relative value and, along with all other indicators, should be used with caution. The balance of payment includes the trade balance, foreign investments and investments by foreigners.

Accounting of a country's economic transactions with foreign countries in a stated period of time is normally one year. The balance of payments for any country is divided into two broad categories: the Current Account representing import and export trade, plus income from tourism, profits earned overseas, and interest payments; and the Capital Account, representing the sum of bank deposits, investments by private investors, and debt securities sold by a central bank or official government agencies.

In economic terms, a balance of payments surplus means a nation has more funds from trade and investments coming in than it pays out to other countries, resulting in an appreciation in the value of its national currency versus currencies of other nations. A deficit in the balance of payments has the opposite effect: an excess of imports over exports, a dependence on foreign investors, and an overvalued currency. Countries experiencing a payments deficit must make up the difference by exporting gold or hard currency reserves, such as the U.S. Dollar, that are accepted currencies for settlement of international debts. In democratic countries the most important objective is to gain and remain in power and this goes without saying. One of the vital equations for achieving success in elections is to have a sound economy. Hence, the broad economic objectives which are set by the government constitute of:

- Economic growth
- Stable price
- Balance on the external account
- Higher employment

In order to achieve these, government uses policy actions pertaining to both the monetary and fiscal instruments viz;

- Monetary policy consists of: (1) Rate of Interest (2) Exchange Rate
- Fiscal policy consists of: (1) Government spending (2) Level structure of taxation

These monetary and fiscal policies has been discussed in detail in the Economic Policy chapter.

Meanwhile, in order to get an idea of how an economic stabilization could be realized with planning, it is worth to take an example from one of the most important emerging economies from the BRIC i.e. India. The study was undertaken by Goldman Sachs and the ten most critical points outlined in the research paper is as under:

1. **Improve governance.** Without better governance, delivery systems and effective implementation, India will find it difficult to educate its citizens, build its infrastructure, increase agricultural productivity and ensure that the fruits of economic growth are well established.

2. **Raise educational achievement.** Among more micro factors, raising India's educational achievement is a major requirement to help achieve the nation's potential. According to our basic indicators, a vast number of India's young people receive no (or only the most basic) education. A major effort to boost basic education is needed. A number of initiatives, such as a continued expansion of Pratham and the introduction of Teach First, for example, should be pursued.

3. **Increase quality and quantity of universities.** At the other end of the spectrum, India should also have a more defined plan to raise the number and the quality of top universities.

4. **Control inflation.** Although India has not suffered particularly from dramatic inflation, it is currently experiencing a rise in inflation similar to that seen in a number of emerging economies. A formal adoption of Inflation Targeting would be a very sensible move to help India persuade its huge population of the (permanent) benefits of price stability.

5. **Introduce a credible fiscal policy.** India should introduce a more credible medium-term plan for fiscal policy. Targeting low and stable inflation is not easy if fiscal policy is poorly maintained. We think it would be helpful to develop some 'rules' for spending over cycles.

6. **Liberalize financial markets.** To improve further the macro variables within the Growth Environment Score (GES) framework, we believe further liberalization of Indian financial markets is necessary.

7. **Increase trade with neighbors.** In terms of international trade, India continues to be much less 'open' than many of its other large emerging nation colleagues, especially China. Given the significant number of nations with large populations on its borders, we would recommend that India target a major increase in trade with China, Pakistan and Bangladesh.

8. **Increase agricultural productivity.** Agriculture, especially in these times of rising prices, should be a great opportunity for India. Better

specific and defined plans for increasing productivity in agriculture are essential, and could allow India to benefit from the BRIC-related global thirst for better quality food.

9. **Improve infrastructure.** Focus on infrastructure in India is legendary, and tales of woe abound. Improvements are taking place, as any foreign business visitor will be aware, but the need for more is paramount. Without such improvement, development will be limited.

10. **Improve Environmental Quality.** The final area where greater reforms are needed is the environment. Achieving greater energy efficiencies and boosting the cleanliness of energy and water usage would increase the likelihood of a sustainable stronger growth path for India.

Perhaps not all these 'action areas' can be addressed at the same time, but it is believed that, in coming years, progress will have to be made in all of them if India is to achieve its very exciting growth potential.

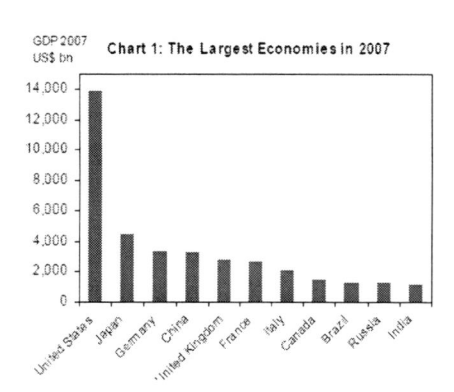

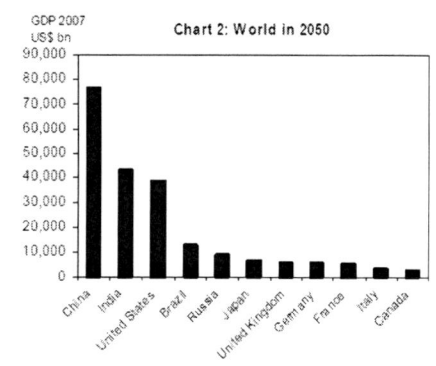

Chart 1: The Largest Economies in 2007

Chart 2: World in 2050

C.6 ECONOMICS INSTITUTIONS

The major international economic institutions are the International Monetary Fund, the World Bank Organization, and the World Trade Organization. These three organizations were all created with the purpose of helping out the world economy, and to lend money to countries on the verge of economic crisis. These three organizations are there to try to help with currency issues between countries, whether it is in trade, exchange, or payments; they are here to alleviate some of the difficulty in the process. The International Monetary Fund (IMF) is principally created to ensure stable exchange rates between the currencies of the various sovereign states. This would have allowed for free convertibility between different currencies. The major problem with the IMF is that it takes over the economies of the countries that it saves form economic crisis. The policies used by the IMF to run a countries economy are controversial, because they create unemployment and lower the standard of living in those countries. The World Bank Organization (World Bank) was created to provide loans to countries that do not have good enough credit to attract private capital, in nation building process.

The period between the First and Second World Wars witnessed a lot of turmoil. The international trade went haywire and countries torn with the war tried to create discrimination and trade restrictions to protect the domestic trade. The international trade went downhill as shown below:

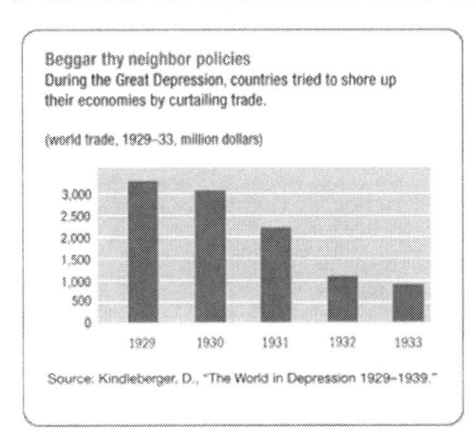

During the Great Depression of the 1930s, countries attempted to shore up their failing economies by sharply raising barriers to foreign trade, devaluing their currencies to compete against each other for export markets, and curtailing their citizens' freedom to hold foreign exchange. These attempts proved to be self-defeating. World trade declined sharply, and employment and living standards plummeted in many countries.

Countries after country resorted to competitive devaluation as the respective governments' tried to stimulate aggregate demand. The un-employment level rose significantly creating further havoc. This breakdown in international monetary cooperation led the IMF's founders to plan an institution charged with overseeing the international monetary system—the system of exchange rates and international payments that enables countries and their citizens to buy goods and services from each other. The new global entity would ensure exchange rate stability and encourage its member countries to eliminate exchange restrictions that hindered trade.

The major economists of the 40s were greatly affected by this global economic crisis. After the end of Second World War, representatives from 44 nations gathered at Bretton Woods and agreed to organize the world economy with the help of the International Monetary Fund (IMF), the International Bank for Reconstruction and Development (IBRD) or World Bank, and the International Trade Organization (ITO). However, in place of ITO what came into being was General agreement on Tariffs and Trade (GATT). The prime objective of International Monetary Fund was to maintain the stability of exchange rates and that of International Bank for Reconstruction and Development or more widely known as World Bank to reconstruct the economy of European countries which has been severely affected due to prolonged war. All the 44 participating countries also agreed the stability and peace of the world cannot be only ensured by maintaining economic revival in Europe but also if the process of economic revival has a broadened scope including countries from the underdeveloped economies. Although, all 44 countries signed the Articles of Agreement to set up an International Monetary Fund, however, the movement momentum and presently the membership stand to 183.

The objectives of International Monetary Fund as stated in Article I depict the following are:

1. To promote international monetary cooperation through a permanent institution to provide the machinery for consultation and collaboration on international monetary problems.

2. To facilitate the expansion and balanced growth of international trade and to contribute thereby to promote and maintenance of high level of employment and real income and to the development of productive resources of all members of all members as primary objectives of economic policy.

3. To promote exchange stability, to maintain orderly exchange arrangements among members, and to avoid competitive exchange depreciation.

4. To assist in the establishment of a multilateral system of payments in respect of current transactions between members and in the elimination of foreign exchange restrictions to hamper the growth of world trade.

5. To give confidence to members by making the fund's resources available to them under adequate safeguards, thus providing them with opportunity to correct maladjustments in their balance of payments without resorting to measures destructive of national or international prosperity.

6. In accordance with the above, to shorten the duration and lessen the degree of disequilibrium in the international balance of payments of members.

P.T. Ellsworth and J. Clark Leith in "The International Economy" have summarized the above objectives into three categories:

- Elimination of exchange control.

- Ensuring reasonable stability of exchange rates.

- Combine exchange rate stability with national independence in monetary and fiscal policy.

The fund agreement of international monetary fund as stated in Article IV requires every member to establish a par value of its currency in terms of either gold or US Dollar. Currencies were defined in terms of both gold and dollar and exchange rates were determined similar to the gold standard. All the signatory members were under statutory obligation to declare a par value corresponding to the gold content of the US Dollar. Most of the countries did declare a par value and those who failed to declare par values maintained *de facto* parities till 1970 when the Bretton Woods system of pegged exchange rates broke down permanently and was replaced by the system of floating exchange rates.

All the member countries were allowed to have transactions with international monetary fund at official par value. The rights of the member countries to draw, contributions and voting power is determined in line with their quotas. The member's quota is determined based on their gold and foreign exchange reserve, national income, international trade, balance of payment. That is why the quotas for different countries vary. However, as a policy all the member country is required to contribute 25 % of their respective quotas to the fund either in gold or in US Dollar and the remaining 75 % is payable in their respectable currencies. However, exceptions could be the low income group countries.

A member's quota subscription determines the maximum amount of financial resources the member is obliged to provide to the IMF. A member must pay its subscription in full upon joining the Fund: up to 25 percent must be paid in SDRs or widely accepted currencies (such as the U.S. dollar, the euro, the yen, or the pound sterling), while the rest is paid in the member's own currency. The quota largely determines a member's voting power in IMF decisions. Each IMF member has 250 basic votes plus one additional vote for each SDR 100,000 of quota. Accordingly, the United States has 37,149.3 votes (17.09 percent of the total), whereas the BRIC countries have quota in the following order: Brazil 3036.1 votes (1.40 percent of total), Russia 5945.4 votes (2.73 percent of total), India 4158.2 votes (1.91 percent of total) and China 8090.1 votes (3.72 percent of total). The number of basic votes will change once the April 2008 reforms become effective. The amount of financing a member can obtain from the IMF (its access limit) is based on its quota. Currently, under stand-by and extended arrangements, a member can borrow up to 200 percent of its quota annually and 600 percent cumulatively. However, access may be higher in exceptional circumstances.

In view of the above it is evident that the voting power of a country is linked with their respective quotas, therefore, it would not be wrong to state that the Western countries dominate the IMF at present. Although, since inception the quotas for the member countries have been revised, but the revisions have primarily contributed in raising the share of developed countries and this does not only depend on the national and international variables but also on the bargaining strength of various countries. Presently, the G7 countries i.e. USA, UK, France, Germany, Canada, Italy and Japan account for approximately half of the voting power and hence in a way control the IMF effectively.

The SDR (Special Drawing Right) is an artificial "basket" currency used by the IMF (International Monetary Fund) for internal accounting purposes. The SDR is also used by some countries as a peg for their own currency, and is used as an international reserve asset.

Recently, the governor of the People's Bank of China, Zhou Xiao chuan, has proposed that the SDR should gradually displace the dollar at the center of the international monetary system and that surplus countries should be able to convert their dollar holdings into SDR-denominated assets. The SDR (Special Drawing Right) is an artificial "basket" currency used by the IMF (International Monetary Fund) for internal accounting purposes. The SDR is also used by some countries as a peg for their own currency, and is used as an international reserve asset.

In 1960 one of the most original analysts of the postwar international monetary system, the Belgian/US economist Robert Triffin, published a small volume with a big thesis called *Gold and the Dollar Crisis*. He argued that the system that had been agreed at Bretton Woods and had just come into operation would not last because its inner workings contained an internal contradiction. Apart from gold, whose supply was small and erratic, the increase in demand for international liquidity could be satisfied only if the reserve center, the United States, ran a payments deficit to supply more dollars to the world. But such deficits were bound to undermine confidence in an unchanged link of the US dollar to gold. The Triffin Dilemma posited that the world therefore confronted a choice between running short of liquidity and undermining confidence in the dollar, which was destined sooner or later to produce a crisis. Analysts argued that the system had other problems, such as the lack of a crisis-proof adjustment mechanism as a result of widespread unwillingness to change exchange rates except as a last resort. But officials decided that the problem they could solve best, or at least the one they would solve first, was the Triffin Dilemma. Their solution was to create a synthetic reserve asset to supplement the supply of gold. Its price was fixed in terms of gold at exactly the same level as $1, so that SDR1 = $1. Because of a continuing disagreement over whether the new reserve asset should be considered money ("paper gold") or credit (since countries receiving assets had to reconstitute a part of their endowments in due course), it was given the anodyne name, Special Drawing Right. Hence we still live with the term SDRs. The first SDRs, 3 billion of them, were created and allocated among members of the IMF in proportion to their quotas on January 1, 1970. The rationale for making, by the standards of the time, such a sizeable allocation was the prospect of a reserve shortage as a result of stringent US monetary policy in 1969.

Further allocations of approximately SDR 3 billion a year were agreed simultaneously for the following two years: The actual allocations were SDR 2.9 billion in 1971 and SDR 3.4 billion in 1972. At the end of that process the SDR constituted some 9.5 percent of the world's stock of non gold reserve assets. However, before the last of these allocations had occurred, the world was no longer short of liquidity. Monetary stringency had led to a US slowdown, and the US Federal Reserve, seeing that this posed a threat to the president's reelection, stepped on the monetary accelerator. This resulted in an explosion of international liquidity and the breakdown of the Bretton Woods system, and in 1972 the IMF convened a Committee of Twenty (C-20), based on the 20 constituency chairs then operative in the Fund, to agree on an appropriate reform of the international monetary system. The state of thought at the time can be gleaned from a conference convened by the IMF in 1970 to discuss the criteria that should govern reserve creation. The prevailing view saw the IMF as essentially controlling the world's reserve base, consisting of a more-or-less fixed supply of gold plus a consciously variable quantity of SDRs. Countries would choose to hold dollars and secondary reserve currencies in a fairly fixed relationship to their holdings of primary reserve assets and they would issue domestic money more or less in proportion to their reserve holdings. Hence by varying its issues of SDRs the IMF could determine the monetary evolution of the world. This being the heyday of monetarism versus Keynesianism, the big bone of contention was whether the IMF should allocate SDRs so as to secure an equilibrium long-run monetary growth rate independent of short-run fluctuations in aggregate demand or whether it should try to engage in short-run countercyclical fine-tuning. The monetarists won, and so the IMF continued to determine the rate of SDR allocations for multiyear "basic periods," based on prospective shortages of reserves.

Chambers of Commerce of the G20 countries announced in 2009 the creation of the "C20 Group" – a business counterpart of the official Group of 20, whose aim is to support them in elaborating solutions to restore economic stability and sustainable growth globally. The purpose of this group is to represent the views of enterprises – particularly small and medium-sized ones – from the G20 countries and make an impact on economic and financial policies discussed at G20 level. Christoph Leitl, Honorary President of EUROCHAMBRES and initiator of the C20 idea, said: "As the G20 grows in importance in addressing the world's economic challenges, it is crucial that they can rely on a 'mirror' business group that will provide the real economy's perspective. We wish to establish a regular exchange of information and consultation mechanisms between the G20 and the C20, which should lead to solutions beneficial to businesses worldwide."

The founding conference of the C20 Group took place in Vienna (Austria) in early 2010, and the first official position of the C20 was presented ahead of the G20 Summit in Canada in June 2010. The Chamber members of the G20 Group are: Argentina, Australia, Brazil, Canada, China, France, Germany, India, Indonesia, Italy, Japan, Mexico, Russia, Saudi Arabia, South Africa, South Korea, Turkey, United Kingdom, United States and Europe (represented by EUROCHAMBRES). The Netherlands and Spain act as Observers.

The Europeans came to the C-20 assuming that its mandate was to secure such a world. But it turned out that European preoccupations were not shared by others. First, the United States was not prepared to consign the advantages it accrued from issuing the world's reserve currency, at least not without much-stronger assurances that it could rely on the rest of the world to adjust when needed, which it sought to achieve by the institution of a "reserve indicator" system. Under such a system each IMF member would have been assigned—there was no agreement on how—a target level of reserves and would have then assumed an obligation to adjust so as to keep its reserves within some limits around this target. Specifically, if reserves hit an upper limit of some specified, proportionate difference from the reserve target, the country would have been obliged either to revalue or to take other adjustment measures. Deficit countries would have been under a symmetrical obligation to adjust if they hit a lower reserve limit.

It was finally conceded in 1973 that the breakdown of the Bretton Woods system was permanent and that the exchange rates of the major currencies would float against one another in the future, the previous practice of valuing the SDR in terms of only one currency, the US dollar, appeared distinctly anomalous. The only viable alternative in a system of predominantly floating exchange rates was to value the SDR as equal to a basket of currencies. In the first instance this basket consisted of the 16 currencies whose issuers each accounted for more than 1 percent of world exports. This basket was subsequently revised to the G-5 currencies, and it is now a basket of four, since the French franc and the Deutschmark have both been merged into the euro. Since 1972 the IMF has used the SDR as its basic unit of account, so that all the Fund's transactions are denominated in SDRs. The IMF has periodically debated whether to create additional SDRs, but with one exception it has always concluded that the additional reserves stemming from the US deficit obviated. In one version of the aid link, newly issued SDRs would have gone to multilateral development banks like the World Bank.

There are now 21.4 billion SDRs in existence. As a proportion of total world (non gold) reserves, this is less than a derisory 0.5 percent. A reserve for shortage would justify additional SDR creation. The lone exception occurred in 1978, when major reserve holders did not wish to increase their dollar holdings. Instead, there was active consideration at that time of creating a substitution account at the Fund. This would have entitled reserve holders to sell dollars to the Fund in exchange for an equivalent amount of SDRs at the current market exchange rate. According to normal practice, the Fund would have thereby obtained an SDR claim on the United States, and hence the United States would have been obliged to pay the Fund sufficient dollars to make up for any subsequent depreciation in the value of the dollar in terms of the SDR as the United States would have profited by any subsequent appreciation of the dollar, which in fact happened.

But the United States wished to have a dollar-denominated debt, and this difference remained to the end. However, there was sufficient suspicion of the dollar at that time to make most reserve holders reluctant to accept more dollars, and so a new SDR allocation was agreed. The basic period agreed was again three years (against the five years that were supposed to be normal), and the issue was to be about SDR 4 billion per year. There has periodically been debate about the value of creating a reserve asset that would principally accrue to those countries with large IMF quotas (the industrial countries) rather than to those in need of additional reserves (largely the developing countries).

In 1997 the IMF agreed on a Fourth Amendment to the Articles, which involved doubling the quantity of SDRs outstanding. The additional allocation of SDR 21.4 billion would have been distributed in such a way as to bring each country's cumulative allocation up to the same percentage as its 1997 quota. Thus the bulk of the allocation would have been distributed to members that had joined after the earlier allocations, principally the former communist countries. However, amending the Articles requires an 85-percent majority approval, and since the United States has a quota of about 17 percent, it effectively has a veto over such actions. Because the US Congress has not yet ratified this amendment (if only because Congress has not previously been asked to ratify it), the amendment has not come into effect and countries have not received the additional SDR allocations that were agreed. This is one of several IMF reforms requiring congressional action that the Obama administration submitted to Congress.

The SDRs were originally distributed in proportion to countries' IMF quotas on the dates of allocation, but since then they have tended to gravitate from developing countries in deficit toward industrial countries in surplus. When a country wishes to use some of its SDRs, it finds a country (or the IMF) that is willing to receive the SDRs and supply a reserve currency (in practice the US dollar) in exchange; SDRs cannot be spent in the market.

When the SDR was first created, countries had a duty to hold, or if necessary rebuild, some proportion of the SDR allocations they had originally received. In 1981 this "reconstitution provision" was abrogated, which is slightly less definitive than being abolished. It was argued that this marked a step toward acceptance of the SDR as money, since countries face no obligation to reestablish their currency holdings, but they are bound to repay credit.

The SDR is currently defined as a basket consisting of:

- US dollar, 63.2 cents;
- Euro, 41.0 euro cents;
- Japanese yen, 18.4 yen; and
- Pound sterling, 9.03 pence.

The percentage weights used for calculating the above figures were 44 percent for the US dollar, 34 percent for the euro, and 11 percent each for the Japanese yen and the pound sterling. The basket is recalculated every five years, most recently on the basis of these weights and market exchange rates for the three months preceding the last SDR recalculation on December 30, 2005. The SDR interest rate is an average of defined, short-term, money-market interest rates of the four currencies in the basket, with similar weights to those used in defining the value of the SDR. This figure is calculated weekly. The creation of a substitution account, which would enable countries to exchange dollars for SDRs, has been proposed at two periods in history. The first was after the breakdown of the Bretton Woods system in 1971–73, when many countries feared for the future value of their dollar holdings. The second was the period of dollar weakness in the late 1970s. The basic proposal was that dollar holders would have the right to present their excess dollar holdings to the IMF, which would then issue an equivalent value of SDRs. If the IMF had maintained its normal practice of transacting with members exclusively in SDRs, this would have resulted in the United States accepting an SDR-denominated liability. US reluctance to accept such liabilities presumably contributed to the failure on both occasions to agree on a substitution account.

There are four major differences between an SDR-centered system and a dollar-centered system such as we have had in recent years. First, there is the issue of elasticity of reserve supply. The supply of dollar reserves depends upon the US balance of payments position and can therefore expand in response to an increase in demand as well as to an exogenously determined increase in the US payments deficit. In contrast, the supply of SDRs depends on an administrative decision of the IMF, and if the supply of competing reserve assets (in practice dollars) has been tied down, the reserve supply will be unresponsive to demand except insofar as those administrative decisions respond. A common view is that the reserve supply should respond automatically to variations in demand—because the alternative would be a destructive attempt to achieve adjustment—but those exogenous variations in supply that may impose global inflation or deflation should be avoided. Opinions have differed sharply as to whether this view pointed to the dollar system or an SDR system being preferable.

Second, the dollar system bestows on the United States what the French, in the days of President de Gaulle and his economic maestro Jacques Rueff, used to describe as the "exorbitant privilege" of paying its debts in its own currency. Unlike every other country, the United States' prospective future deficit is not limited by the assets it currently holds plus what the international capital market will lend it. But note that it is a requirement that debts be settled by a transfer of assets rather than by an increase in liabilities that would resolve this asymmetry.

Third, the two systems have different implications as to the pattern of payments imbalances and therefore the debt profiles of various countries. Under a dollar-centered system, increases in reserve supply come from an increase in the gross debt of the United States. In principle this increase in gross debt could be financed entirely by increased borrowing by the rest of the world from the United States, so that there would be no net increase in US debt. But in practice one expects that while a part of the reserve increase will be borrowed, a part will also take the form of increased current account surpluses outside the United States and therefore an increased US current account deficit. To the extent that this is true, the US net international investment position will go into higher debt. In contrast, an SDR-centered system that distributes SDRs in exact proportion to the increases in demand for reserves would not require any country to increase its net debt. The increased allocation of SDRs a country receives will be an asset that offsets the country's increased liability to the SDR account. In particular, there would be no need for the United States to increase its net indebtedness to feed the rest of the world's increasing demand for reserves.

Fourth, the mirror image of the last point is what economists refer to as "seigniorage." This refers to the fact that the issuer has a gain, or at least a potential gain, from issuing the zero-interest asset of money or the low-interest asset of reserves. It is clear that the United States gains by making a high-interest loan that is used to buy low-interest reserves from it: Its gain is the interest differential. If the reserve-holding country chooses to run a current account surplus to build up its reserves instead, this is presumed to be as disagreeable as taking the high-interest loan, since for an optimal solution the welfare effects of these two decisions must be equated at the margin. But it is not clear that the corresponding current account deficit is valued as much by the United States as the capital outflow, as is implicitly assumed in high theory. If that is not true, then there is a potential social gain available from creating reserves through the SDR system instead of the dollar system.

Three paths can be envisaged for giving the SDR a greater role in the future. One proposal would turn the SDR into a privately held asset. A second would reform the international monetary system and put the SDR at its center, very much along the lines pursued in the C-20. A third would increase the supply of SDRs while retaining a predominantly dollar-centered system. The creation of a substitution account might accompany any of these systems, though it would be essential only in the second.

From time to time there have been proposals to allow private parties to hold SDRs. One advantage from the standpoint of the official sector is that this would potentially make SDRs directly usable by official actors in intervention, which is by its nature a transaction between the official and private sectors. At present SDRs have to be converted into an intervention currency before they can be used in intervention, which presumably makes them less attractive to official holders. If private parties were permitted to hold SDRs, they might be held either to facilitate transactions or as an asset. Although it would in principle be possible to transact in SDRs even if a country were pegging its currency to a reserve currency like the dollar, this would be pointless: Private transactions in SDRs are likely to be restricted to cases in which the country is seeking to peg its currency to (or intervening so as to limit its variation in terms of) the SDR. This suggests that the SDR is unlikely to take off as a privately held asset, even if this were legal, unless a significant number of central banks decide to stabilize their currencies in terms of the SDR rather than in terms of some bilateral exchange rate or alternative basket. Such a development appears highly desirable, especially for countries whose trade is not dominated by transactions with a single major monetary bloc.

The conditions in which the private parties find it convenient to hold assets in the form of SDRs would be only if many of the world's long-term assets were SDR-denominated, which would mean that they were denominated in terms of a basket of principal currencies (with specific weights) rather than in any individual currency. This would not help those who issue assets in countries with currencies that are already used to denominate debt. However, it may be attractive either to those who issue assets in countries whose currencies have not traditionally been used to denominate debt contracts or to those who want to undertake activities that straddle several currencies. Until now there has been almost no use of the SDR to denominate private debt contracts, although there is no obstacle to such denomination. Because there have been no private SDR-denominated contracts, there has been no pressure to allow private parties to hold SDRs. But there would be real social advantages to the widespread use of the SDR to denominate the debts of those whose currencies do not move closely with one of the major currencies. The fact that this has not yet occurred may be due to an "infant market" problem—no one has an incentive to be an early user of an asset whose appeal comes from its use by others—rather than any inherent unattractiveness of the proposal.

Another way of enhancing the future role of the SDR is to make it the center of the international monetary system, as proposed in the C-20. The C-20 argued that this implied making it the principal reserve asset.

The prima facie meaning of this phrase is that nearly all reserve holdings would consist of SDRs. In fact, however, the significant economic meaning of the phrase as interpreted by the C-20 is that the evolution of the SDR stock would determine the growth rate of total reserves, which would require merely that the total reserve stock be a fairly constant multiple of the quantity of SDRs. This implies some form of asset settlement: requiring countries that acquire reserve currencies to convert these into SDRs rather than to hold onto them, since otherwise the total reserve stock would be influenced by the reserve-composition policies of member countries. It would also be necessary to create a substitution account to allow countries to convert their reserve-currency holdings above some limit into SDRs. The C-20 declared that the SDR would be the numeraire, in terms of which each currency would express its central value (at that time it was assumed there would be such a thing). The contemporary equivalent of this proposal would be that countries should declare reference rates in terms of the SDR, ensuring that the countries whose currencies compose the SDR declare rates that are collectively consistent. It rapidly became clear in the C-20 that the United States would agree to proposals to make the SDR the center of the international monetary system only if there were some mechanism of exerting strong adjustment pressures on countries in addition to asset settlement. It is not difficult to see why. Asset settlement by nature places pressure on deficit countries. In the absence of comparable pressure on surplus countries, all a surplus country would need to do to avoid adjustment pressure is to not adjust, throwing the entire burden of adjustment onto deficit countries.

To avoid this danger the United States designed and proposed the reserve indicator system described previously. An obligation to take adjustment actions, including revaluing exchange rates in the absence of alternative concrete actions, provoked visceral objections from countries that had repeatedly witnessed speculators enriched at the expense of their taxpayers when reserve levels had given warnings of impending exchange rate changes. This was a major reason why the C-20 failed to agree on the design of a new international monetary system. There seems to be no technical reason why the world should not adopt such a system at the present time, presumably modified by the presence of floating exchange rates, which would therefore limit the SDR's numeraire role to expressing reference rates. Since countries would not be setting their own exchange rates, they could not be enjoined to revalue if reserves hit an indicator level, so this obligation would have to be modified to that of changing their macroeconomic, e.g., fiscal, policy.

The fundamental respects in which the present world differs from that envisaged by the C-20 are that (a) today the exchange rates of almost all systemically significant countries float and (b) the main reserve asset is the dollar and not the SDR (a consequence of which is the absence of asset settlement). It has just been argued that one could retain floating exchange rates within a system otherwise similar to that envisaged by the C-20. In this section I examine whether one could also enhance the role of the SDR within a system that retains both of the key features of present arrangements. Suppose that in the present world one were to make regular allocations of SDRs of a size that would satisfy demand for greater reserve holdings. As noted earlier, there are several key ways in which such a system would differ from the present dollar-based system: It may change the elasticity of reserve supply, it may alter the pattern of payment imbalances, and the distribution of seigniorage may differ. Consider first the issue of reserve supply. Suppose that the IMF curtailed the rate of SDR expansion in the hope of combating inflation. Countries would be entitled to accumulate dollars instead, and if the IMF had cut the rate of SDR growth to a level that did not satisfy the growth of demand for reserves, one would expect countries simply to shift back their reserve holding patterns to accumulate more dollars in view of the fewer SDRs. As long as countries retain the right to accumulate more dollars at the margin, it is unrealistic to expect to control the rate of reserve growth by varying the rate of the creation of SDRs. However, a critical difference from the reformed monetary regime envisaged by the C-20 is that a country that felt reserve growth to be excessive would be able to defend itself by allowing its exchange rate to appreciate without violating the letter or spirit of its international obligations.

This system would avoid the need for the United States to maintain a deficit to enable the supply of liquidity to grow. If in fact the rate of SDR creation satisfied the reserve-accumulation objectives of all countries, it would be possible to envisage the elimination of global imbalances. The only exception would be if countries were anxious for current account surpluses because they preferred to maintain an export surplus rather than simply to build up reserves. The obverse of the obligation to adjust is the distribution of the benefit of seigniorage. Countries would reap this in proportion to their IMF quotas. If the Asian countries maintained high reserve-accumulation objectives relative to the size of their IMF quotas, then they would still need to earn or borrow a part of their additional reserves, but a part would accrue free of the need to adjust, as of right. Presumably the traditional powers in the IMF, primarily European countries, would receive seigniorage benefits that outweighed their reserve-accumulation objectives.

The long-proposed reforms to IMF quotas would reduce but not eliminate this discrepancy, since they do not envisage rewarding the Asian countries for their high reserve-accumulation objectives. The role of a substitution account in a dollar-centered system would be entirely to increase the portfolio choices available to reserve holders. It would enable a reserve holder to convert some of its dollar holdings into SDRs, and vice versa if the substitution account were designed to permit this. There would be no ex ante profit in such switches since the market determines the exchange rate and the SDR's interest rate is consistent with this, nor there any market effects of official switches. It would of course be necessary to determine whether liabilities to the substitution account should be SDR denominated or subject to some ad hoc alternative. But in neither case would the creation of a substitution account impose ex ante changes in wealth.

One of the proposals endorsed by the G-20 leaders in London in April 2009 was for a renewed SDR issue of $250 billion of SDRs. This would be the first issue to be approved since 1978. The call was made despite the fact that the total reserve stock (excluding gold, which hardly counts as a reserve asset these days) has increased even faster than its natural comparators (trade and "world GDP," which should be called GWP) in recent years. But the fact that the world is now in a severe recession outweighed the rapid growth in dollar reserves and convinced the G-20 leaders that the world would benefit from an increase in purchasing power. At least when the world is in a severe recession, as now, it appears that current leaders are dominated by a desire to apply Keynesian pump-priming rather than subscribing to the 1970s monetarist logic that SDRs should act strictly as a reserve supplement. But even after an increase that appears massive in comparison with previous SDR issues, SDRs would only account for approximately 5 percent of the world's total non gold reserve stock, as opposed to the 9.5 percent that prevailed after completion of the first basic period in 1972. Reserves increased by 1,938 percent between 1975 and the end of 2008, in comparison with a 1,758 percent increase in visible trade and an expansion in nominal world GDP of 868 percent. It would not be technically difficult for the IMF to issue liabilities such as bonds denominated in SDRs, as has been proposed recently by a number of emerging-market economies. Indeed, the important issues raised by these proposals for the IMF to issue bonds concern not denomination but the limited maturity of bonds versus the indeterminate duration of a loan under the New Arrangements to Borrow. The attraction seen in the former is that fixed maturity implies that countries would be able to make money available to the IMF during this time of crisis without jeopardizing their future leverage to increase their representation in the Fund.

If in fact the rate of SDR creation satisfied the reserve-accumulation objectives of all countries, it would be possible to envisage the elimination of global imbalances. However, as mentioned above all member countries are eligible to utilize the resources of international monetary fund. In lieu of the support from IMF these countries are required to carry out a balance of payment adjustments. This requirement is known as conditionality and it is a reflection of IMF principles that financing and adjustment should be parallel. Although, every member country has the right to borrow 25 % of the quota, provided the IMF conditions that have been finally negotiated are abided. Broadly speaking IMF conditions encompasses the following:

I. Devaluation of currency in order to narrow the gap between the official and market exchange rates.

II. Reduction in government expenditure with an objective to reduce inflationary pressures.

III. Reduction in fiscal deficit below 4 %, proportional to GDP in a phased manner.

However, the breakdown of Bretton Woods's system in 1970s and the oil price shock resulted in the review of this conditionality during 1978-

79 by the member countries with an objective to motivate member countries to approach the international monetary fund proactively much before the balance of payment issues become grave. These were known as 'economic stabilization programs' having the following basic conditions:

- Liberalization of foreign exchange and import controls.

- Devaluation of official exchange rate.

- Inflation control program with the help of fiscal tools such as – control of government deficit through controlling expenditure, control of wages, abolish price control and promote free market, control bank credit by raising interest rates and reserve requirements.

- Encourage foreign direct investment by incorporating various incentives to promote international commerce.

A large number of countries have taken assistance from the international monetary fund to seek additional foreign exchange in order to overcome the balance of payment situations. All these nations were required to adapt some conditionality per negotiation with IMF. Use of conditionality resulted in direct surveillance into the macro-economic policies of these nations. Countries who have been the beneficiaries of IMF and also experienced conditionality imposed by IMF resented the intrusion of international monetary fund into economic territory. Michael P. Todaro and Stephen C. Smith in their "Economic Development" have stated that the balance of payment problem in many countries may be structural and long – term with the result that short term stabilization policies may easily lead to long run development crisis. Joseph Stiglitz in his book "Globalization and its Discontents" has also criticized the functioning of international monetary fund. According to him, "A half century after its founding, it is clear that the IMF has failed in its mission. It has not done what it was supposed to do – provide funds for countries facing an economic downturn, to enable the country to restore itself to close to full employment. In spite of the fact that our understanding of economic process has increased enormously during the last fifty years, and in spite of IMF's effort during the past quarter century, crises around the world have been more frequent and deeper. By some reckoning, close to hundred countries have faced the crisis. Worse, many of the policies that the IMF pushed, in particular, premature capital liberalization, have contributed to global instability. And once a country was in crisis, IMF funds and programmes not only failed to stabilize the situation but in many cases actually made the matter worse, especially for the poor." Although it is normally said that the conditionality are negotiated between the borrowing country and the IMF but in reality the negotiations are one-sided as in the case of any borrowings. It is a accepted fact that IMF conditionality are more than simple exercise of power and more often goes beyond economics into the areas of political domain.

Devaluation of pound sterling in 1967 and dollar crisis in 1971 led to the demise of Bretton Woods's system and emergence of the hybrid system in 1976 during Jamaica summit. Samuelson and Nordhaus in their book Economics have used the term 'System of Hybrid Exchange Rates'. The main features are as follows:

a. A country may allow their currencies to float freely as the US. According to this approach, a country allows markets to determine the currency value and does not interfere.

b. Few countries decided to have a managed but flexible exchange rate e.g. Japan, Canada, and UK. In this system the country tries to reduce volatility of currency fluctuations by selling or buying. Hence, it is like a systematic intervention to maintain the value at an appropriate level.

c. Smaller countries decide to peg their currency to a major currency or to a basket of currencies.

d. Some countries join together to form a currency block in order to stabilize exchange rates among themselves. Most important example of this could be the European Monetary System.

e. Besides different measures to stabilize currency valuation, almost all countries intervene at times when markets tend to become chaotic or may give rise to uncontrolled inflation.

International Bank for Reconstruction and Development (IBRD) was created during the Bretton Woods conference to assist the war-ravaged economies of Europe. By 1950, due to the success of Marshall Plan this objective was met to a large extent. Hence, in 1960, International Development Association (IDA) was set up to provide loans on concessional terms to countries with low per capita income, whereas, IBRD provides loan on commercial terms to the borrowing countries. The basic difference being IDA loans have a longer repayment period and are normally interest free. Together with IBRD and IDA comprise World Bank (although there also exists a close affiliate of the World Bank that is International Finance Corporation – IFC).

The objectives of World Bank as stated in Article I depict the following are:

- To assist in the reconstruction and development of the territories of its members by facilitating the investment of capital for productive purposes.

- To promote foreign private investment by means of a guarantees, internal resources etc.

- To promote the long range balanced growth of international trade and the maintenance of equilibrium in balance of payments by encouraging international investment thereby assisting in raising productivity, the standard of living and conditions of labour in the territories of the member countries.

- To encourage loans made or guaranteed so that more useful and urgent projects, large and small alike, will be dealt with first.

- To conduct its operations so as to bring about a smooth transition from a war-time economy to a peace-time economy.

Although, one may see that international monetary fund (IMF) and the World Bank have an overlapping role; but the basic difference is that IMF is more concerned with the macro-economic management while WB is more concerned with micro, project-based lending. A.P. Thirlwall in his Growth and Development: With Special Reference to Developing Economics has tried to clarify the distinct roles of both the economic organizations:

Sl. No.	International Monetary Fund	World Bank
1	Overseas the international monetary system and promotes international monetary cooperation.	Seeks to promote the economic development and structural reform in developing countries.
2	Promotes exchange stability and orderly exchange relations among its members	Assists developing countries through long-term financing of development projects and programmes.
3	Assists members in temporary balance of payment difficulties by providing short to medium financing, thus providing them with the opportunity to correct maladjustment in their balance of payments.	Provides special financial assistance to the poorest developing countries through the International Development Association (IDA).
4	Supplements the reserves of its members by allocating SDRs if there is a long term global need.	Stimulates private enterprises in developing countries through its affiliate, the International Finance Corporation (IFC).
5	Draws its financial resources principally from the quota subscription of its members.	Acquires most of its financial resources by borrowing on the international bond market.

According to Michael P. Todaro and Stephen C. Smith in their book "Economic Development", the increasing convergence in the approaches of the IMF and the World Bank that is now being witnessed is on account of the "growing recognition that the successful resolution of both external and internal problems requires the simultaneous coordination of macroeconomics and microeconomics policies."

The General Agreement on Tariffs and Trade (GATT) was negotiated during the UN Conference on Trade and Employment and was the outcome of the failure of negotiating governments to create the International Trade Organization (ITO). GATT was formed in 1947 and lasted until 1994, when it was replaced by the World Trade Organization in 1995. The original GATT text (GATT 1947) is still in effect under the WTO framework, subject to the modifications of GATT 1994.

The foundation of the post-WWII capitalist world was laid in a quite New Hampshire town on July 1944. Gathering under the auspices of the United Nations Monetary and Financial Conference, Ministers from the Allied Nations, apart from the Soviet Union, set out to revive and maintain their economic system over as much of the world they could. They created three successful institutions to accomplish their aims: the International Monetary Fund (IMF), the International Bank for

Reconstruction and Development (IBRD), also called the World Bank, and the General Agreement on Tariffs and Trade (GATT).

With the European economy in tatters by the utter destruction caused by the war, the unscathed United States was the only nation able to rescue capitalism once the War was over. Before the War, almost every country in the world had erected trade barriers to protect their own economies from the devastating crisis sweeping across the world in the wake of the Wall Street Crash. These protectionist measures had contributed to the Great Depression, making export of goods to other countries just as impossible as producing for non-existent domestic markets. There was no chance of rebuilding the war-shattered capitalist economy unless international trade could be re-created.

GATT was established to break down trade barriers (in the form of tariffs, quotas, preferential trade agreements between countries, etc) to make the flow of commodities and capital less restricted by national government influence. GATT explained how the new order would function with three principles for negotiating trade agreements: reciprocity, non-discrimination, and national security.

Reciprocity is the principle that nations should offer an equivalent exchange for the benefits they gain. In practice however, reciprocity is meaningless unless the negotiating nations have, in fact, equal or near equal economic relationships. For example, the U.S. exports food to Somalia, but Somalia exports very little to the U.S. Thus, Somalia is obliged to lower tariffs on U.S. food imports, but the U.S. can offer little benefits to Somalia in return. The end result is that wealthy, productive nations have a great deal to gain with foreign markets lowering tariffs, while poor nations have little to gain when the markets of the wealthy are already dominated by local producers, while their own markets at home are flooded by the wealthy nations. This makes it impossible to build up their own industries since they have no opportunity to compete with the imported goods.

The second principle of GATT, called **"non-discrimination"**, was intended to protect against the corruption that would come about if there were a myriad of different tariffs applying to commodities that come from different countries. Multi-lateral trade agreements were thus necessary for the exchange of particular commodities. In liberal-speak, "non-discrimination" means that once a member reduced a tariff on some commodity for any country that reduction applied to all member countries. Poor nations were again shafted – multi-lateral trade concessions made between western nations to lower tariffs on automobiles for example, made little impact in most South American nations. Tariffs in the West remained high for textiles, tropical fruit, etc, because it wasn't advantageous to the West to lower these tariffs. The markets of Western nations are more lucrative than those of poor nations; therefore lowering tariffs into western markets is a very big concession, while lowering tariffs into Southern nations is much smaller by comparison. Thus "non-discrimination" in practice applied primarily to the West – they strive to not "discriminate" among one another, but for the most part the rest of the world is not included.

Further still, GATT established a series of exceptions to reciprocity and non-discrimination. Maintaining **national security** means many things. In Article 1, paragraph 2, it means that the U.S., British, and others, re-established their old imperial preferences in colonies; while Article 14 explains that non-tariff barriers that discriminate between nations can be erected. Article 19 makes it clear that if the lowering of any tariff proved to be too harmful for national businesses, it could be rescinded. Article 21 states that "Nothing in this Agreement shall be construed …" to negatively impact what any nation defines as a risk to its own "security". Further, in Article 24, allowances are made specifically against "non-discrimination" – i.e. the establishment of regional trade alliances that exclude other member nations (i.e. the European Union, FTA, ASEAN, etc.). By Article 25, GATT explains that two negotiating nations can use a two-thirds vote between them to "waive an obligation imposed upon a contracting party by this Agreement".

Originally GATT was set up as a temporary body to facilitate trade negotiations. The International Trade Organization (ITO) had instead been created to break down trade barriers, govern trade during negotiations, and resolve trade disputes. The ITO Charter, adopted at the United Nations Conference on Trade and Development (UNCTAD) in 1948, included (among other "leftist" principles) a provision that all nations should maintain full employment. This provision outraged the U.S. and U.K.; both calling it socialistic and a violation of national sovereignty. In 1950, the U.S. government refused to ratify the agreement, and the ITO died.

Instead, the U.S. supported GATT in an expanded role. In the GATT agreement of 1947, 23 nations had signed on; by 1949 10 more nations agreed to comply; all together claiming they governed four-fifths of global trade. While GATT members negotiated separately on numerous occasions, the entire group held eight organized rounds of trade negotiations. At the first round in Geneva (1947), tariffs were cut by 20% on around three-fourths of commodity imports In the four rounds that followed: Annecy (1949), Torquay (1950-51), Geneva (1955-56) and (1960-61), tariff cuts never amounted to more than 3%, covering less than a tenth of commodity imports. Those controlling GATT thus resolved a new approach: across the board cuts in tariffs, with exception negotiations to follow. The last three rounds of GATT, very much extended, did exactly this: the "Kennedy Round" (1962-67), the Tokyo Round (1973-79), and the Uruguay Round (1986-94).

The last round of GATT negotiations, the Uruguay Round, marked the end of GATT, and the beginning of a new corporate era: the WTO. 128 nations were signatories at its creation in 1994. The WTO began life on 1 January 1995, but its trading system is half a century older. Since 1948, the General Agreement on Tariffs and Trade (GATT) had provided the rules for the system. (The second WTO ministerial meeting, held in Geneva in May 1998, included a celebration of the 50th anniversary of the system.)

The Uruguay Round which lasted from 1986 to 1994 and led to the WTO's creation. Whereas GATT had mainly dealt with trade in goods, the WTO and its agreements now cover trade in services, and in traded inventions, creations and designs (intellectual property). There are a number of ways of looking at the WTO. It is an organization for liberalizing trade. It is a forum for governments to negotiate trade agreements. It's a place for them to settle trade disputes. It operates a system of trade rules.

Essentially, the WTO is a place where member governments go, to try to sort out the trade problems they face with each other. The first step is to talk. The WTO was born out of negotiations, and everything the WTO does is the result of negotiations. The bulk of the WTO's current work comes from the 1986-94 negotiations called the Uruguay Round and earlier negotiations under the General Agreement on Tariffs and Trade (GATT). The WTO is currently the host to new negotiations, under the "Doha Development Agenda" launched in 2001. Where countries have faced trade barriers and wanted them lowered, the negotiations have helped to liberalize trade. But the WTO is not just about liberalizing trade, and in some circumstances its rules support maintaining trade barriers — for example to protect consumers or prevent the spread of disease.

At its heart are the WTO agreements, negotiated and signed by the bulk of the world's trading nations. These documents provide the legal ground-rules for international commerce. They are essentially contracts, binding governments to keep their trade policies within agreed limits. Although negotiated and signed by governments, the goal is to help producers of goods and services, exporters, and importers conduct their business, while allowing governments to meet social and environmental objectives.

The system's overriding purpose is to help trade flow as freely as possible — so long as there are no undesirable side-effects — because this is important for economic development and well-being. That partly means removing obstacles. It also means ensuring that individuals, companies and governments know what the trade rules are around the world, and giving them the confidence that there will be no sudden changes of policy. In other words, the rules have to be "transparent" and predictable.

The third important role of WTO's work relates to trade relations that often involve conflicting interests. Agreements, including those painstakingly negotiated in the WTO system, often need interpreting. The most harmonious way to settle these differences is through some neutral procedure based on an agreed legal foundation. That is the purpose behind the dispute settlement process written into the WTO agreements.

The functioning of WTO during the last thirteen years revealed numerous flaws from the point of developing countries:

- It has been observed by various economists that extreme inequality exist within the structure of WTO. According to Subir Gokarn in his article "Guilty until Proven Innocent" in Business Standard (1999), "the contents of agreements is determined by the leverage that developed countries can exert over developing countries; bribing them to agree and threatening to penalize them in other ways if they do not. Thus the basic agreements and subsequent amendments are stacked in favour of developed countries." The two prominent aspect of inequality that stands out are – (1) During Uruguay round of negotiations, a single undertaking framework was adopted and it was required to be accepted by all countries irrespective of their level of economic development. This obviously placed the developing economies in much disadvantageous position contrary to the basic objectives. (2) All WTO members are required to adhere to the same Intellectual Property Rights (IPR) as per the Trade Related Aspects of Intellectual Property Rights (TRIPS) agreement. Since, the standards were set based on the system in developed countries, hence, the effective burden concerning adjustments according to TRIPS falls primarily on the developing countries with no commensurate benefits.

- WTO has affected loss of autonomy in policy formulation particularly for developing economies. The agreements have actually acted in limiting their scope to safeguard their economic policy policies related to direct tools viz; tariffs, subsidies and other protectionist instruments for their domestic enterprises.

- Non-tariff barriers (NTBs) that have come up with WTO have disturbed exports from developing countries. For example, EU has set high standards for pesticides residues for various fruits. Besides this, EU has also imposed various anti-dumping and safeguard duties. Under non-tariff barrier, the developed countries have also imposed barriers through the use of child labour clause, sanitary and phytosanitary measures and the insistence of eco-friendly labour for imports of goods into their countries.

- The dispute settlement mechanism of WTO is biased and not suitable for developing economies. The influence of US on the functioning of WTO is clearly visible as the provision of United States Trade Act of 1974 was held by the WTO panel. This act allows US to take unilateral action against other trading partners. This makes a mockery of the multilateral structure of the WTO. According to Biswajit Dhar in his "Unilateral Sanctions under WTO" in The Economic Times, "By providing legitimacy to the controversial provisions of the Trade Act of 1974, the WTO has allowed USA to impose Sections 301 to 310 on countries that are seen as violating US trading interests even when the WTO has emerged as the organization responsible for ensuring fair trade."

- The sensitive issues concerning labour standard and environment were forced during the Seattle meeting. As far as the question of child labour is concerned the demand is a fair one, but it ignores the harsh reality of the developing economies which still lack the educational infrastructure. Although, child labour is also prevalent in developed countries as well, however, developing countries are not able to take trade measures against them. Similarly, linking trade to environment would be undesirable from the point of developing countries. According to Arun Kumar in his "India at the Seattle Meeting" – no one can be opposed to sustainable development but those who wish to link trade to sustainable development have not defined sustainability or demonstrated a convincing link between trade and development.

The Doha Development Round or Doha Development Agenda (DDA) is the current trade-negotiation round of the WTO which commenced in November 2001. Its objective is to lower trade barriers around the world, which allows countries to increase trade globally. As of 2008, talks have stalled over a divide on major issues, such as agriculture, industrial tariffs and non-tariff barriers, services, and trade remedies. The most significant differences are between developed countries led by the European Union (EU), the United States (USA), and Japan and the major developing countries led and represented mainly by India, Brazil, China, and South Africa. There is also considerable contention against and between the EU and the U.S. over their maintenance of agricultural subsidies—seen to operate effectively as trade barrier.

The current WTO Doha Ministerial started in 2001 was declared the Development Round, and was marked by a core concern: that the multilateral trading system should benefit the developing countries that constitute over three quarters of WTO members. The Doha declaration pledged to enable developing countries to 'secure a share in the growth of world trade commensurate with the needs of their economic development' through two key routes:

- Improving market access to Northern markets for developing countries by reducing import tariffs that prevent increase prices and distort competitiveness

- Phasing out domestic and export subsidies, that enable the over-production of goods at very low prices, often leading to the dumping of these goods at prices that are cheaper than those of locally produced goods

The most strategic area identified for reform at Doha was agriculture, followed by non-agricultural market access trade in services, developing country issues (Special and Differential Treatment); aid for trade. Yet, in the intervening period, Northern countries (Denmark, Finland, Iceland, Norway, and Sweden) have proved unwilling to open up their agricultural markets, without a commitment from developing countries to lower their own barriers in services and non-agricultural goods. Rich countries also want to limit the scope of Special and Differential Treatment Measures (SDT) measures that would soften the impact of tariff reductions for developing countries. Thus, the promise of Doha as a catalyst for development has largely not been met.

Several countries have called for negotiations to start again. Brazil and Pascal Lamy (Director General WTO) have led this process. Lula, president of Brazil, called several countries leaders to urge them to renew negotiations. Lamy visited India to discuss possible solutions to the impasse. The declaration at the end of the G-20 summit of world leaders in London in 2009 included a pledge to complete the Doha round.

In early 2010, Brazil and Lamy have focused on the role of the United States in overcoming the deadlock. Brazilian President Lula has urged Barack Obama to end the trade dispute between Brazil and the US over cotton subsidies following his increase in tariffs on over 100 US goods. Lamy has highlighted the difficulty of obtaining agreement from the US without the Presidential fast track authority and biennial elections. One of the consequences of the economic crisis of 2008 - 2009 is the desire of political leaders to shelter their constituents from the increasingly competitive market experienced during market contractions. Lamy hopes that the drop in trade of 12% in 2009, quoted as the largest annual drop since the Second World War, could be countered by successful conclusion of the Doha round. The Copenhagen Consensus, which evaluates solutions for global problems regarding the cost-benefit ratio, in 2008 ranked the Doha Development Agenda (DDA) as the second-best investment for global welfare.

A short summary of GATT and WTO rounds would provide an overall picture:

1. **Geneva Round (Switzerland):** Started in 1947 and participated by 23 countries. Major achievement was signing of GATT and 45,000 tariff concessions which led to affect the trade worth US $ 10 billion.

2. **Annecy Round (France):** Started in 1949 and participated by 13 countries. Major achievement was that countries exchanged approximately 5000 tariff concessions.

3. **Torquay Round (UK):** Started in 1950 and participated by 38 countries. Major achievement was reduction of 1948 tariff levels by 25 % and exchange of 8700 tariff concessions.

4. **Geneva Round (Switzerland):** Started in 1956 and participated by 26 countries. Major achievement was tariff reduction worth US$ 2.5 billion.

5. **Dillon Round (Geneva):** Started in 1960 and participated

by 26 countries. Major achievement was tariff concessions of approximately US$ 4.9 billion.

6. **Kennedy Round (Geneva):** Started in 1964 and participated by 62 countries. Major achievement was tariff concessions of approximately US$ 40 billion.

7. **Tokyo Round (Japan):** Started in 1973 and participated by 102 countries. Major achievement was tariff reduction worth US$ 300 billion.

8. **Uruguay Round (Uruguay/Morocco):** Started in 1986 and participated by 123 countries. Major achievement was creation of WTO and tariff reductions in agricultural products and subsidies. Additionally, trade accessibility of textile and clothing from developing countries. It also secured a consensus on Trade related Intellectual Property Rights among the developing countries.

9. **Doha Development Round (Qatar, Mexico, Hong Kong, Switzerland, France, and Germany):** Started in 2001 and participated by 141 countries. Although, intense negotiations were held primarily between USA, China and India in order to agree on modalities but these did not yield any result. Some of the major issues under discussion are labour standards, environmental issues, patent law etc. Still not concluded.

PART D

ECONOMIC & BUSINESS SCENARIOS

D.1 ECONOMICS, BUSINESS & INDUSTRY

In order to realize a stable economic growth, any government would have explicit or implicit financial strategy as a guide to its policy actions. For example the government may have set an internal growth of 5-6 % real growth with 2 % inflation rate per annum with fluctuations up to 3 % and unemployment rate not exceeding 9 %. In addition to these, the balance of payment on current account should remain within 1 % either on surplus or deficit side. However, in a market economy it is impossible to expect a stable performance on all four economic objectives due to the dynamics of multiplier effect and investment accelerator. Therefore, the government has to prioritize these economic indicators in importance as perceived by the electorate. This prioritization changes with time and so does the economic policy particularly if the timing is close to elections.

Consider that prioritization of government has been to enhance growth, create more jobs to reduce unemployment. To achieve these objectives an expansionary fiscal policy has been deployed coupled with an expansionary monetary policy. This means that the government spending exceeds tax revenues and the PLC money has been expanding rapidly as the result of lower interest rates and the level of investment is greater than the level of saving. PLC money is created by financial institutions such as banks and finance houses whereas, Central bank money is issued as coins and notes. An example of PLC money is a cheque drawn on a bank. Since, multiplier effect works through all sectors of the economy, hence majority of the firms would experience high sales forecast, and professionals would expect higher wages and shareholders higher dividends. The thumb rule is:

- When banks increase their lending, PLC money is created.
- When banks reduce their lending, PLC money is destroyed.

Therefore, companies and individuals are able to get finances easily from banks in an expanding economy. However, as the economy moves towards, fuller employment, bottlenecks may appear on the supply side because, an economy has an installed capacity and there is a lead time to expand and accommodate the increased volumes. Suppliers may start to demand for price increase and similarly the skilled labour as well. The companies' productivity would be affected as it starts to operate under wage pressures. Companies try to maintain their margins by increasing the prices above the retail price index. These input feed directly to the bottom line and return on capital employed increases. The manufacturing key ratios are:

- ◊   Margin x Asset Utilization = ROCE

- ◊   (Profit / Sales) x (Sales /Asset) = Return on Capital Employed

It is evident that the government would recognize that prices are going up and in order to slow the economy down, the option could be to raise the rate of interest to contain the monetary policy. Suppose due to inertia there is not much difference in the prices and after a lead time the rate of interest is further increased. Now the multiplier effect would begin to work in reverse direction and slow down the sales, profits and return on capital employed and after a time lag the price increase slows down.

Consider a typical example of an industry of manufacturing type which consists of manpower, capital equipment, raw materials and finished products. Every year a business plan is prepared in order to formulate the future business operandi. Basically, the business plan is based on sales forecast would consist of – cash flow, inventory levels and finally expected return on capital employed & dividend per share. In an industry, there is a complex interplay between various functions e.g. the finance function would like the revenues as planned, the production will like the plant utilization as per the plan. But the fact still remains that the business plan is based on the forecast and the market conditions are not fixed, they are likely to undergo change. The market may swing either in positive direction or in negative direction. Financially, the problem is if the market swings negatively and results in fewer sales than planned. This would result in increased inventory and the liquidity will decrease. If the trend continues then, the situation would deteriorate the company's balance sheet. Hence, the management will be left with no other option but to destock i.e. convert stocks into cash by cutting the rate of production below the current level of sales.

Therefore, the market swing plays an important role creating difference between the planned and the actual. If we think about 'natural law', we know this also extends to such laws as 'gravity'. What goes up must come down. No market will go down or up forever. Also, that a rising market will soon become a falling market and then back to a rising market once again. That is cyclic. So the bottom line here is that all the events that occur around us, being cyclic in nature, are also directly and indirectly connected to the markets. And by understanding these 'cyclic' events, one can anticipate with a high degree of accuracy when to expect a market top or bottom.

In reality, there are many cycles of different time periods at work at the same time. And each market is affected by different cycles from one another. For example, grains have planting and harvesting cycles based on season and other factors that would not match exactly the seasonal factors of raising and harvesting cattle. Yet there would be an indirect relationship between the grains and cattle, seasonally, due to cattle's need to feed. Because there are several cycles at play in any given market, these individual cycles will either work with or against each other at various points along their axis due to their different time periods. In other words, at one point in time several cycles may be moving up while some are moving down. These additive and opposing forces will result in a value that does not match any of the individual component cycles, resulting in a 'distorted' cycle pattern.

It is impossible to forecast exactly when changes will take place but it is normally known that changes will happen. The swing is the key. Its effect is multiplied by company stocks or inventory. Taken together these are major source of instability for all mature economies. Government can moderate but not eradicate this effect. There is no such thing as a stable economy.

The economic cycle or business cycle is the result of the interaction of the income multiplier and accelerator effect. The income multiplier is driven by the fact that one person's expenditure is another person's income. In a complex open economy such United States, U.K., India, there are considerable withdrawals i.e. losses to tax, savings and imports.

The GDP multiplier can be defined as: Inverse of (% taken in tax + % spent on imports + % saved). Therefore, the value of GDP multiplier will fall if the population saves more, imports more or pay more taxes per capita. Similarly, the accelerator principle suggests that greater than expected growth in sales when existing plant is operating at close to capacity, generates a surge in capacity creation. The significance of the principle is that it suggests investment spending will be erratic. For a steady growth in investment spending, there has to be continuous increase in the rate of growth of final sales. The existence of withdrawals suggests that such conditions are unlikely except during the upswing of the market business cycle. Investment in factories, building and plant and equipment has strong income multiplier and investment accelerator effect. In view of the above, it is important to have an accurate forecast to the maximum possible extent keeping in mind several market factors.

Traditionally, business economics provided the baseline macroeconomic forecasts that drive divisional sales estimates and annual budget and earnings projections. A long-term trend forecast of GNP growth covering the planning horizon and an annual cyclical forecast for the first year of the business plan are the main inputs into the planning process. However, the potential contributions of business economics to the planning process are expanding far beyond this traditional role, as strategic planners develop more sophisticated planning systems in response to a more complex and more global competitive economic environment.

The growing sophistication of strategic planning systems, and the consequent expansion of the potential contributions of business economics, can be seen from the four classic phases of strategic planning viz. development, testing, implementation and maintenance. The strategic planning process typically passes through four phases of increasing sophistication and effectiveness. The effectiveness of the planning process improves dramatically as a company graduates through testing and undertakes a thorough analysis of the external business environment.

Annual forecasts of key macroeconomic variables needed to project revenues, costs and capital needs for a year are all that are required to support the planning process. When longer product and investment lead times make it necessary to extend the planning horizon, multiyear forecasts of these same macroeconomic variables are required.

In order to increase precision in forecasting, it is essential to understand the opportunities and threats in the external business environment in which they must compete. It is also in this development phase of planning that strategic business units (SBU's) are created as the basic planning organizations throughout the company, and that contingency planning is undertaken as an integral part of the planning process.

The potential contributions of business economics also take a quantum leap forward as the company enters the implementation phase of strategic planning as this requires comprehensive analysis of the external business environment that will serve as the analytical foundation for the company's strategic plans. This analysis plays a critical role in revealing the strategic opportunities and threats facing the firm over the planning horizon and in identifying the company's relative competitive strengths and weaknesses. The multiyear forecasts of key macroeconomic variables must now be coupled with in-depth analyses of the industry, of competitors and of the many socio-political issues that could significantly impact the company's competitive position. In addition, the decentralization of planning responsibilities to the SBUs and the development of contingency plans greatly increase the number of customers for the business economist and the demands of each.

The last phase is characterized by the integration of strategic planning and operations management. The strategic planning process is supported throughout the company with the organizational structures, business systems and company values necessary to translate the strategies into effective operating decisions. The linking of strategic planning and operations management, results in another substantial increase in planning effectiveness.

As indicated above, two major uses exist for these inputs: the development of the strategic plans; and the implementation of those plans. These inputs are used to identify opportunities and threats in the external environment, and to assess and account for the company's internal competitive strengths and weaknesses in formulating the business plans. Strategic business plan uses these inputs to establish cost, productivity and other business plan goals; to provide internal consistency checks on the plans and projections of individual SBUs; and to test the sensitivity of alternative plans to critical assumptions and uncertainties. Other inputs from forecasting based on business economics is to help create the organizational structures and incentive systems appropriate for the strategies of each strategic business units.

A comprehensive analysis of the external business environment is required to support the development of strategic plans. This analysis of the external environment must include the macroeconomic forecast, and analyses of the industry, competitors and relevant regulatory and trade issues.

The macroeconomic forecast that drives industry demand and overall cost levels is critical at every phase of planning, but even more so in last phase where the forecast is an integral part of an analytical effort to understand and plan for an uncertain future rather than a discreet set of data points for cranking out budget and earnings projections. Long-term, trend forecasts spanning the planning horizon (typically five years) of growth in GNP, disposable income, personal consumption expenditures, employment, inflation, interest and exchange rates and energy and other raw materials prices are all essential inputs into the strategic planning process. These are essential not only as basic drivers of demand and cost, but also as determinants of competitive advantage and changing business opportunities and threats that may arise out of changes in economic environment.

For many companies today, these macroeconomic forecasts must take on a global dimension, which does not mean simply generating forecasts for the various regions of the world in which the company operates. Global companies need integrated, worldwide design, research, production and marketing strategies to compete successfully. The strategic business planning is essential to understand the implications of developments in one region of the world for interdependent operations in others, and how the economies of the different regions of the world are linked together through global financial and product markets. For example, forecasts of slowing U.S. consumption and growing exports to reduce the huge U.S. trade deficit must be accompanied by the implications for demand, imports and growth in large trade-surplus nations such as Germany and Japan, the newly industrialized countries (NICs) and the debt-ridden countries of South America.

Macroeconomic forecasting in planning systems sometimes includes limited industry forecasting and analysis. The analysis of the competitive structure of the industry in which the company (SBUs) competes is also an important input. Analyses of the number and size distribution of sellers and buyers in the industry, potential new entrants, capacity utilization and expansion, economies of scale, entry barriers, vertical integration, diversification, distribution channels and downstream component suppliers all are undertaken to provide strategic business planners with the information they need to plan effectively. These analyses help to understand the nature of competition in the industry; identify current and future business opportunities and risks; and assess the long-term profit potential of alternate strategies.

As an illustration of such industry analysis, the projected increase in North American automobile production capacity by over two million units by the early 1990s as a result of new entry of foreign producers and expansion by existing producers will add to worldwide excess capacity, increase competitive pressure and produce declining real automobile prices for at least the next several years. This industry environment will result in limited profit opportunities for manufacturers that cannot reduce their costs substantially or successfully differentiate their products.

The in-depth analysis of competitors is the most distinguishing characteristic of a business planning process which also culminates into a forecast. This analysis yields critical insights into the company's strengths and weaknesses relative to its leading competitors. When coupled with the identification of opportunities and threats in the external environment, the analytical foundation for the development of the company's strategic plans is in place.

The strategic business planning extends far beyond the traditional analyses of monetary and fiscal policies that are an integral part of the macroeconomic forecast. It is necessary to analyze the impact on the company of a broad array of safety, health, environmental, energy and industrial policies (e.g., plant closing legislation). These regulations can have an important impact on the demand for the company's product, its cost and performance and on the company's relative competitive position. The tools of the business economist are especially helpful in analyzing the impact of regulation on product cost and performance as viewed by the consumer, who may well discount any social benefits in his purchase decision. Even more importantly, the business economist must analyze the differential competitive effects these regulations can have on individual competitors or between current and potential competitors or domestic and foreign competitors.

Environmental regulations that limit plant or product emissions illustrate the full range of public policy analysis required of the business economist. These regulations add to the cost of the product and often reduce its performance, while the social benefits in terms of cleaner air are not adequately valued by the individual consumer because of a classic free-rider problem. These regulations also often benefit existing firms, which may be "grandfathered-in" under the regulations, over new entrants that are required to install the best available (and most expensive) technology. They also often disadvantage domestic firms relative to foreign producers who face less stringent or perhaps no regulation. If economies of scale are significant in reducing emissions, large manufacturers also may be advantaged over smaller producers.

Trade policy has become a critical element in strategic planning for international companies. Trade policy also can have an important impact on the competitive position of domestic companies. A company cannot avoid international competition by restricting its operations to its home market. Indeed, such a strategy may only increase the company's exposure to global competitive risks by limiting its access to international product and financial hedging strategies.

Trade restraints, local content and export requirements, exchange rate policies and nontariff barriers to trade all can have significant effects on a company's competitive position and on its efforts to implement an integrated, global strategy.

Business strategy based on economic forecasting and market trend can provide substantial assistance to design internal organizational structures that will ensure the effective implementation of the strategic plans. Following the dictum that "structure follows strategy," General Motors, after extensive analysis, undertook a massive reorganization in 1984. General Motors had developed strategies to shorten product lead times, to increase the differentiation of its vehicles and to improve quality and lower cost through better coordination among product design, engineering and manufacturing. Implementing this strategy, however, required a new, less centralized organizational structure to improve the coordination and speed of decision making. Thus, the company created two new car groups (C-P-C and B-O-C) that were given total responsibility for engineering, manufacturing and marketing their products and that were held accountable for the quality and performance of their vehicles and for the profitability of their operations.

It is absolutely important to identify and assess the risks created by uncertainty in the external business environment and evaluate the strategic alternatives for responding to these risks. Exchange rates, which cannot be forecasted with great reliability, provide an excellent example of the need to assess and plan for uncertainty. The only thing that can be forecasted accurately is that current exchange rates will change, sometimes making, for example, the U.S. an attractive location for production and export of a product, and sometimes making it an attractive import market. A company, however, cannot effectively respond to the business opportunities created by changing currency values unless it has planned for these changes well in advance. If it has not, it will not be in a position to take advantage of them when they occur. By the time the product is modified or overseas production or distribution facilities are developed to take advantage of export opportunities created by a weak currency, the exchange rate may well have changed again. A company that has planned its product, production and distribution systems for continuously fluctuating exchange rates, on the other hand, will be able to move quickly enough to take advantage of the competitive opportunities created by changing currency values.

Another area requiring substantial improvement to be more useful to strategic planners is the global analysis of the external environment provided for companies competing in worldwide industries. To be successful in such industries, these companies require global strategies for coordinating and effectively utilizing their worldwide research, design, and production and marketing networks. Because of the strategic interdependence of these operations throughout the world, business planners need to know what the implications of economic, industry, competitive and policy developments in one region of the world are for the rest of the world. Independent forecasts and analyses of these regions, which pass for global analyses in most companies, do not provide the strategic insights needed to develop an internally consistent set of global plans for effectively utilizing the company's worldwide resources.

A final area requiring much improvement is the treatment of public policy issues in the strategic planning process. From its origins, strategic planning has called for the analysis of both the economic and socio-political environments facing the firm. The reality of strategic business planning is that, even in advanced planning, the focus is almost exclusively on the economic environment. The assessment of the company's socio-political environment is left to the public affairs specialists who operate largely in isolation from those developing the company's business plans in most companies.

The integration of strategic business and public affairs planning is essential to both business success and to the realization of broader social goals. Without such integration, social and economic issues are not adequately addressed at the operating levels where the most effective solutions can often be found, and business plans often are frustrated by unanticipated regulation or other forms of social control.

The basic challenge is to keep pace with the advances in the company's planning system to ensure that the planners have and fully understand the economic environment they need to respond effectively to a more complex, less stable and increasingly global business environment.

D.2 FDI & BUSINESS TRENDS

Amid a sharpening financial and economic crisis, global FDI inflows fell from a historic high of $1,979 billion in 2007 to $1,697 billion in 2008, a decline of 14%. The slide continued into 2009, with added momentum: preliminary data for 96 countries suggest that in the first quarter of 2009, inflows fell a further 44% compared with their level in the same period in 2008. A slow recovery is expected in 2010, but should speed up in 2011. The crisis has also changed the investment landscape, with developing and transition economies' share in global FDI flows surging to 43% in 2008.

The decline posted globally in 2008 differed among the three major economic groupings – developed countries, developing countries and the transition economies of South-East Europe and the Commonwealth of Independent States (CIS) – reflecting an initial differential impact of the current crisis. In developed countries, where the financial crisis originated, FDI inflows fell in 2008, whereas in developing countries and the transition economies they continued to increase.

This geographical difference appears to have ended by late 2008 or early 2009, as initial data point to a general decline across all economic groups. The 29% decline in FDI inflows to developed countries in 2008 was mostly due to cross-border M&A sales that fell by 39% in value after a five-year boom ended in 2007. In Europe, cross-border M&A deals plummeted by 56% and in Japan by 43%. Worldwide mega deals – those with a transaction value of more than $1 billion – have been particularly strongly affected by the crisis.

In the first half of 2008 developing countries weathered the global financial crisis better than developed countries, as their financial systems were less closely interlinked with the hard-hit banking systems of the United States and Europe. Their economic growth remained robust, supported by rising commodity prices. Their FDI inflows continued to grow, but at a much slower pace than in previous years, posting a 17%

to $621 billion. By region, FDI inflows increased considerably in Africa (27%) and in Latin America and the Caribbean (13%) in 2008, continuing the upward trend of the preceding years for both regions. However, in the second half of the year and into 2009, the global economic downturn caught up with these countries as well, adversely affecting FDI inflows. Inflows to South, East and South-East Asia witnessed a 17% expansion to hit a high of $298 billion in 2008, followed by a significant decline in the first quarter of 2009. A similar pattern prevailed in the transition economies of South-East Europe and the CIS, with inflows rising by 26% to $114 billion in 2008 (a record high), but then plunging by 47% year-on-year in the first quarter of 2009. Dramatic changes in FDI patterns over the past year have caused changes in the overall rankings of the largest host and home countries for FDI flows. While the United States maintained its position as the largest host and home country in 2008, many developing and transition economies emerged as large recipients and investors: they accounted for 43% and 19% of global FDI inflows and outflows, respectively, in 2008. A number of European countries saw their rankings slide in terms of both FDI inflows and outflows. The United Kingdom lost its position as the largest source and recipient country of FDI among European countries. Japan improved its outward position.

FDI flows increased to structurally weak economies in 2008, including Least Developed Countries (LDCs), Landlocked Developing Countries (LLDCs) and Small Island Developing States (SIDS) by 29%, 54% and 32% respectively. However, due to the distinctive characteristics of these three groups of economies, including their dependence on a narrower range of export commodities that were hard hit by falling demand from developed countries, the current crisis has exposed their vulnerabilities in attracting inward FDI. These economies may therefore, wish to consider promoting FDI in industries which are less prone to cyclical fluctuations, such as agriculture-related industries, particularly food and beverages, as part of a diversification strategy.

In late 2008 and the first few months of 2009, significant declines were recorded in all three components of FDI inflows: equity investments, other capital (mainly intercompany loans) and reinvested earnings. Equity investments fell along with cross-border M&As. Lower profits by foreign affiliates drove down reinvested earnings, contributing to the

46% drop in FDI outflows from developed countries in the first quarter of 2009. In some cases, the restructuring of parent companies and their headquarters led to repayments of outstanding loans by foreign affiliates and a reduction in net intra-company capital flows from TNCs to their foreign affiliates. Critically, the proportionate decline in equity investments today is larger than that registered during the previous downturn.

Since mid-2008, divestments, including repatriated investments, reverse intra-company loans and repayments of debt to parent firms, have exceeded gross FDI flows in a number of countries. For instance, divestments amounted to $110 billion in the case of FDI outflows from Germany, accounting for 40% of its gross FDI flows in 2008. In the first half of 2009, nearly one third of all cross-border M&A deals involved the disposal of foreign firms to other firms (whether based in a host, home or third country). This depressed FDI flows further. While divestments are not uncommon (affecting between one quarter and four fifths of all FDI projects), they became especially noticeable during a crisis. Indeed the motivations for divestment have been heightened during this crisis as TNCs seek to cut operating costs, shed non-core activities, and in some cases take part in industry-wide restructuring. Greenfield Investments (new investments and expansion of existing facilities) were resilient overall in 2008, but have also succumbed to the crisis since late 2008. Available cross-border M&A data by sector indicate that companies in a limited number of industries increased their FDI activities in 2008. Industries exhibiting rising cross-border M&A sales (by value) during the year included food, beverages and tobacco, buoyed by the $52 billion purchase of Anheuser Busch (United States) by Stichting Interbrew (Belgium); precision instruments; mining, quarrying and petroleum; motor vehicles and other transportation equipment; business services; other services; agriculture, hunting, forestry and fisheries; coke, petroleum and nuclear fuel; and public administration and defence. In general, the primary sector witnessed a growth of 17% in the value of M&A sales in 2008; whereas manufacturing and services – which account for the largest proportion of world inward FDI stocks – reported declines of 10% and 54% respectively.

The financial and economic crisis had varying impacts on FDI carried out by special funds, such as Sovereign Wealth Funds (SWFs) or private equity funds. Private equity funds were hit especially hard, as the financial crisis struck at their lifeblood: easy capital, which shrank as lenders became more risk conscious. Cross-border M&As by these funds fell to $291 billion in 2008, or by 38%, from a peak of $470 billion in 2007. The main reason for the sharp decline was that the financing of leveraged buyouts – that contributed most to the dynamic growth of cross-border M&As by these funds in previous years – nearly dried up in the second half of 2008. SWFs, on the other hand, recorded a rise in FDI in 2008, despite a fall in commodities prices, the export earnings of which often provide them with finance. Compared with 2007, the value of their cross-border M&As – the predominant form of FDI by SWFs – was up 16% in 2008, to $20 billion, a small amount in proportion to the size of FDI and other assets under their management. This increase bucked the downward trend in global FDI as a whole. However, during the course of 2008, the sharp economic downturn in developed countries and the worldwide slump in stock prices led to large losses in SWFs' investments (partly because of a high concentration of investments in financial and business services industries), which depressed the pace of growth of their cross-border M&A deals. Moreover, the large size of SWFs and their perceived non-economic intentions have aroused concerns in a number of countries. To counter this concern, in October 2008 a number of SWFs agreed on a set of Generally Accepted Principles and Practices (GAPP) – the so called Santiago Principles. Prospects for further increases in cross-border M&As by SWFs have deteriorated dramatically, judging by data on M&As for the first half of 2009.

Sovereign Wealth Funds are pools of money derived from a country's reserves, which are set aside for investment purposes that will benefit the country's economy and citizens. The funding for a sovereign wealth fund (SWF) comes from from central bank reserves that accumulate as a result of budget and trade surpluses, and even from revenue generated from the exports of natural resources. The types of acceptable investments included in each SWF vary from country to country; countries with liquidity concerns limit investments to only very liquid public debt instruments. Some countries have created SWFs to diversify their revenue streams. For example, the United Arab Emirates (UAE) relies on oil exports for its wealth; therefore, it devotes a portion of its reserves to an SWF that invests in other types of assets that can act as a shield against oil-related risk. The amount of money in these SWF is substantial. The estimated value of all SWFs is pegged at $2.5 trillion.

Today, there are some 82,000 TNCs worldwide, with 810,000 foreign affiliates. These companies play a major and growing role in the world economy. For example, exports by foreign affiliates of TNCs are estimated to account for about a third of total world exports of goods and services, and the number of people employed by them worldwide totaled about 77 million in 2008 – more than double the total labour force of Germany. However, their international stature has not insulated them from the worst global recession in a generation. The 4.8% reduction in inward FDI stock worldwide was reflected in the decline in value of gross product, sales and assets, as well as employment of TNCs' foreign affiliates in 2008, a marked contrast to huge double-digit growth rates in 2006 and 2007. UNCTAD's *World Investment Prospects Survey (WIPS) 2009–2011* shows that TNCs' FDI plans have been affected by the global economic and financial crisis in the short term. In contrast to the previous survey, when only 40% of companies reported being affected by the crisis, in 2009 as many as 85% of TNCs worldwide blamed the global economic downturn for influencing cutbacks in their investment plans; and 79% blamed the financial crisis directly. Both of these aspects, separately and combined, have diminished the propensity and ability of TNCs to engage in FDI.

The economic and financial crisis has had a strong impact both industry-wide and at the individual company level. This is reflected in declining profits, increasing divestments and layoffs, and forced restructuring. The rate of internationalization of the largest TNCs slowed down markedly in 2008, while their overall profits fell by 27%. Even so, the 100 largest TNCs worldwide continue to represent a sizable proportion of total international production by the universe of TNCs. Over the three years from 2006 to 2008 these 100 companies accounted for, on average, 9%, 16% and 11% respectively, of estimated foreign assets, sales and employment of all TNCs. And their combined value-added accounted for roughly 4% of world GDP, a share that has remained relatively stable since 2000.

In terms of the sectoral composition of the top 100 list for 2007, the majority of the largest TNCs continued to be in manufacturing. General

Electric, Toyota Motor Corporation, and Ford Motor Company were among the biggest manufacturers. TNCs from the services sector, however, have been steadily increasing their share among the top 100. There were 26 companies on the 2008 list, as opposed to 14 in 1993, with Vodafone Group and Electricité de France among the biggest. Primary sector

TNCs — such as Royal Dutch/Shell Group, British Petroleum Company, and ExxonMobil Corporation — ranked high in the list, buoyed by swelling foreign assets. As for TNCs from developing countries, 7 featured in the list, among them large diversified companies such as Hutchison Whampoa and CITIC Group, as well as important electronics manufacturers like LG Corporation and Samsung Electronics. The operations of the 50 largest financial TNCs were more geographically spread in 2008 than ever before; however it is not clear what the ultimate consequences of the hiatus of late 2008 and early 2009 will be.

With massive government interventions in banking and financial services, some developed-country governments have become the largest or sole shareholders in several of the biggest financial TNCs. This dramatic change, together with the downfall of some of the largest financial TNCs, will strongly reshape FDI in financial services in the coming years.

Global FDI prospects are set to remain gloomy in 2009, with inflows expected to fall below $1.2 trillion. However, recovery of these flows is expected to begin slowly in 2010 to reach up to $1.4 trillion, and will gather momentum in 2011 when the level could approach an estimated $1.8 trillion – almost the same as in 2008. In the short run, with the global recession extending into 2009 and slow growth projected for 2010, as well as the drastic fall of corporate profits, FDI is expected to be low. TNCs appear hesitant and bearish about expanding their international operations. This is confirmed by the results of *WIPS:* a majority (58%) of large TNCs reported their intentions to reduce their FDI expenditures in 2009 from their 2008 levels, with nearly one third of them (more than 30%) even anticipating a large decrease. Considering the 44% fall in actual FDI inflows worldwide in the first quarter of 2009, compared to the same period last year, 2009 could end with much lower flows than in 2008.

The medium-term prospects for FDI are more optimistic. TNCs responding to *WIPS* expect a gradual recovery in their FDI expenditures in 2010, gaining momentum in 2011; half of them even foresee their FDI in 2011 exceeding the 2008 level. The United States, along with China, India, Brazil and the Russian Federation (the so-called **BRIC** countries) are likely to lead the future FDI recovery, as indicated by the responses of large TNCs to *WIPS*. Industries that are less sensitive to business cycles and operate in markets with stable demand (such as agribusiness and many services), and those with longer term growth prospects (such as pharmaceuticals) are likely to be the engine for the next FDI boom. Furthermore, in the immediate aftermath of the crisis, when the global economy is on its way to recovery, the exit of public/government funds from ailing industries will possibly trigger a new wave of cross-border M&As.

In 2008 and the first half of 2009, despite concerns about a possible rise in investment protectionism, the general trend in FDI policies remained one of greater openness, including lowering barriers to FDI and lowering corporate income taxes. During 2008, 110 new FDI-related measures were introduced, of which 85 were more favourable to FDI. Compared to 2007, the percentage of less favourable measures for FDI remained unchanged. The trend of scrutinizing foreign investments for national security reasons continued. Regulations to this end were adopted in some OECD countries. They expanded the scope of compulsory notification rules or enabled governments to block acquisitions of stakes in domestic companies. There was also a continuing trend towards nationalization of foreign-owned entities in extractive industries, particularly in parts of Latin America. The majority of policy measures specific and/or related to investment, taken by G-20 countries in the period November 2008 to June 2009 were non-restrictive towards foreign inward and domestic outward investment. In fact, a substantial number of the policy changes surveyed were in the direction of facilitating investment, including outward investment. There were, however, also a few policy measures that restrict private (including foreign) investment in certain highly sensitive sectors, or introduce new criteria and tests for investments that cause national security concerns.

So far, the current financial and economic crisis has had no major impact on FDI policies per se, since FDI is not the cause of this crisis. However, some national policy measures of a more general scope (national bailout programmes, economic stimulus packages) introduced in response to the crisis is likely to have an impact on FDI flows and TNC operations in an indirect manner. They may have a positive effect on inward FDI, as they could help stabilize, if not improve, the key economic determinants of FDI. On the other hand, concerns have been expressed that country policy measures could result in investment protectionism by favoring domestic over foreign investors, or by introducing obstacles to outward investment in order to keep capital at home.

There are also signs that some countries have begun to discriminate against foreign investors and/or their products in a "hidden" way using gaps in international regulations. Examples of "covert" protectionism include favoring products with high "domestic" content in government procurement (particularly huge public infrastructure projects), de facto preventing banks from lending for foreign operations, invoking "national security" exceptions that stretch the definition of national security, or moving protectionist barriers to sub national levels that are outside the scope of the application of international obligations (e.g. in matters of procurement).

Looking to the future, a crucial question is which FDI policies host countries will apply once the global economy begins to recover. The expected exit of public funds from flagship industries is likely to provide a boost to private investment, including FDI. This could possibly trigger a new wave of economic nationalism to protect "national champions" from foreign takeovers. International Investment Agreements (IIAs) have a role to play in ensuring predictability, stability and transparency of national investment regimes. Investment insurance and other home-country measures that encourage outward investment are cases in point where continued international cooperation can be useful. All of these developments, as well as impacts of the crisis on FDI flows and TNC activities have had different effects on the pattern of FDI by region.

FDI inflows into **Africa** rose to $88 billion in 2008 – another record level, despite the global financial and economic crisis. The main FDI recipients included many natural-resource producers that have been attracting large shares of the region's inflows in the past few years, but also some additional commodity-rich countries. Developed countries were the leading sources of FDI in Africa, although their share in the region's FDI stock has fallen over time. A number of African countries adopted policy measures to make the business environment in the region more conducive to FDI. However the region's overall investment climate still presents a mixed picture.

South, East and South-East Asia continued to register strong growth in FDI inflows in 2008 (17%), to reach a new high of $298 billion. Inflows into the major economies in the region varied significantly: they surged in China, India and the Republic of Korea; continued to grow in Hong Kong (China); dropped slightly in Malaysia and Thailand; and fell sharply in Singapore and Taiwan. Outward FDI from South, East and South-East Asia rose by 7%, to $186 billion, due mainly to large outflows from China. In contrast, FDI outflows from other major economies in the region generally slowed down in early 2009, as the crisis has largely reduced the ability and motivation of many TNCs from these economies to invest abroad. Some countries introduced changes in national policies and legislation favourable to FDI, for instance by raising or abolishing FDI ceilings or streamlining approved procedures. Available data in early 2009 point to a significant downturn in FDI flows to the region, and cast doubts about FDI growth prospects in the short term. Inflows to China and India are inevitably affected by the crisis, too, but their medium to long-term prospects remain promising. China and India retain their positions among the most attractive locations for FDI.

FDI inflows into West Asia increased in 2008 for the sixth consecutive year. They totaled $90 billion, representing a 16% increase. This was largely due to the significant growth of inflows to Saudi Arabia, especially to real estate, petrochemicals and oil refining. In contrast, FDI growth was negative in the second and third largest recipient countries: Turkey and the United Arab Emirates. FDI outflows from West Asia declined by 30% in 2008, to $34 billion, largely due to the significant fall in the value of net cross-border M&A purchases by West Asian TNCs. The trend towards a more liberal FDI related policy continued in 2008 in a number of countries. Examples include reductions in the rate of tax levied on foreign companies, privatization of State-owned enterprises, liberalization of the exchange rate regime, improved access to financing by investors and investment facilitation. Since the third quarter of 2008, a sharp fall in oil prices and the steadily worsening outlook for the world economy have dampened the prospects for FDI inflows in 2009.

In Latin America and the Caribbean, FDI inflows increased in 2008 by 13% to $144 billion. The growth was uneven among the sub regions: it was up by 29% in South America and down by 6% in Central America and the Caribbean. Natural-resource-related activities continued to be the main attraction for FDI in South America, and they are increasingly becoming a significant FDI target in Central America and the Caribbean. In contrast, FDI to the manufacturing sector declined due to a sharp drop in flows to Central America and the Caribbean. FDI outflows from Latin America and the Caribbean increased in 2008 by 22% to $63 billion, due to soaring outflows from South America, which offset the decline in outflows from Central America and the Caribbean. A number of the countries in the region took measures to strengthen national champions. In the region as a whole, FDI inflows and outflows are expected to decline in 2009, as the impacts of the economic and financial crisis spread across the region.

FDI inflows to South-East Europe and the CIS increased for the eighth consecutive year, reaching $114 billion – a record level – in spite of financial turmoil and conflicts in certain parts of the region. The inflows continued to be unevenly distributed, with three countries (the Russian Federation, Kazakhstan and Ukraine, in that order) accounting for 84% of the region's total. Outward FDI flows in 2008, dominated by Russian TNCs, maintained their upward trend. In 2008, countries in both sub regions continued to liberalize their FDI regulations in certain industries such as electricity generation, banking, retail and telecommunications. Conversely, some natural-resource-rich countries introduced certain policy changes less favorable to foreign investors, such as strengthening their control over natural resources through legislation. The slowdown of economic growth in all the countries of the region, and the fall in commodity prices, coupled with the near-exhaustion of major privatization opportunities, is likely to lead to a strong decline in FDI.

As the economic and financial crisis and the accelerating economic downturn seriously affected all of the world's major economies, FDI flows to and from developed countries fell sharply in 2008, after reaching a historic peak in 2007. Inflows amounted to $962 billion, down by 29% from the previous year, and these declines occurred in all major host countries except the United States. The fall in inward FDI was more pronounced in the manufacturing and services sectors, while the consolidation process in mining and quarrying and the increasing participation of large companies from developing countries (notably from China) contributed to the rise of FDI in the primary sector.

FDI policy environments in developed countries in 2009 were influenced by the continuing public debate about the cross-border investments of SWFs, and by concerns of new investment protectionism in developed countries in reaction to the financial and economic crisis. Some developed countries adopted or amended rules concerning the review of foreign investment on national security grounds, while others adopted measures aimed at further liberalization of their investment regimes. FDI to and from developed countries is continued to fall further in 2009 because of the continuing effects of the financial crisis and weaker economic growth in these economies, but is expected a gradual recovery in their FDI expenditures in 2010, which may gain momentum in 2011; or even their FDI in 2011 exceeding the 2008 level.

So far, no signs of a significant direct impact of the crisis on the policy and legal environment for FDI have been observed. However, there are concerns regarding the implications of the new policies of nationalization and State control, as well as of signs of rising protectionism, for global capital flows. For the Governments of both developed and developing countries, it is important to resist the temptation of "quick-fix" solutions, and to maintain an overall favourable business and investment climate. In this regard, investment promotion agencies can play a proactive role in both retaining existing TNC activities and stimulating new investments.

According to World Economic Situation and Prospects 2010 (UN Publication) the world economy continued to improve in the first half of 2010, leading to a slight upward revision in the United Nations outlook for global growth. The pace of the recovery is too weak, however, to close the global output gap left by the crisis. The recovery is also uneven across countries. While growth prospects for some developing countries are encouraging, economic activity is lack lustre in developed economies and below potential elsewhere in the developing world. Important weaknesses in the global economy remain. Despite the large amounts of liquidity injected into the financial system, credit growth remains feeble in major developed economies and the process of financial deleveraging is still ongoing. Unemployment rates are expected to remain elevated for a protracted period in most developed economies. In developing countries, many workers have been pushed into vulnerable employment and the number of working poor may still increase further in the immediate outlook. Fiscal positions are deteriorating rapidly, particularly among developed countries. This is limiting the space for further policy support needed to sustain the recovery in many economies. Escalated concerns about risks associated with sovereign debts in some economies have also become a new source for financial instability. Continued macroeconomic stimulus remains crucial for solidifying and broadening the recovery, but should become more focused on boosting employment growth. A balance between the continued need for sustaining the recovery and the need for fiscal consolidation in the medium run is a key policy challenge for many developed countries. International policy coordination needs to be strengthened in order to put the world economy on a robust, sustainable and more balanced growth path, and for reforming both the national and international financial systems.

D.3 TRENDS IN BUSINESS INVESTMENT

Agriculture is central to the provision of food and the eradication of poverty and hunger. Not only does it provide significant mass and rural employment, it is also a major contributor to national economic growth and a considerable foreign exchange earner for many developing countries. Given the fundamental importance of agriculture to most developing economies, its chronic neglect by many of them has been of utmost concern for some time. However, several factors, which are not mutually exclusive, have resulted in a recent upswing in domestic private and foreign participation in agricultural industries in a significant number of developing countries.

Most of these factors are of a structural nature, and are expected to drive agricultural investment in the foreseeable future. In this context foreign participation, as well as domestic investment, can play a critical part in agricultural production in developing countries, boosting productivity and supporting economic development. The main drivers of agricultural investment include the availability of land and water in target locations, combined with fast growing demand and rising imports of food crops in various countries, including both the more populous emerging countries, such as Brazil, China, India and the Republic of Korea, and land and water-scarce developing regions, such as member States of the Gulf Cooperation Council (GCC). International demand for agricultural commodities has been further spurred by other factors, such as bio-fuel initiatives around the world, resulting in a spate of investments in developing countries in the cultivation of sugarcane, grains (such as maize) and oilseeds (such as soya beans), as well as non-food crops such as Jatropha. These trends are intertwined with a rapid rise in food prices over the past few years and subsequent shortages in commodities such as rice, which has spawned a number of "new investors", and also triggered a number of speculative direct investments in agriculture and land.

FDI in agriculture is on the rise, although its total size remains limited (inward FDI stock in 2007 was $32 billion) and is small relative to other industries. At the turn of the 1990s, world FDI flows in agriculture remained less than $1 billion per year, but by 2005–2007, they had tripled to $3 billion annually. Moreover, TNCs established in downstream segments of host-country value chains (e.g. food processing and supermarkets) also invest in agricultural production and contract farming, thereby multiplying the actual size of their participation in the industry. In fact, after a rapid rate of growth in the early 2000s, FDI flows in the food and beverages industry alone (i.e. not including other downstream activities) exceeded $40 billion in 2005–2007.

Although the share of FDI in agriculture remains small as a share of total FDI in developed, developing and transition economies as a whole, in some Least Developed Countries (LDCs), including Cambodia, the Lao People's Democratic Republic, Malawi, Mozambique and the United Republic of Tanzania, the share of FDI in agriculture in total FDI flows or stocks is relatively large. This is also true for some non-LDCs, such as Ecuador, Honduras, Indonesia, Malaysia, Papua New Guinea and Viet Nam. The high share in these countries is due to factors such as the structure of the domestic economy, availability of agricultural land (mostly for long-term lease), and national policies (including promotion of investment in agriculture).

FDI is relatively large in certain cash crops such as sugarcane, cut flowers and vegetables. The bulk of inward FDI in developing regions is aimed at food and cash crops. There is also a growing interest in crops for bio fuel production through projects related to oil-seed crops in Africa and sugarcane in South America, for instance. In terms of the main produce targeted by foreign investors in developing and transition economies, some regional specialization is apparent. For example, South American countries have attracted FDI in a wide range of products such as wheat, rice, sugarcane, fruits, flowers, soya beans, meat and poultry; while in Central American countries, TNCs have focused mostly on fruits and sugarcane. In Africa, foreign investors have shown a particular interest in staple crops such as rice, wheat and oil crops; but there is also TNC involvement in sugarcane and cotton in Southern Africa, and in floriculture in East Africa. In South Asia, foreign investors have targeted the large-scale production of rice and wheat, while their activities in other Asian regions are concentrated more in cash crops, meat and poultry. Finally, TNCs in the transition economies are largely involved in dairy products, although more recently they are also seeking to invest in wheat and grains.

Contract farming is a significant component of TNCs' participation in agricultural production, in terms of its geographical distribution, intensity of activity at the country level, coverage by commodities and types of TNCs involved. In this context contract farming can be defined as non-equity contractual arrangements entered into by farmers with TNC affiliates (or agents on behalf of TNCs) whereby the former agree to deliver to the latter a quantity of farm outputs at an agreed price, quality standard, delivery date and other specifications. It is an attractive option for TNCs, because it allows better control over product specifications and supply than spot markets. At the same time it is less capital intensive, less risky and more flexible than land lease or ownership. From the perspectives of farmers, contract farming can provide predictable incomes, access to markets, and TNC support in areas such as credit and know-how.

TNCs engaged in contract farming activities and other non-equity forms are spread worldwide in over 110 countries across Africa, Asia and Latin America. For example, in 2008 the food processor Nestle (Switzerland) had contracts with more than 600,000 farms in over 80 developing and transition economies as direct suppliers of various agricultural commodities. Similarly, Olam (Singapore) has a globally spread contract farming network with approximately 200,000 suppliers in 60 countries (most of them developing countries). Contract farming is not only widespread, but also intensive in many emerging and poorer countries. For instance, in Brazil, 75% of poultry production and 35% of soya bean production are sourced through contract farming, including by TNCs. In Viet Nam the story is similar, with 90% of cotton and fresh milk, 50% of tea and 40% of rice being purchased through farming contracts. In Kenya, about 60% of tea and sugar are produced through this mode.

Moreover, contract faming arrangements cover a broad variety of commodities, from livestock through staple food produce to cash crops. For example, Olam sources globally for 17 agricultural commodities (including cashew nuts, cotton, spices, coffee, cocoa and sugar). Similarly, agricultural crops make up two thirds of Unilever's (United Kingdom/

Netherlands) raw materials, and include palm and other edible oils, tea and other infusions, tomatoes, peas and a wide range of other vegetables. These are sourced from 100,000 smallholder farmers and larger farms in developing countries, as well as third-party suppliers. Contractual farming arrangements enable different types of TNCs in the downstream stages of agribusiness value chains, including food manufacturers, bio-fuel producers, retailers and many others, to secure agricultural inputs from local farmers in different host countries.

The 25 largest agriculture-based TNCs (i.e. companies which are primarily located in the *agricultural production* segment of agribusiness, such as farms and plantations) differ from the top agriculture-related TNCs (i.e. those primarily in *upstream* or *downstream* stages of these value chains): the former have a significant number of developing-country firms among their ranks, while the latter do not. In terms of foreign assets, the number of agriculture-based TNCs is split almost evenly between developed and developing-country firms, indicating that firms from developing countries are also emerging as important players in global food and non-food agricultural production. However, developed-country firms still dominate among agriculture-related TNCs. Twelve out of the top 25 agriculture-based TNCs are headquartered in developing countries and 13 in developed countries. Indeed, the top position in the list is occupied by a developing-country TNC, Sime Darby Berhad (Malaysia), while United States firms (Dole Food and Del Monte) occupy the second and third positions.

The universe of agriculture-related TNCs includes food processors/manufacturers, retailers, traders and suppliers of inputs. These TNCs are usually larger than agricultural TNCs. For example, the world's largest food and beverages TNC, Nestle (Switzerland), controls $66 billion in foreign assets, and the largest food retailer, Wal-Mart (United States), controls $63 billion. In contrast, the largest agricultural TNC, Sime Darby (Malaysia), has only $5 billion of foreign assets. The list of the largest TNC input suppliers to agriculture comprises only developed-country firms. In food processing, 39 of the top 50 firms are headquartered in developed countries. Compared to other TNCs in agribusiness, those in food and beverages are very large: the nine largest, all headquartered in developed countries, control about $20 billion of foreign assets each;

together, they represent more than two thirds of the foreign assets of the top 50 firms.

Retailing and supermarket TNCs also play a major role in international agricultural supply chains. The majority of the 25 largest TNCs in this industry (22) are again from developed countries. Apart from traditional TNCs involved in agriculture, newcomers, such as State owned enterprises, Sovereign Wealth Funds and international institutions, are increasingly active in agriculture. The main drivers of (or motives for) the new investors are the intertwined twins of threat and opportunity. For example, Agricapital (a State-owned fund based in Bahrain) is investing in food crops overseas to support its government's food security policies. At the same time, supplying food to the world's burgeoning markets is seen as a lucrative opportunity by other actors, thereby spurring international investment in agriculture by companies and funds such as Vision 3 (United Arab Emirates) and Goldman Sachs (United States).

There are indications that South-South investment in agricultural production is on the rise, and that this trend is set to continue in the long term. Investors from developing countries became major sources of cross-border takeovers in 2008. Their net cross-border M&A purchases, amounting to $1,577 million, accounted for over 40% of the world total ($3,563 million). Examples of South-South investment projects include Sime Darby's (Malaysia) $800 million investment in a plantation in Liberia in 2009; Chinese investments and contract farming in commodities such as maize, sugar and rubber in the Mekong region, especially in Cambodia and the Lao People's Democratic Republic; the regional expansion of Zambeef (Zambia) into Ghana and Nigeria; and the expansion by Grupo Bimbo (Mexico) across Latin America and the Caribbean.

In addition to commercial investment in agriculture – a common feature of developed and developing-country TNCs – in the wake of the food crisis, food security has also become a major driver of new investors. These include companies and funds (some State-owned or backed) from a variety of countries, especially the Republic of Korea and GCC countries. To varying degrees, the governments of these source countries have decided that investment in target host countries, giving them control over crop production and export of the output back to their home economy, is the most effective way of ensuring food security for their populations. For many of these countries, the most crucial factor or driver behind outward FDI in agriculture is not land per se, but rather the availability of water resources to irrigate the land. Most of their investment is in other developing countries.

The scale of South-South FDI driven by food security concerns is not easy to determine because many relevant deals have only recently been signed, although others are being considered or in negotiation. Of the definite larger scale investments involving land acquisitions (i.e. outright ownership and long-term leases) undertaken thus far, the largest investing countries from the South include Bahrain, China, Qatar, Kuwait, the Libyan Arab Jamahiriya, Saudi Arabia, the Republic of Korea and the United Arab Emirates. The most important developing host countries are in Africa, with Ethiopia, Sudan and the United Republic of Tanzania among the foremost FDI recipients.

A precisely quantified evaluation of the impact of TNC involvement in agriculture on important development aspects, such as contribution to capital formation, technology transfer and foreign market access, is impeded by the limited availability of relevant hard data available from international sources. The actual impacts and implications vary enormously across countries and by types of agricultural produce. In addition, they are influenced by a range of factors, including the type of TNC involvement, the institutional environment and the level of development of the host country. A number of salient observations of TNCs' involvement in agriculture for developing countries nevertheless emerge.

Overall, TNC involvement in developing countries has promoted the commercialization and modernization of agriculture. TNCs are by no means the only – and seldom the main – agent driving this process, but they have played an important role in a significant number of countries. They have done so not only by investing directly in agricultural production, but also through non-equity forms of involvement in agriculture, mostly contract farming. Indeed, non-equity forms of participation have been on the rise in recent years. In many cases, they have led to significant transfers of skills, know-how and methods of production, facilitated access to credit and various inputs, and given access to markets to a very large number of small farmers previously involved mostly in subsistence farming.

Although TNC involvement in agriculture has contributed to enhanced productivity and increased output in a number of developing countries, there is lack of evidence on the extent to which their involvement has allowed the developing world to increase its production of staple foods and improve food security. Available evidence points to TNCs being mostly involved in cash crops (except for the recent rise of South-South FDI in this area). Such a finding reveals the development challenges for developing countries in promoting TNC participation in their agricultural industry to improve food security. However, food security is not just about food supply. TNCs can also have an impact on food access, stability of supply and food utilization and, in the longer run; their impacts on these aspects of food security are likely to prove more important for host economies.

Positive impacts of TNC involvement in agriculture are not gained automatically by developing countries. While TNCs have at times generated employment and improved earnings in rural communities, no clear trend is discernible. To the extent that TNCs promote modernization of agriculture and a shift from subsistence to commercial farming, their long-term impact is likely to accelerate the long-term reduction in farm employment while raising earnings. Only a limited number of developing countries have also been able to benefit from transfers of technologies. In particular, the R&D and technological innovations of the large TNCs are typically not geared towards the staple foods produced in many developing countries.

Apart from the potentially large benefits that developing countries can derive from TNC participation in their agriculture, past experiences and evidence indicate that governments need to be sensitive to the negative impacts that can arise. A particular concern is that of the asymmetry in the relationship between small farmers and a restricted number of large buyers, which raises serious competition issues. Recent experiences also underscore that developing-country governments need to be aware of the environmental and social consequences of TNCs involvement in agriculture, even though there is no clear and definite pattern of impact.

Case studies show that TNCs have the potential to bring environmentally sound production technologies, but their implication in extensive farming has also raised concerns, together with their impact on biodiversity and water usage. Similarly, TNCs' involvement raises significant social and political issues whenever they own or control large tracts of agricultural land. The expansion of agricultural production is vital for developing countries, both to meet rising food needs and to revitalize the sector. Therefore, policymakers need to promote more investment in this sector, both private and public, and domestic and foreign. Given the financial and technological constraints in many developing countries, policymakers should devise strategies for agricultural development and consider what role TNCs could play in implementing them.

The challenge is considerable, as agriculture is a sensitive industry. There is a need to reflect the interests of all stakeholders, especially local farmers, and include them, as far as possible, in the policy deliberation and formulation process. The key challenge for policymakers in developing countries is to ensure that TNC involvement in agricultural production generates development benefits. Both FDI and contractual arrangements between TNCs and local farmers can bring specific benefits to the host country, such as transfer of technology, employment creation and upgrading the capacities of local farmers, together with higher productivity and competitiveness. Therefore, policies need to be designed with a view to maximizing these benefits. It is equally important for policymakers to address social and environmental concerns with regard to TNC involvement. Social and environmental impacts need to be assessed carefully, and particular attention paid to possible implications for domestic agricultural development and food security in the long run. Negotiations with foreign investors should be transparent with regard to the land involved and the purpose of production, and local landholders should be encouraged to participate in the process. Policies should be designed to protect traditional land tenure rights of local farmers in order to avoid abuses of what might be considered underutilized or underdeveloped land, and to make possible local farmers' access to courts in case of dispossession. Care needs to be taken to secure the right to food for the domestic population and to protect the rights of indigenous peoples.

Numerous developing countries have started to actively encourage

FDI in agricultural production. A survey jointly undertaken by UNCTAD and the World Association of Investment Promotion Agencies (WAIPA) on the role of Investment Promotion Agencies (IPAs) in attracting FDI in agricultural production revealed that the majority of respondents, in particular those in developing countries, promote FDI in this sector. Moreover, these respondents anticipate a still greater role for FDI in this area in the future. TNCs are mainly expected to make new technologies, finance and inputs available to the sector and to improve access to foreign markets for cash crops.

Overall, developing countries are relatively open to TNC involvement in agricultural production, although there are considerable differences between individual countries based on cultural, socio-economic and security-related considerations. The most frequently found restriction for foreign investment in agricultural production relates to land ownership, but in many cases foreign investors are allowed to lease land. Aside from promoting FDI in agricultural production, host countries should pay particular attention to promoting contractual arrangements between TNCs and local farmers, such as contract farming, which would enable the latter to enhance their capacities and become part of national or international food value chains. However, in pursuing such strategies host countries should be aware that, in general, TNCs are more interested in contractual arrangements concerning the production of cash crops.

This means that promoting contract farming for alleviating the food crisis remains a big challenge. In this context, governments should address the specific obstacles for efficient cooperation between TNCs and local farmers, such as

- Lack of capacity of smallholders to supply products in a consistent and standardized manner;

- Lack of availability of adequate technology;

- Lack of capital;

- Remoteness of production and capacity for timely delivery;

- Limited role of farmer organizations; and

- Lack of adequate legal instruments for dispute settlement.

Various policy options exist for tackling these bottlenecks. Among them are education and training programmes for local farmers, the provision of government-led extension services, the establishment of standards and certification procedures, the granting of financial aid, matchmaking services to connect local farmers to TNCs, support for the establishment of farmer organizations, and improving the domestic court systems to increase legal security. Governments could also consider the development of model contracts to protect the interests of farmers in negotiating with TNCs.

Notwithstanding some reservations about FDI in agricultural production, host countries should not underestimate the potential of this form of TNC involvement for enhancing development objectives. In particular, in light of the recent interest in outward FDI to secure domestic food supply there is potential for host countries to benefit from such investment for their own staple food needs, provided that the amount of production is shared between home and host countries. The challenge for host countries is to match inward FDI with existing domestic resources, such as abundant labour and available land, and to create positive synergies to promote long-term agricultural development and increase food security.

Key instruments for maximizing the contribution of FDI to sustainable agricultural and rural development are the domestic legislative framework and, especially as far as major land acquisitions are involved, investment contracts between the host government and foreign investors. These contracts should be designed in such a way as to ensure that benefits for host countries and smallholders are maximized. Critical issues to be considered include, in particular,

- Entry regulations for TNCs,
- The creation of employment opportunities,
- Transfer of technology and R&D,
- Welfare of local farmers and communities,

- Production sharing,
- Distribution of revenues,
- Local procurement of inputs,
- Requirements of target markets,
- Development of agriculture related infrastructure, and
- Environmental protection.

To ensure food security in host countries as a result of FDI in staple food production by "new" investors, home and host countries could consider output-sharing arrangements. Before concluding an investment contract with foreign investors, governments should conduct an environmental and social impact assessment of the specific project. After the investment has been made, monitoring and evaluating its impact on the host country's overall development process is critical. IIAs can be an additional means to promote TNC participation in agricultural production, but careful formulation is crucial with a view to striking a proper balance between the obligations to protect and promote foreign investment, on the one hand, and policy space for the right to regulate, on the other hand. This is particularly important in the case of agriculture, as the sector is highly regulated and sensitive, and government agricultural policies may be controversial and subject to change.

There are several other policy areas relating to a broader economic agenda that are determinants for TNC participation in agricultural production and their development impact in the host country. These therefore should be integrated into host-country strategies aimed at attracting TNCs to agricultural production. Among them are those related to infrastructure development, competition, trade and R&D. Infrastructure development is critical as a means of trade facilitation for agricultural goods. This includes improving existing transportation systems, investing in trade facilitation, providing sufficient post-harvest storage facilities and renovating outdated water irrigation infrastructure. Given the high costs involved and the limited Official Development Assistance (ODA) available, policymakers may wish to require TNCs to contribute to infrastructure development when permitting large-scale projects. Since farmers are generally the weakest link in the supply chain, competition policy can play a vital role in protecting them against potential abuses arising from the dominant position enjoyed by TNCs.

Tariffs and non-tariff barriers as well as subsidies may substantially influence TNC involvement in agricultural production. These kinds of policy measures in developed countries could discourage investment and contract farming in developing countries where the subsidizing country and the potential developing host country produce identical agricultural products or close substitutes. Reducing subsidies in developed countries could encourage FDI to poor countries.

Economies of scale are another challenge, particularly for small developing countries. In their case, regional integration can be an important instrument in making them more attractive for TNCs involved in agricultural production and exports. Host countries should also consider the role of R&D activities and intellectual property rights for increasing agricultural production and adapting the development of seeds and agricultural products to local and regional conditions. Policies should aim at domestic capacity-building to develop strong counterparts to TNCs in the host country – private or public.

In this regard, Public-Private Partnerships (PPPs) for R&D can serve as models for fostering innovation, for adapting the development of seeds and products to local and regional conditions, for making agricultural R&D more responsive to the needs of smallholders and to the challenges of sustainability, for reducing costs, and for mitigating the commercial and financial risks of the venture through risk sharing between the partners. In the wake of recent food price hikes and export restrictions by agricultural exporter countries, some food-importing countries have established policies aimed at the development of overseas food sources for their domestic food security. Despite some concerns that these policies may aggravate food shortage in host countries, they have the potential for increasing global food production and mitigating food shortages in both home and host developing countries. Past attempts by some governments to invest in overseas agriculture have not always met their expectations. Indeed, there are lessons to be learnt.

In addition to outward FDI, home countries could consider whether overseas food production in the form of contract farming may be a viable and less controversial alternative to FDI. Besides focusing on agricultural production itself, another option is to invest in trading houses and in logistical infrastructure such as ports. Agriculture and food security have gained considerable importance on the international policy agenda, both at the multilateral and regional level. A major development was the establishment of the United Nations High-Level Task Force on the Global Food Security Crisis (HLTF) in April 2008. The aim of the HLTF was to create a prioritized plan of action for addressing the global food crisis and coordinate its implementation. The HLTF thus developed the Comprehensive Framework for Action (CFA) – a framework for setting out the joint position of HLTF members on proposed actions to address the current threats and opportunities resulting from food price rise; create policy changes to avoid future food crises, and contribute to country, regional and global food and nutritional security. A number of initiatives to boost agricultural productivity have also been taken at the regional level, including the Comprehensive Africa Agriculture Development Programme (CAADP) under the New Partnership for Africa's Development (NEPAD).

The G-8 Summit in L'Aquila, Italy, in July 2009 made a commitment to mobilizing $20 billion over the next three years for a comprehensive strategy for sustainable global food security and for advancing by end 2009 the implementation of a Global Partnership for Agriculture and Food Security. When deciding how to make best use of these new ODA funds, consideration could be given to agricultural development strategies that combine public investments with maximizing benefits from TNC involvement. With regard to possible future international initiatives, consideration should be given to developing a set of core principles concerning major land acquisitions, including rules on transparency, respect for existing land rights, the right to food, protection of indigenous peoples and social and environmental sustainability.

TNC participation in agriculture in developing countries through FDI, contract farming and other forms has helped a number of pioneering countries, including Brazil, China, Kenya and Vietnam; meet the challenge of boosting investment in their agriculture, thereby making the industry a lynchpin for economic development and modernization. The route has not been easy, with costs and benefits arising from

TNC involvement. For most developing countries many development challenges still remain in the quest for agricultural development, food security and modernization. Among these challenges is how to build and reinforce domestic, regional and international value chains, as well as harness technology in agriculture. It is clear that for LDCs and other poor countries, in Africa and elsewhere, a "new green revolution" is urgent, and an essential question to ask is whether TNCs can play a role in its fulfillment.

The investment trend reveals a real and rising interest by TNCs – from the South as well as the North – for investment in developing countries' agricultural industries. Moreover, a large proportion of this interest is in poorer regions, such as Africa. TNCs vary along the value chain, but overall they have the technological and other assets available to support developing countries' strategies towards intensifying take-up of the green revolution. There are numerous examples partnerships and alliances with farmers, public research entities and others. More needs to be done, but the building blocks are in place for striking a new "grand bargain" to harness the green revolution in the service of Africa's poor and hungry, as well as the wider objectives of development. Central to this programme are, first, investing in trade and investment facilitation and, secondly, creating institutional arrangements such as PPPs to advance the green revolution in the region by encouraging and boosting critical flows of capital, information, knowledge and skills from partners to the countryside. An important initiative in this regard would be the establishment of seed and technology centers in the form of PPPs, mandated with the task of fostering channels to adapt relevant seed and farming technologies to make them suitable to local conditions, distributing seeds to farmers, and, in the longer term, building and deepening indigenous capacity and stable deep-rooted economy with sustainable industrialization.

PART E

GLOSSARY

E.1 ECONOMICS & BUSINESS MANAGEMENT TERMS

- Absolute advantage: A country has an absolute advantage if its output per unit of input of all goods and services produced is higher than that of another country.

- Accelerator Principle: the growth in output that would induce a continuation in net investment.

- Accounting: The recording, classifying, summarizing, and interpreting of events of a financial character. These events can include income, expenses and cash flow.

- Accounts Payable: Trade accounts of businesses representing amounts owed for goods or services received. Accounts Receivable: Trade accounts of businesses representing amounts due for goods sold or services rendered.

- Accrual-Basis Accounting: An accounting system in which income is recorded when it is earned rather than when it is paid, and expenses are recorded when an obligation is established rather than when the money is paid.

- Acid-test ratio: Also called the quick ratio, the ratio of current assets minus inventories, accruals, and prepaid items to current liabilities.

- Ad valorem: (in Latin: to the value added) – a tax based on the value (or assessed value) of property.

- Addendum: An attachment or exhibit to a written document, such as a contract.

- Age Discrimination in Employment Act (ADEA): A federal law that prohibits employers from discriminating against individuals age 40 or more. This law generally applies to companies with 20 or more employees.

- Agent: A person granted the authority to act on behalf of another person or entity, known as the "principal." The actions and decisions of the agent can be binding on the principal.

- Aggregate demand: it is the sum of all demand in an economy. This can be computed by adding the expenditure on consumer goods and services, investment and not exports.

- Aggregate supply is the total value of the goods and services produced in a country, plus the value of imported goods less the value of exports.

- Aging schedule: A table of accounts receivable broken down into age categories (such as 0-30 days, 30-60 days, and 60-90 days), which is used to see whether customer payments are keeping close to schedule.

- Alternative Dispute Resolution (ADR): An approach to conflict resolution designed to avoid court proceedings. ADR traditionally encompasses two main forms: arbitration and mediation.

- Alternative minimum tax: This tax is created to ensure that high-income individuals, corporations, trusts, and estates pay at least some minimum amount of tax, regardless of deductions, credits or exemptions. Alternative minimum tax operates by adding certain tax-preference items back into adjusted gross income. While it was once only important for a small number of high-income individuals who made extensive use of tax shelters and deductions, more and more people are being affected by it.

- Americans with Disabilities Act (ADA): A federal law that prohibits discrimination against those with physical or mental disabilities in employment, public services and public places, such as restaurants, hotels and shops. The ADA requires companies with 15 or more employees to make reasonable accommodations to enable qualified disabled employees to perform their job.

- Amortization: Paying off debt in regular installments over a period of time, or deducting certain capitalized expenditures over a specified period of time.

- Appreciation: The increase in the value of an asset.

- Arbitration: A form of alternative dispute resolution in which a neutral third party (an arbitrator) considers the competing parties' arguments and evidence and renders a decision or award. Arbitration can be binding or non-binding.

- Asset: Any possession that has value in an exchange. Anything of monetary value that is owned by a person. Assets include real property, personal property, and enforceable claims against others (including bank accounts, stocks, mutual funds etc.)

- Asymmetric Information: is where one party in a transaction has less information than the other.

- Audit: A review or examination of an individual's or organization's records to determine legal compliance or proper record keeping.

- Average propensity to consume: is the proportion of income the average family spends on goods and services.

- Average propensity to save: is the proportion of income the average family saves (does not spend on consumption).

- Average total cost: is the sum of all the production costs divided by the number of units produced.

- Award: A decision rendered by a court or arbitrator that one party in a dispute is owed money and that the other party or parties are liable.

- Balance of Payment: is the summation of imports and exports made between one countries and the other countries that it trades with.

- Balance of trade: The difference in value over a period of time between a country's imports and exports.

- Balance Sheet: Also called the statement of financial condition, it is a summary of the assets, liabilities, and owners' equity.

- Bankruptcy: State of being unable to pay debts. Thus, the ownership of the firm's assets is transferred from the stockholders to the bondholders.

- Barter system: System where there is an exchange of goods without involving money.

- Base year: In the construction of an index, the year from which the weights assigned to the different components of the index is drawn. It is conventional to set the value of an index in its base year equal to 100.

- Bear: An investor with a pessimistic market outlook; an investor who expects prices to fall and so sells now in order to buy later at a lower price. A Bear Market is one which is trending downwards or losing value.

- Bid price: The highest price an investor is willing to pay for a stock.

- Bill of Exchange: A written, dated, and signed three-party instrument containing an unconditional order by a drawer that directs a drawee to pay a definite sum of money to a payee on demand or at a specified future date. Also known as a draft. It is the most commonly used financial instrument in international trade.

- Bond: A certificate of debt (usually interest-bearing or discounted) that is issued by a government or corporation in order to raise money; the bond issuer is required to pay a fixed sum annually until maturity and then a fixed sum to repay the principal.

- Bonds: Securities issued by the U.S. government, corporations, federal agencies, or state or local municipalities.

- Bonus: A cash award granted to employees by the employer, usually based on personal and/or company performance. Bonuses can also come in the form of extra vacation time, gifts and other nonmonetary awards.

- Boom: A state of economic prosperity.

- Breach of Contract: A violation of or failure to perform according to the terms and conditions of an agreement.

- Break even: This is a term used to describe a point at which revenues equal costs (fixed and variable).

- Break-even analysis: An analysis of the level of sales at which a project would make zero profit.

- Bretton Woods: An international monetary system operating from 1946-1973. The value of the dollar was fixed in terms of gold, and every other country held its currency at a fixed exchange rate against the dollar; when trade deficits occurred, the central bank of the deficit country financed the deficit with its reserves of international currencies. The Bretton Woods system collapsed in 1971 when the US abandoned the gold standard.

- Budget: A detailed schedule of financial activity, such as an advertising budget, a sales budget, or a capital budget.

- Budget: A summary of intended expenditures along with proposals for how to meet them. A budget can provide guidelines for managing future investments and expenses. The budget deficit is the amount by which government spending exceeds government revenues during a specified period of time usually a year.

- Bull: An investor with an optimistic market outlook; an investor who expects prices to rise and so buys now for resale later. A bull market is one in which prices are rising.

- Business Plan: A planning document that describes a company, its market, its management team, its potential, its competitors, and all other relevant information about its business and its prospects.

- Call money: Price paid by an investor for a call option. There is no fixed rate for call money. It depends on the type of stock, its performance prior to the purchase of the call option, and the period of the contract. It is an interest bearing band deposits that can be withdrawn on 24 hours notice.

- Capital: (1) Assets less liabilities, representing the ownership interest in a business, (2) a stock of accumulated goods, especially at a specified time and in contrast to income received during a specified time period, (3) accumulated goods devoted to the production of goods, and (4) accumulated possessions calculated to bring income.

- Capital account: Part of a nation's balance of payments that includes purchases and sales of assets, such as stocks, bonds, and land. A nation has a capital account surplus when receipts from asset sales exceed payments for the country's purchases of foreign assets. The sum of the capital and current accounts is the overall balance of payments.

- Capital Asset Pricing Model: A way to show the prices of securities and other risk-free assets.

- Capital budget: A plan of proposed capital outlays and the means of financing them for the current fiscal period. It is usually a part of the current budget. If a Capital Program is in operation, it will be the first year thereof. A Capital Program is sometimes referred to as a Capital Budget.

- Capital Expenditures: Business spending on additional plant equipment and inventory.

- Capital gains tax: Tax paid on the gain realized upon the sale of an asset. It is a tax on profits from the sale of capital assets, such as shares. A capital loss can be used to offset a capital gain, reducing any tax you would otherwise have to pay.

- Capital: Wealth in the form of money or property owned by a person or business and human resources of economic value. Capital is the contribution to productive activity made by investment is physical capital (machinery, factories, tools and equipments) and human capital (eg general education, health). Capital is one of the three main factors of production other two are labour and natural resources.

- Cartel: An organization of producers seeking to limit or eliminate competition among its members, most often by agreeing to restrict output to keep prices higher than would occur under competitive conditions. Cartels are inherently unstable because of the potential for producers to defect from the agreement and capture larger markets by selling at lower prices.

- Cash: The value of assets that can be converted into cash immediately.

- Cash Discount: An incentive offered by the seller to encourage a buyer to pay within a stipulated time. For example, if the terms are 1%/10/net 30, the buyer may deduct 1 percent from the amount of the invoice (if paid with 10 days); otherwise the full amount is due within 30 days.

- Cash Equivalents: Investments of high liquidity and safety with a known market value and a very short-term maturity. Examples include Treasury bills and money market funds.

- Cash Flow: An accounting presentation showing how much of the cash generated by a business remains after both expenses (including interest) and principal repayment on loans are paid. A projected cash flow statement indicates whether the business will have cash to pay its expenses, loans, and make a profit. Cash flows can be calculated for any given period of time, normally done on a monthly basis or yearly basis.

- Cash flow from operations: The sum of net income plus non-cash expenses that were deducted in calculating net income.

- CDs: CDs, or certificates of deposit, are interest-bearing debt instruments issued by banks with maturities from a few weeks to several years.

- Census: Official gathering of information about the population in a particular area. Government departments use the data collected in planning for the future in such areas as health, education, transport, and housing.

- Central bank: Major financial institution responsible for issuing currency, managing foreign reserves, implementing monetary policy, and providing banking services to the government and commercial banks.

- Centrally planned economy: A planned economic system in which the production, pricing, and distribution of goods and services are determined by the government rather than market forces. Former Soviet Union, China, and most other communist nations are examples of centrally planned economy.

- CIF, abbrev: Cost, Insurance and Freight: Export term in which the price quoted by the exporter includes the costs of ocean transportation to the port of destination and insurance coverage.

- Circulation: The number of copies that a publication distributes or sells. Also refers to the number of people who have an opportunity to observe a piece of outdoor advertising, such as a billboard or poster.

- Classical economics: The economics of Adam Smith, David Ricardo, Thomas Malthus, and later followers such as John Stuart Mill. The theory concentrated on the functioning of a market economy, spelling out an explanation of consumer and producer behaviour in particular markets and postulating that in the long term the economy would tend to operate at full employment because increases in supply would create corresponding increases in demand.

- Close: The point during the sales process when the customer agrees to buy a product or service.

- Closed economy: A closed economy is one in which there are no foreign trade transactions or any other form of economic contacts with the rest of the world.

- Closing: Actions and procedures required to effect the successful conclusion of a business transaction, such as a real estate purchase or loan consummation.

- Cold Call: An unscheduled contact, either on the phone or in person, between a seller and a prospective customer.

- Collateral: Something of value pledged to support the repayment of an obligation or loan. Examples include real estate and certificates of deposit.

- Collateral Document: A legal document covering the item(s) pledged as collateral on a loan.

- Collateral security: Additional security a borrower supplies to obtain a loan.

- Commercial Policy: encompassing instruments of trade protection employed by countries to foster industrial promotion, export diversification, employment creation, and other desired development-oriented strategies. They include tariffs, quotas, and subsidies.

- Common Law: Law made by judges in individual cases, rather than by the legislature.

- Comparative advantage: The ability to produce a good at a lower cost, relative to other goods, compared to another country. With perfect competition and undistorted markets, countries tend to export goods in which they have a Comparative Advantage and hence make gains from trading.

- Compensation: Direct and indirect monetary and nonmonetary rewards given to employees based on the value of the job, their personal contributions and their performance.

- Compound interest: Interest paid on the original principal and on interest accrued from time it became due.

- Compromise: The settlement of a dispute or claim.

- Conditionality: The requirement imposed by the International Monetary Fund that a borrowing country undertake fiscal, monetary, and international commercial reforms as a condition to receiving a loan for balance of payments difficulties.

- Consideration: The inducement to a contract. Some right, interest, profit, or benefit accruing to one party, or some forbearance, detriment, loss, or responsibility given, suffered, or undertaken by the other.

- Consumer Surplus: is the difference between the price a consumer pays and what they were prepared to pay.

- Contingency Fee: A common legal fee arrangement that relies on the collection of monetary damages for the plaintiff before any legal fees are owed. Most common in litigation (such as in personal injury lawsuits), it allows the client to receive legal services while paying the attorney little or no money up front.

- Contingent Liability: A potential obligation that may be incurred dependent upon the occurrence of a future event. Two examples are: (1) the liability of a guarantor of a promissory note if the primary borrower fails to pay as agreed and (2) the liability that would be incurred if a pending lawsuit is resolved in the other party's favor.

- Controlled Circulation: Publications, generally business oriented, delivered only to readers who have some special qualifications. Generally, these publications are free to the qualified recipients, who must complete registration questionnaires in order to receive them.

- Copyright: An exclusive ownership interest in an artistic or literary work. The term "literary work" includes computer software and other information stored in electronic form. Copyright is often noted by the following example: "Copyright© 2010 by ASHUTOSH.com."

- Copyright: A legal right (usually of the author or composer or publisher of a work) to exclusive publication production, sale, distribution of some work. What is protected by the copyright is the "expression," not the idea. Notice that taking another's idea is plagiarism, so copyrights are not the equivalent of legal prohibition of plagiarism.

- Corporate bonds: Debt instruments issued by corporations, as distinct from ones issued by a government agency, typically interest-bearing with a fixed maturity.

- Corporation: A form of organization that provides its owners and shareholders with certain rights and privileges, including protection from personal liability, if proper steps are followed. Corporations may take a number of forms, depending on the goals and objectives of the founders. Corporations are regarded as "persons" in the eyes of the law and may thus sue and be sued, own property, borrow money and hire employees.

- Correlation coefficient: Denoted as "r", a measure of the linear relationship between two variables. The absolute value of "r" provides an indication of the strength of the relationship. The value of "r" varies between positive 1 and negative 1, with -1 or 1 indicating a perfect linear relationship, and r = 0 indicating no relationship. The sign of the correlation coefficient indicates whether the slope of the line is positive or negative when the two variables are plotted in a scatter plot.

- Cost benefit analysis: A technique that assesses projects through a comparison between their costs and benefits, including social costs and benefits for an entire region or country. Depending on the project objectives and its the expected outputs, three types of CBA are generally recognized: financial; economic; and social. Generally cost-benefit analyses are comparative, i.e. they are used to compare alternative proposals. Cost-benefit analysis compares the costs and benefits of the situation with and without the project; the costs and benefits are considered over the life of the project.

- Cost of Goods Sold: This term represents the cost of buying raw materials and producing the goods that a company sells. It also includes the cost of the company's labor force and overhead costs.

- Countervailing duties: Duties (tariffs) that are imposed by a country to counteract subsidies provided to a foreign producer.

- Credit Rating: A formal evaluation of an individual or a company's credit history and capability of repaying debt.

- Credit Score: A statistical summary of the individual pieces of information on a credit report. A credit score predicts how likely it is that a company or individual will repay debts. Lenders use credit scores to determine whether to extend credit and at what interest rate. Also called a risk score.

- Cross Elasticity of Demand: The change in the quantity demanded of one product or service impacting the change in demand for another product or service. E.g. percentage change in the quantity demanded of a good divided by the percentage change in the price of another good (a substitute or complement)

- Crowding out: The possible tendency for government spending on goods and services to put upward pressure on interest rates, thereby discouraging private investment spending.

- Currency appreciation: An increase in the value of one currency relative to another currency. Appreciation occurs when, because of a change in exchange rates; a unit of one currency buys more units of another currency. Opposite is the case with currency depreciation.

- Currency board: Form of central bank that issues domestic currency for foreign exchange at fixed rates.

- Currency substitution: The use of foreign currency (e.g., U.S. dollars) as a medium of exchange in place of or along with the local currency (e.g., Rupees, Baht, Dinar).

- Current account: Part of a nation's balance of payments which includes the value of all goods and services imported and exported, as well as the payment and receipt of dividends and interest. A nation has a current account surplus if exports exceed imports plus net transfers to foreigners. The sum of the current and capital accounts is the overall balance of payments.

- Current Ratio: The ratio of the company's current assets to its current liabilities. A current ratio of less than 1-to-1 typically indicates a poor credit risk. A current ratio of greater than 2-to-1 typically indicates a good credit risk.

- Customer: Someone who has bought or made the decision to buy a product or service.

- Customs duty: Duty levied on the imports of certain goods. Includes excise equivalents. Unlike tariffs, customs duties are used mainly as a means to raise revenue for the government rather than protecting domestic producers from foreign competition.

- Cyclical Industry: An industry that has natural high and low sales periods based on the time of year, season or other factors.

- Damages: A cash compensation ordered by a court or arbitrator to offset losses or suffering caused by another's fault or negligence. Damages are a typical request made of a court or arbitrator when persons sue for breach of contract or tort.

- Debenture: Debt instrument evidencing the holder's right to receive interest and principal installments from the debtor.

- Debt Financing: The provision of long term loans to small business concerns in exchange for debt securities or a note.

- Deed of Trust: A document that, when properly delivered, transfers a security interest in real property.

- Defaults: The nonpayment of principal and/or interest on the due date as provided by the terms and conditions of a promissory note or loan agreement.

- **Demand Letter:** A letter from a lawyer on behalf of a client that demands payment or some other action. Demand letters often threaten litigation if the other party does not perform.

- **Demographic:** A descriptive classification for consumers, such as age, sex, income, education, household size, home ownership or other defining characteristics.

- **Depreciation:** An accounting procedure that spreads the cost of purchasing an asset over the useful lifetime of the asset.

- **Direct Mail:** Marketing or advertising materials sent directly to a prospective customer via the Postal Service or a private delivery company.

- **Direct Marketing:** The process of sending promotional messages directly to individual consumers, rather than via a mass medium. Includes methods such as direct mail and telemarketing.

- **Disability Benefits:** Benefits paid to an employee who cannot work because of disability, usually limited to what is not covered by workers compensation. Disability benefits are usually a percentage of the employee's prior income and generally run for a limited time.

- **Doing Business As (DBA):** A situation in which a business owner operates a company under a different name than the one under which it is incorporated. The owner typically must file a fictitious name statement or similar document with the appropriate county or state agency.

- **Deflation:** It is a reduction in the level of national income and output, usually accompanied by a fall in the general price level.

- **Developed country:** is an economically advanced country whose economy is characterized by a large industrial and service sector and high levels of income per head.

- Developing country, less developed country, underdeveloped country or third world country: a country characterized by low levels of GDP and per capita income; typically dominated by agriculture and mineral products and majority of the population lives near subsistence levels.

- Direct investment: Foreign capital inflow in the form of investment by foreign-based companies into domestic based companies. Portfolio investment is foreign capital inflow by foreign investors into shares and financial securities. It is the ownership and management of production and/or marketing facilities in a foreign country.

- Direct tax: A tax that you pay directly, as opposed to indirect taxes, such as tariffs and business taxes. The income tax is a direct tax, as are property taxes. See also Indirect Tax.

- Double taxation: Corporate earnings taxed at both the corporate level and again as a stockholder dividend.

- Dumping: this occurs when goods are exported at a price less than their normal value, generally meaning they are exported for less than they are sold in the domestic market or third country markets, or at less than production cost.

- Duopoly: A market structure in which two producers of a commodity compete with each other.

- EBITDA: Earnings before interest, taxes, depreciation, and amortization.

- Entrepreneur: One who assumes the financial risk of the initiation, operation, and management of a given business undertaking.

- Econometrics: The application of statistical and mathematical methods in the field of economics to test and quantify economic theories and the solutions to economic problems.

- Economic Development: The process of improving the quality of human life through increasing per capita income, reducing poverty, and enhancing individual economic opportunities. It is also sometimes defined to include better education, improved health and nutrition, conservation of natural resources, a cleaner environment, and a richer cultural life.

- Economic Growth: An increase in the nation's capacity to produce goods and services. Quantitative measure of the change in size/volume of economic activity, usually calculated in terms of gross national product (GNP) or gross domestic product (GDP).

- Economic infrastructure: The underlying amount of physical and financial capital embodied in roads, railways, waterways, airways, and other forms of transportation and communication plus water supplies, financial institutions, electricity, and public services such as health and education. The level of infrastructural development in a country is a crucial factor determining the pace and diversity of economic development.

- Economic integration: The merging to various degrees of the economies and economic policies of two or more countries in a given region. See also common market, customs union, free-trade area, trade creation, and trade diversion.

- Economic Policy: A statement of objectives and the methods of achieving these objectives (policy instruments) by government, political party, business concern, etc. Some examples of government economic objectives are maintaining full employment, achieving a high rate of economic growth, reducing income inequalities and regional development inequalities, and maintaining price stability. Policy instruments include fiscal policy, monetary and financial policy, and legislative controls (e.g., price and wage control, rent control).

- Elasticity of demand: The degree to which consumer

demand for a product or service responds to a change in price, wage or other independent variable. When there is no perceptible response, demand is said to be inelastic.

- Excess capacity: Volume or capacity over and above that which is needed to meet peak planned or expected demand.

- Excess demand: the situation in which the quantity demanded at a given price exceeds the quantity supplied. Opposite: excess supply.

- Exchange control: A governmental policy designed to restrict the outflow of domestic currency and prevent a worsened balance of payments position by controlling the amount of foreign exchange that can be obtained or held by domestic citizens. Often results from overvalued exchange rates.

- Exchange rate: The price of one currency stated in terms of another currency, when exchanged.

- Export incentives: Public subsidies, tax rebates, and other kinds of financial and nonfinancial measures designed to promote a greater level of economic activity in export industries.

- Exports: The value of all goods and nonfactor services sold to the rest of the world; they include merchandise, freight, insurance, travel, and other nonfactor services. The value of factor services (such as investment receipts and workers' remittances from abroad) is excluded from this measure. See also merchandise exports and imports.

- Equal Employment Opportunity (EEO): Federal legislation prohibiting employment discrimination based on age, race, sex, religion or ethnic background.

- Equity: An ownership interest in a business: For

example, stock in a corporation represents equity in the corporation.

- Equity Financing: The provision of funds for capital or operating expenses in exchange for capital stock, stock purchase warrants, and/or options in the business financed, without any guaranteed return, but with the opportunity to share in the company's profits.

- Employee Stock Ownership Plan (ESOP): A retirement-type plan in which a trust holds stock in the employees' names. Employees receive cash from the stock only when they leave the company or perhaps when the company is sold.

- Exit Interview: An interview conducted at the end of an employee's term of employment to obtain employment feedback and to remind the employee of his or her confidentiality obligations.

- Externalities: A cost or benefit not accounted for in the price of goods or services. Often "externality" refers to the cost of pollution and other environmental impacts.

- Fair Use: A legal doctrine that authorizes use of copyrighted materials for certain purposes without the copyright owner's permission.

- Financial Reports: Reports concerning the financial aspects of a business, such as:

- (1) Balance Sheet - A report of the status of a firm's assets, liabilities and owner's equity at a given time.

- (2) Income Statement - A report of revenue and expense which shows the results of business operations or net income for a specified period of time.

- (3) Cash Flow - A report which analyzes the actual or projected source and disposition of cash during a past or future accounting period.

- Financing: New funds provided to a business, either by way of equity infusion, or loans.

- Fixed Costs: Costs of doing business, such as rent and utilities that remain generally the same regardless of the amount of sales of goods or services.

- Flow Chart: A graphical representation for the definition, analysis, or solution of a problem, in which symbols are used to represent operations, data, flow, equipment, etc.

- Foot Traffic: Consumer activity produced by visitors at stores, trade show exhibits or by popular retail locations.

- Foreclosure: The act by the mortgagee or trustee upon default, in the payment of interest or principal of a mortgage of enforcing payment of the debt by selling the underlying secured property.

- Franchising: A relationship in which the franchisor provides a licensed privilege to the franchise to do business and offers assistance in organizing, training, merchandising, marketing, and managing in return for a consideration. Examples of franchises include Burger King and Taco Bell.

- Fiscal deficit: is the gap between the government's total spending and the sum of its revenue receipts and non-debt capital receipts. The fiscal deficit represents the total amount of borrowed funds required by the government to completely meet its expenditure.

- Fiscal Policy: is the use of government expenditure and taxation to try to influence the level of economic activity. An expansionary (or reflationary) fiscal policy could mean: cutting levels of direct or indirect tax increasing government expenditure The effect of these policies would be to encourage more spending and boost the economy. A contractionary (or deflationary) fiscal policy could be: increasing taxation - either direct or indirect cutting government expenditure These policies would reduce the level of demand in the economy and help to reduce inflation.

- Fixed Annuities: Investment contract sold by an insurance company that guarantees fixed payments, either for life or for a specified period, to the annuitant. The insurer takes both the investment risk and the mortality risk.

- Fixed Costs: A cost incurred in the general operations of the business that is not directly attributable to the costs of producing goods and services. These "Fixed" or "Indirect" costs of doing business will be incurred whether or not any sales are made during the period, thus the designation "Fixed", as opposed to "Variable".

- Fixed exchange rate: The exchange value of a national currency fixed in relation to another (usually the U.S. dollar), not free to fluctuate on the international money market.

- Foreign aid: The international transfer of public funds in the form of loans or grants either directly from one government to another (bilateral assistance) or indirectly through the vehicle of a multilateral assistance agency like the World Bank. See also tied aid, private foreign investment, and nongovernmental organizations.

- Foreign Direct Investment (FDI): Overseas investments by private multinational corporations.

- Foreign exchange reserves: The stock of liquid assets denominated in foreign currencies held by a government's monetary authorities (typically, the finance ministry or central bank). Reserves enable the monetary authorities to intervene in foreign exchange markets to affect the exchange value of their domestic currency in the market. Reserves are invested in low-risk and liquid assets, often in foreign government securities.

- Free trade: in which goods can be imported and exported without any barriers in the forms of tariffs, quotas, or other restrictions. Free trade has often been described as an engine of growth because it encourages countries to specialize in activities in which they have comparative advantages, thereby increasing their respective production efficiencies and hence their total output of goods and services.

- Free-trade area: a form of economic integration in which there exists free internal trade among member countries but each member is free to levy different external tariffs against non-member nations.

- Free-market exchange rate: rate determined solely by international supply and demand for domestic currency expressed in terms of, say, U.S. dollars.

- Fringe benefit: A benefit in addition to salary offered to employees such as use of company's car, house, lunch coupons, health care subscriptions etc.

- Gains from trade: The addition to output and consumption resulting from specialization in production and free trade with other economic units including persons, regions, or countries.

- General Agreement on Tariffs and Trade (GATT): An international body set up in 1947 to probe into the ways and means of reducing tariffs on internationally traded goods and services. Between 1947 and 1962, GATT held seven conferences but met with only moderate success. Its major success was achieved in 1967 during the so-called Kennedy Round of talks when tariffs on primary commodities were drastically slashed and then in 1994 with the signing of the Uruguay Round agreement. Replaced in 1995 by World Trade Organization (WTO).

- Gross Domestic Product (GDP): Gross Domestic Product: The total of goods and services produced by a nation over a given period, usually 1 year. Gross Domestic Product measures the total output from all the resources located in a country, wherever the owners of the resources live.

- Gross national product (GNP): is the value of all final goods and services produced within a nation in a given year, plus income earned by its citizens abroad, minus income earned by foreigners from domestic production. The Fact book, following current practice, uses GDP rather than GNP to measure national production. However, the user must realize that in certain countries net remittances from citizens working abroad may be important to national well being. GNP equals GDP plus net property income from abroad.

- Globalization: The process whereby trade is now being conducted on ever widening geographical boundaries. Countries now trade across continents and companies also trade all over the world.

- Guarantee: A promise to step in and perform another's obligation if that person should fail or default.

- Guarantor: A person who makes a legally binding promise either to pay another person's obligation or to perform another person's duty if that person defaults or fails to perform.

- High-Yield Bonds: A bond that has a rating of BB or lower and pays a higher yield to compensate for the greater credit risk.

- Human capital: Productive investments embodied in human persons. These include skills, abilities, ideals, and health resulting from expenditures on education, on-the-job training programs, and medical care.

- Imperfect competition: A market situation or structure in which producers have some degree of control over the price of their product. Examples include monopoly and oligopoly. See also perfect competition.

- Imperfect market: A market where the theoretical assumptions of perfect competition are violated by the existence of, for example, a small number of buyers and sellers, barriers to entry, non homogeneity of products, and incomplete information. The three imperfect markets commonly analyzed in economic theory are monopoly, oligopoly, and monopolistic competition.

- Import substitution: A deliberate effort to replace major consumer imports by promoting the emergence and expansion of domestic industries such as textiles, shoes, and household appliances. Import substitution requires the imposition of protective tariffs and quotas to get the new industry started.

- Incentive Stock Options (ISOs): Stock options granted to employees that are taxed as capital gains rather than income if the employee meets the required holding period before selling them. Also called statutory stock options and qualified stock options.

- Income Statement: A record of the financial performance of a company over a period of time. It records all the income generated by the business during the period and deducts all its expenses for the same period to arrive at net income, or the profit for the period.

- Independent Contractor: A worker who works on a specific project for a specified period of time. Independent contractors are not subject to tax withholdings and usually don't receive benefits granted to full-time employees.

- Infringement (of copyright): Any unauthorized use of a copyrighted work other than fair use.

- Infringement (of patent): Violation of a patent through production, use or sale of a patented invention or its functional equivalent without the patent holder's permission.

- Infringement (of trademark): Unauthorized use of a protected trademark or service mark or use of a confusingly similar mark.

- Inquiries:. Consumer response to a company's advertising, or to other promotional activities such as coupons. Used to measure the effectiveness of promotions.

- Inserts: Extra printed pages inserted loosely into printed pieces. Often inserts are advertising supplements to a newspaper or magazine.

- Insolvency: The inability of a borrower to meet financial obligations as they mature, or having insufficient assets to pay legal debts.

- Interest: (1) An amount paid a lender for the use of funds, or (2) cost of using credit or another person's or company's money. Interest is usually calculated as a rate per a period of time, typically a year.

- Interest Rate: Percentage of a sum of money charged for the use of the money. Borrowing $100 for one year at a 10 percent simple interest rate would cost $10.

- Internet: A network of networks, built upon a set of widely used software protocols that links millions of computers around the world. Services such as email and the Web use the Internet to transfer data.

- Intranet: A private corporate network built with Internet-based protocols and software applications.

- Invoice: A bill prepared by the seller of goods or services. Invoices tell purchasers how much they owe.

- Income inequality: The existence of disproportionate distribution of total national income among households whereby the share going to rich persons in a country is far greater than that going to poorer persons (a situation common to most LDCs). This is largely due to differences in the amount of income derived from ownership of property and to a lesser extent the result of differences in earned income. Inequality of personal incomes can be reduced by progressive income taxes and wealth taxes. This is measured by the Gini coefficient.

- Index of industrial production: A quantity index that is designed to measure changes in the physical volume or production levels of industrial goods over time.

- Inflation: is the percentage increase in the prices of goods and services.

- Indirect tax: A tax you do not pay directly, but which is passed on to you by an increase in your expenses. For instance, a company might have to pay a fuel tax. The company pays the tax but can increase the cost of its products so consumers are actually paying the tax indirectly by paying more for the merchandise.

- Interdependence Interrelationship: between economic and noneconomic variables. Also, in international affairs, the situation in which one nation's welfare depends to varying degrees on the decisions and policies of another nation, and vice versa. See also dependence.

- International commodity agreement: Formal agreement by sellers of a common internationally traded commodity (coffee, sugar) to coordinate supply to maintain price stability.

- International Labor Organization (ILO): One of the functional organizations of the United Nations, based in Geneva, Switzerland, whose central task is to look into problems of world labor supply, its training, utilization, domestic and international distribution, etc. Its aim in this endeavor is to increase world output through maximum utilization of available human resources and thus improve levels of living.

- International Monetary Fund (IMF): An autonomous international financial institution that originated in the Bretton Woods Conference of 1944. Its main purpose is to regulate the international monetary exchange system, which also stems from that conference but has since been modified. In particular, one of the central tasks of the IMF is to control fluctuations in exchange rates of world currencies in a bid to alleviate severe balance of payments problems.

- International poverty line: An arbitrary international real income measure, usually expressed in constant dollars (e.g., $270), used as a basis for estimating the proportion of the world's population that exists at bare levels of subsistence.

- Joint Venture: An agreement between two or more partners ("joint venturers") to pursue collaboratively a particular project or business, with a sharing of profits or losses.

- Judgment: Judicial determination of the existence of an indebtedness or other legal liability.

- Judgment by Confession: The act of debtors permitting judgment to be entered against them for a given sum with a statement to that effect, without the institution of legal proceedings.

- Jurisdiction: The authority of a court to hear and decide a case. For a decision to be valid, a court must have both "subject matter jurisdiction" (the ability to hear the type of case at issue) and "personal jurisdiction" (authority over the parties).

- Land reform: A deliberate attempt to reorganize and transform existing agrarian systems with the intention of improving the distribution of agricultural incomes and thus fostering rural development. Among its many forms, land reform may entail provision of secured tenure rights to the individual farmer, transfer of land ownership away from small classes of powerful landowners to tenants who actually till the land, appropriation of land estates for establishing small new settlement farms, or instituting land improvements and irrigation schemes.

- Lease: A contract by which a tenant (the "lessee") takes possession of office space, furniture, equipment or other property for a specified rent and specified amount of time. At the end of a lease, the property reverts back to its owner (the "lessor").

- Lessee: The renter or tenant.

- Lessor: The landlord or owner.

- Letter of Credit: A document issued by a bank guaranteeing payment of a customer's debt up to a set amount over a set period of time. Letters of credit are used extensively in international trade.

- Letter of Intent (LOI): An agreement, usually nonbinding, documenting the general terms of a proposed business relationship. Often used as a prelude to a binding, definitive agreement.

- Liability: Any debt or obligation due now or potentially in the future. Liability is synonymous with legal responsibility.

- Lien: A charge upon or security interest in real or personal property maintained to ensure the satisfaction of a debt or duty ordinarily arising by operation of law.

- Limited Liability Company (LLC): A flexible business structure, popular with small businesses, offering owners the advantage of limited personal liability and the choice of being taxed like a partnership or a corporation.

- Limited Liability Partnership (LLP): A type of partnership recognized in many states that protects individual partners from personal liability for negligent acts committed by other partners and employees not under their direct control. Some states restrict this type of partnership to professionals, such as lawyers, accountants and architects.

- List Broker: A person or company who prepares, rents and maintains mailing lists.

- Litigation: Lawsuits instituted through the judicial process.

- Loan Agreement: An agreement for the borrowing of money, typically containing pertinent terms, conditions, covenants and restrictions.

- Logo: A symbol that a company uses to represent itself or its brand.

- Long-Term Debt: Obligations or liabilities that a company owes in one year or more.

- Long-Term Government Bonds: Securities issued by the US government and debt issues of federal agencies having a maturity of 10 years or more.

- Macroeconomics: The branch of economics that considers the relationships among broad economic aggregates such as national income, total volumes of saving, investment, consumption expenditure, employment, and money supply. It is also concerned with determinants of the magnitudes of these aggregates and their rates of change over time.

- Market economy: A free private – enterprise economy governed by consumer sovereignty, a price system, and the forces of supply and demand.

- Market failure: A phenomenon that results from the existence of market imperfections (e.g., monopoly power, lack of factor mobility, significant externalities, lack of knowledge) that weaken the functioning of a free-market economy--it fails to realize its theoretical beneficial results. Market failure often provides the justification for government interference with the working of the free market.

- Market-friendly approach: World Bank notion that successful development policy requires governments to create an environment in which markets can operate efficiently and to intervene selectively in the economy in areas where the market is inefficient (e.g., social and economic infrastructure, investment coordination, economic "safety net").

- Market mechanism: The system whereby prices of stocks & shares, commodities or services freely rise or fall when the buyer's demand for them rises or falls or the seller's supply of them decreases or increases.

- Market prices: Prices established by demand and supply in a free-market economy.

- Merchandise exports and imports: All international changes in ownership of merchandise passing across the customs borders of the trading countries. Exports are valued f.o.b. (free on board). Imports are valued c.i.f. (cost, insurance, and freight).

- Merchandise trade balance: Balance on commodity exports and imports.

- Microeconomics: The branch of economics concerned with individual decision units--firms and households--and the way in which their decisions interact to determine relative prices of goods and factors of production and how much of these will be bought and sold. The market is the central concept in microeconomics.

- Middle-income countries (MICs): LDCs with per capita income above $785 and below $9,655 in 1997 according to World Bank measures.

- Mixed economic system: Economic systems that are a mixture of both capitalist and socialist economies. Most developing countries have mixed systems. Their essential feature is the coexistence of substantial private and public activity within a single economy.

- Monetary policy: The regulation of the money supply and interest rates by a central bank in order to control inflation and stabilize currency. If the economy is heating up, the central bank (such as RBI in India) can withdraw money from the banking system, raise the reserve requirement or raise the discount rate to make it cool down. If growth is slowing, it can reverse the process - increase the money supply, lower the reserve requirement and decrease the discount rate. The monetary policy influences interest rates and money supply.

- Money supply: the total stock of money in the economy; currency held by the public plus money in accounts in banks. It consists primarily currency in circulation and deposits in savings and checking accounts. Too much money in relation to the output of goods tends to push interest rates down and push inflation up; too little money tends to push rates up and prices down, causing unemployment and idle plant capacity. The central bank manages the money supply by raising and lowering the reserves banks are required to hold and the discount rate at which they can borrow money from the central bank. The central bank also trades government securities (called repurchase agreements) to take money out of the system or put it in. There are various measures of money supply, including M1, M2, M3 and L; these are referred to as monetary aggregates.

- Monopoly: A market situation in which a product that does not have close substitutes is being produced and sold by a single seller.

- Marketing Plan: A company plan for marketing products and services and increasing sales.

- Market Share: The percentage of a product category's sales, in dollars or units, that a particular brand, product line or company controls.

- Marketing Communications: The process and techniques involved in marketing, promoting or selling products or services through creative, visual or written communications.

- Maturity: In general, the period and date when payment of a loan is due. As applied to securities and commercial paper, the period and date when payment of principal is due.

- Maturity Extension: Extension of payment beyond the original date established for repayment of a loan.

- Mediation: A form of alternative dispute resolution in which a neutral party (a mediator) seeks to promote and negotiate a settlement between opposing parties in a dispute. There is no mechanism to compel the parties to settle; they must voluntarily agree to any settlement.

- Medium: A type of publication or communications method that conveys news, entertainment and advertising to an audience. Examples include newspapers, television, magazines, radio, billboards and the Internet.

- Merger: Typically, a combination of two or more corporations into one corporation.

- Mortgage: An instrument giving legal title to secure the repayment of a loan made by the mortgagee (lender).

- Mortgage-Backed Bonds: Securities backed by mortgages.

- Municipal bonds: Debt obligation of a state or local government entity. The funds may support general government needs or fund special projects. The interest on these bonds is typically exempt from federal income taxes, and most state and local taxes.

- Multi-Fiber Arrangement (MFA) A set of nontariff bilateral quotas established by developed countries on imports of cotton, wool, and synthetic textiles and clothing from individual LDCs.

- Multinational corporation (MNC) An international or transnational corporation with headquarters in one country but branch offices in a wide range of both developed and developing countries. Examples include General Motors, Coca-Cola, Firestone, Philips, Volkswagen, British Petroleum, Exxon etc. Firms become multinational corporations when they perceive advantages to establishing production and other activities in foreign locations. Firms globalize their activities both to supply their home-country market more cheaply and to serve foreign markets more directly. Keeping foreign activities within the corporate structure lets firms avoid the costs inherent in arm's-length dealings with separate entities while utilizing their own firm-specific knowledge such as advanced production techniques.

- National debt: Treasury bills, notes, bonds, and other debt obligations that constitute the debt owed by the federal government. It represents the accumulation of each year's budget deficit.

- Public debt: Borrowing by the Government of India internally as well as externally. The total of the nation's debts: debts of local and state and national governments is an indicator of how much public spending is financed by borrowing instead of taxation.

- Nongovernmental organizations (NGOs) Privately owned and operated organizations involved in providing financial and technical assistance to LDCs. See foreign aid.

- Nontariff trade barrier: A barrier to free trade that takes a form other than a tariff, such as quotas or sanitary requirements for imported meats and dairy products.

- Nondisclosure Agreement (NDA): A contract in which a person or business agrees to maintain the confidentiality of proprietary information or trade secrets and not disclose such information without authorization. Employees, consultants, business partners and investors are often asked to sign nondisclosure agreements.

- Nonexempt Employee: Employees who are protected by wage laws that mandate payment for every hour of overtime worked.

- Nonprofit Corporation: A form of corporation in which no stockholder or trustee shares in profits or losses and which usually exists to accomplish some charitable or educational function. These organizations are exempt from corporate income taxes, and donations to these groups may be tax deductible.

- Nonqualified Stock Options (NSOs): Nonqualified stock options may be granted to employees, consultants, contractors and others. When nonqualified stock options are exercised the holder must pay ordinary income tax on them, even if the shares have not yet been sold.

- Notes Receivable: A secured or unsecured receivable evidenced by a note.

- Official development assistance (ODA): Net disbursements of loans or grants made on concessional terms by official agencies of member countries of the Organization for Economic Cooperation and Development (OECD).

- Official exchange rate: Rate at which the central bank will buy and sell the domestic currency in terms of a foreign currency such as the U.S. dollar.

- Open economy: is an economy that encourages foreign trade and has extensive financial and nonfinancial contacts with the rest of the world in areas such as education, culture, and technology. See also closed economy.

- Opportunity cost: is the implied cost of not doing something that could have led to higher returns.

- Organization for Economic Cooperation and Development (OECD):An organization of 20 countries from the Western world including all of those in Europe and North America. Its major objective is to assist the economic growth of its member nations by promoting cooperation and technical analysis of national and international economic trends.

- Overvalued exchange rate: An official exchange rate set at a level higher than its real or shadow value Overvalued rates cheapen the real cost of imports while raising the real cost of exports. They often lead to a need for exchange control.

- Partnership: A legal relationship existing between two or more persons or entities contractually associated as joint principals in a business.

- Patent: A patent secures to an inventor the exclusive right to make, use and sell an invention for a designated period of time.

- Pay Period: The frequency with which payroll is processed and paychecks are issued.

- Power of Attorney: A written authorization that lets one person act as an agent for another and to make binding decisions for the principal. A power of attorney can be limited to specific types of decisions or it can be general.

- Perfect competition: A market situation characterized by the existence of very many buyers and sellers of homogeneous goods or services with perfect knowledge and free entry so that no single buyer or seller can influence the price of the good or service.

- Performance budget: is a budget format that relates the input of resources and the output of services for each organizational unit individually. Sometimes used synonymously with program budget. It is a budget wherein expenditures are based primarily upon measurable performance of activities.

- Political economy: The attempt to merge economic analysis with practical politics--to view economic activity in its political context. Much of classical economics was political economy, and today political economy is increasingly being recognized as necessary for examination of development problems.

- Portfolio investment: Financial investments by private individuals, corporations, pension funds, and mutual funds in stocks, bonds, certificates of deposit, and notes issued by private companies and the public agencies of LDCs. See also private foreign investment.

- Poverty gap: The sum of the difference between the poverty line and actual income levels of all people living below that line.

- Poverty line: A level of income below, which people are deemed poor. A global poverty line of $1 per person per day was suggested in 1990 (World Bank 1990). This line facilitates comparison of how many poor people there are in different countries. But, it is only a crude estimate because the line does not recognize differences in the buying power of money in different countries, and, more significantly, because it does not recognize other aspects of poverty than the material, or income poverty.

- Preferred Stock: A class of stock with a liquidation preference before payment is made to the common stock holders. Preferred stock is the security most used by venture capital investors.

- Prime Rate: Interest rate which is charged business borrowers having the highest credit ratings, for short term borrowing.

- Price elasticity of supply: The responsiveness of the quantity of a commodity supplied to a change in its price, expressed as the percentage change in quantity supplied divided by the percentage change in price.

- Parent Company: A company that owns a majority stake (51 percent or more) of another company's shares. It may have its own operations, or it may have been set up solely for the purpose of owning the operating company.

- Price: The monetary or real value of a resource, commodity, or service. The role of prices in a market economy is to ration or allocate resources in accordance with supply and demand; relative prices should reflect the relative scarcity of different resources, goods, or services.

- Price elasticity of demand: The responsiveness of the quantity of a commodity demanded to a change in its price, expressed as the percentage change in quantity demanded divided by the percentage change in price.

- Profit Sharing: Employee incentives in which a company distributes or receives a portion of the business's profits to employees.

- Proprietorship: The most common legal form of business ownership; about 85 percent of all small businesses are proprietorships. The liability of the owner is unlimited in this form of ownership.

- Proxy: A right given to an agent, most often in the context of shareholder voting in corporations.

- Public Domain: A copyright term that means a particular work is free for all to use without permission. Works in the public domain include those that were never copyrighted, those for which the copyright has expired and public documents.

- Publicity: Information with news value used to promote a product, service or idea in the media.

- Public Relations: Communication with various sectors of the public to influence their attitudes and opinions in the interest of promoting a person, product or idea.

- Purchase Order: A form that contains pricing, quantity and other purchasing information.

- Qualified Opinion: Audit opinion that states, except for the effect of a matter to which a qualification relates, the financial statements are fairly presented in accordance with Generally Accepted Accounting Principles (GAAP).

- Quasi-Reorganization: Type of reorganization in which, with shareholder approval, the management revalues assets and eliminates the deficit (increased by asset devaluations if any) by charging it to other equity accounts without the creation of a new corporate entity or without court intervention.

- Quota: is a physical limitation on the quantity of any item that can be imported into a country, such as so many automobiles per year.

- Repo rate: This is one of the credit management tools used by the Reserve Bank to regulate liquidity in South Africa (customer spending). The bank borrows money from the Reserve Bank to cover its shortfall. The Reserve Bank only makes a certain amount of money available and this determines the repo rate. If the bank requires more money than what is available, this will increase the repo rate - and vice versa.

- Revenue expenditure: This is expenditure on recurring items, including the running of services and financing capital spending that is paid for by borrowing. This is meant for normal running of governments' maintenance expenditures, interest payments, subsidies and transfers etc. It is current expenditure which does not result in the creation of assets. Grants given to State governments or other parties are also treated as revenue expenditure even if some of the grants may be meant for creating assets.

- Revenue receipts: Additions to assets that do not incur an obligation that must be met at some future date and do not represent exchanges of property for money. Assets must be available for expenditures. These include proceeds of taxes and duties levied by the government, interest and dividend on investments made by the government, fees and other receipts for services rendered by the govern.

- Return on Investment: The amount of profit (return) based on the amount of resources (funds) used to produce it. Also, the ability of a given investment to earn a return for its use.

- Stabilization policies: A coordinated set of mostly restrictive fiscal and monetary policies aimed at reducing inflation, cutting budget deficits, and improving the balance of payments.

- Subsidy: A payment by the government to producers or distributors in an industry to prevent the decline of that industry (e.g., as a result of continuous unprofitable operations) or an increase in the prices of its products or simply to encourage it to hire more labor (as in the case of a wage subsidy). Examples are export subsidies to encourage the sale of exports; subsidies on some foodstuffs to keep down the cost of living, especially in urban areas; and farm subsidies to encourage expansion of farm production and achieve self-reliance in food production.

- Shareholder Agreement: A written agreement between a corporation and its shareholders governing the nature of the relationship and the conduct of certain corporate activities.

- Stock Option: A right to buy a given amount of company stock at a given price for a given period of time.

- Sublease: The act of a tenant leasing the property it is leasing to yet another tenant, called a sub lessee.

- Subsidiary: A company owned by a parent company, a subsidiary is a separate legal entity listed as a corporation or LLC that is required to file its own taxes.

- Tax avoidance: A legal action designed to reduce or eliminate the taxes that one owes.

- Tax base: the total property and resources subject to taxation.

- Tax evasion: An illegal strategy to decrease tax burden by underreporting income, overstating deductions, or using illegal tax shelters.

- Terms of trade: The ratio of a country's average export price to its average import price; also known as the commodity terms of trade. A country's terms of trade are said to improve when this ratio increases and to worsen when it decreases, that is, when import prices rise at a relatively faster rate than export prices.

- T-Notes: T-Notes are negotiable debt obligations of the US government with maturities of 1 to 10 years.

- Treasury Bill: A short-term debt issued by a national government with a maximum maturity of one year. Treasury bills are sold at discount, such that the difference between purchase price and the value at maturity is the amount of interest.

- Trademark: A name, phrase, logo, image or combination of images used to identify and distinguish a business from others in the marketplace.

- Value Added Taxation (VAT): A form of indirect sales tax paid on products and services at each stage of production or distribution, based on the value added at that stage and included in the cost to the ultimate customer.

- Venture Capital: Money used to support new or unusual commercial undertakings; equity, risk or speculative capital.

- Working Capital: Excess of current assets over current liabilities.

- World Bank: An international financial institution owned by its 181 member countries and based in Washington, D.C. Its main objective is to provide development funds to the Third World nations in the form of interest-bearing loans and technical assistance. The World Bank operates with borrowed funds.

- World Trade Organization (WTO): The World Trade Organization is a global international organization dealing with the rules of trade between nations. It was set up in 1995 at the conclusion of GATT negotiations for administering multilateral trade negotiations.

- Z-SCORE: ALTMAN, EDWARD developed the "ALTMAN Z-SCORE" by examining 85 manufacturing companies. Later, additional "Z-Scores" were developed for private manufacturing companies (Z-Score - Model A) and another for general/service firms (Z-Score - Model B). A "Z-Score" is only as valid as the data from which it was derived i.e. if a company has altered or falsified their financial records/books, a "Z-Score" derived from those "cooked books" is of lesser use. ALTMAN Z-SCORE reliably predicts whether or not a company is likely to enter into bankruptcy within one or two years: If the Z-Score is 3.0 or above – bankruptcy is not likely. If the Z-Score is 1.8 or less - bankruptcy is likely. A score between 1.8 and 3.0 is the gray area, i.e., a high degree of caution should be used. Probabilities of bankruptcy within the above ranges are 95% within one year and 70% within two years; obviously, a higher Z-Score is desirable. It is best to assess each individual company's Z-Score against that of the industry. In low margin industries it is possible for Z-Scores to fall below the above. In such cases a trend comparison to the industry over consecutive time periods may be a better indicator.

E.2 Economics & Business Management Acronym Listing

A/D	Advance/Decline Line
AAGR	Average Annual Growth Rate
AAOIFI	Accounting and Auditing Organization for Islamic Financial Institutions
AAR	Average Annual Return
ABA	American Bankers Association
ABB	Activity Based Budgeting
ABCP	Asset-Backed Commercial Paper
ABM	Activity Based Management
ABS	Automated Bond System
ACATS	Automated Customer Account Transfer Service
ACB	Adjusted Cost Base
ACRS	Accelerated Cost Recovery System
ACT	Automated Confirmation Transaction Service
AD&D	Accidental Death And Dismemberment Insurance
ADR	American Depositary Receipt
ADTV	Average Daily Trading Volume
AER	Annual Equivalent Rate
AFFE	Acquired Fund Fees And Expenses
AGI	Adjusted Gross Income
AGM	Annual General Meeting
AIB	American Institute Of Banking
AIP	Automatic Investment Plan
AIR	Assumed Interest Rate
ALCO	Asset-Liability Committee
AMC	Asset Management Company
AML	Anti-Money Laundering
AMLF	Asset-Backed Commercial Paper Money Market Fund Liquidity Facility
ANSI	American National Standards Institute
AP	Accounts Payable
APR	Annual Percentage Rate
APT	Arbitrage Pricing Theory
APV	Adjusted Present Value
APY	Annual Percentage Yield
AR	Accounts Receivable

ARC	Accounts Receivable Conversion
ARM	Adjustable-Rate Mortgage
ARR	Accounting Rate of Return
ASCOT	Asset Swapped Convertible Option Transaction
ASI	Accumulative Swing Index
ASR	Accelerated Share Repurchase
ATM	Automated Teller Machine
ATS	Automatic Transfer Service
AUM	Assets Under Management
BDC	Business Development Company
BIMBO	Buy-In Management Buyout
BOP	Balance Of Payments
BOT	Balance Of Trade
BPS	Basis Point
CADS	Cash Available For Debt Service
CAGR	Compound Annual Growth Rate
CAPEX	Capital Expenditure
CCA	Capital Cost Allowance
CCC	Cash Conversion Cycle
CCD	Compulsory Convertible Debenture
CD	Certificate Of Deposit
CDA	Capital Dividend Account
CDO	Collateralized Debt Obligation
CDPU	Cash Distribution Per Unit
CEPS	Cash Earnings Per Share
CF	Cash Flow
CFAT	Cash Flow After Taxes
CFROI	Cash Flow Return on Investment
CGE	Capital Gains Exposure
CLO	Collateralized Loan Obligation
CMB	Cash Management Bill
CMBS	Commercial Mortgage-Backed Securities
CML	Capital Market Line
CMO	Collateralized Mortgage Obligation
CO	Certificate Of Origin
COD	Cash On Delivery
COUGRs	Certificate Of Government Receipts
CPA	Certified Public Accountant
CPFF	Commercial Paper Funding Facility
CPG	Consumer Packaged Goods
CPI	Consumer Price Index
CPR	Conditional Prepayment Rate
CROGI	Cash Return on Gross Investment

CV	Coefficient Of Variation
DAT	Direct Access Trading
DCF	Discounted Cash Flow
DDM	Dividend Discount Model
DECS	Dividend Enhanced Convertible Stock
DIP	Debtor In Possession
DJ-AIGCI	Dow Jones AIG Commodity Index
DJIA	Dow Jones Industrial Average
DJTA	Dow Jones Transportation Average
DJUA	Dow Jones Utility Average
DLOM	Discounts For Lack Of Marketability
DMI	Directional Movement Index
DNI	Distributable Net Income
DPP	Direct Participation Program
DPS	Dividend Per Share
DRD	Dividends Received Deduction
DRIP	Dividend Reinvestment Plan
DSCR	Debt-Service Coverage Ratio
DSPP	Direct Stock Purchase Plan
DTI	Debt-To-Income Ratio
EBIAT	Earnings Before Interest After Taxes
EBIDA	Earnings Before Interest, Depreciation And Amortization
EBIT	Earnings Before Interest & Tax
EBITAE	Earnings Before Interest, Tax, Amortization And Exceptional Items
EBITAL	Earnings Before Interest, Taxes, Depreciation, Amortization And Special Losses
EBITD	Earnings Before Interest, Tax and Depreciation
EBITDA	Earnings Before Interest, Taxes, Depreciation and Amortization
EBITDAR	Earnings Before Interest, Taxes, Depreciation, Amortization, and Restructuring or Rent Costs
EBITDAX	Earnings Before Interest, Taxes, Depreciation, Depletion, Amortization and Exploration Expenses
EBT	Earnings Before Tax
EDP	Electronic data processing
EMI	Equated Monthly Installment
EPS	Earnings per share
ERP	Enterprise Resource Planning
ESO	Employee Stock Option
ESOP	Employee Stock Ownership Plan
EV	Enterprise Value
FASB	Financial Accounting Standards Board
FCPA	Foreign Corrupt Practices Act
FICA	Federal Insurance Contributions Act

FOB	Free-on-board
GAAP	Generally accepted accounting principles
GAAS	Generally Accepted Auditing Standards
GDI	Gross Domestic Income
GDP	Gross Domestic Product
GDR	Global Depositary Receipt
GDS	Gross Debt Service Ratio
GNP	Gross National Product
IAFE	International Association of Financial Engineers
IAS	International Accounting Standards
IBAN	International Bank Account Number
IBF	International Banking Facility
ICB	International Competitive Bidding
ICCH	International Commodities Clearing House
IDR	International Depository Receipt
IRR	Internal Rate Of Return
IRS	Internal Revenue Service
JIT	just-in-time inventory
LCM	lower cost or market
LIFO	last-in, first-out
MACRS	modified accelerated cost recovery system
NAV	Net Asset Value
NAVPS	Net Asset Value Per Share
NCAVPS	Net Current Asset Value Per Share
NDP	Net Domestic Product
NI	Net Income
NIMS	Net Interest Margin Securities
NNP	Net National Product
NOI	Net Operating Income
NOPAT	Net Operating Profit After Tax
NOPLAT	Net Operating Profit Less Adjusted Taxes
NPV	Net Present Value
NSF	Not sufficient funds
OCF	Operating Cash Flow
OIBDA	Operating Income Before Depreciation And Amortization
OMO	Open Market Operations
P&L	Profit and Loss Statement
P/E	Price-earnings
PBT	Profit Before Tax
ROA	Return On Assets
ROAE	Return On Average Equity
ROCE	Return On Capital Employed
ROE	Return On Equity

ROI	Return on investment
ROIC	Return On Invested Capital
RONA	Return On Net Assets
RONIC	Return On New Invested Capital
ROR	Return On Revenue
RORAC	Return On Risk-Adjusted Capital
ROS	Return On Sales
ROTA	Return On Total Assets
RPI	Retail Price Index
SEC	Securities and Exchange Commission
SYD	Sum-of-the-years-digits (depreciation method)
WEBS	World Equity Benchmark Series
WEO	World Economic Outlook
WGC	World Gold Council
WPI	Wholesale Price Index
WTO	World Trade Organization
YOY	Year Over Year
YTD	Year To Date
YTM	Yield To Maturity
YTW	Yield To Worst
ZBB	Zero-Based Budgeting

E.3 BUSINESS MANAGEMENT: FINANCIAL RATIOS

The Balance Sheet and the Statement of Income are essential, but they are only the starting point for successful financial management. Ratio Analysis enables the business owner/manager to spot trends in a business and to compare its performance and condition with the average performance of similar businesses in the same industry. Ratio analysis may provide the all-important early warning indications concerning financial health of the business and may help the management in taking suitable decisions in accordance with the economic environment in order to stabilize the situation.

Balance Sheet Ratio Analysis

Important Balance Sheet Ratios measure liquidity and solvency (a business's ability to pay its bills as they come due) and leverage (the extent to which the business is dependent on creditors' funding). They include the following ratios:

Liquidity Ratios

These ratios indicate the ease of turning assets into cash. They include the Current Ratio, Quick Ratio, and Working Capital.

Current Ratios

The Current Ratio is one of the best known measures of financial strength. It is figured as shown below:

> Current Ratio = Total Current Assets / Total Current Liabilities

The main question this ratio addresses is: "Does the business have enough current assets to meet the payment schedule of its current debts with a margin of safety for possible losses in current assets, such as inventory shrinkage or collectable accounts?" A generally acceptable current ratio is 2 to 1. But whether or not a specific ratio is satisfactory depends on the nature of the business and the characteristics of its current assets and liabilities. The minimum acceptable current ratio is obviously 1:1, but that relationship is usually playing it too close for comfort.

If the business's current ratio is too low, it may be raised by:

- Paying some debts.

- Increasing current assets from loans or other borrowings with a maturity of more than one year.

- Converting non-current assets into current assets.

- Increasing your current assets from new equity contributions.

- Putting profits back into the business.

Quick Ratios

The Quick Ratio is sometimes called the "acid-test" ratio and is one of the best measures of liquidity. It is figured as shown below:

$$\text{Quick Ratio} = \text{Cash} + \text{Government Securities} + \text{Receivables} / \text{Total Current Liabilities}$$

The Quick Ratio is a much more exacting measure than the Current Ratio. By excluding inventories, it concentrates on the really liquid assets, with value that is fairly certain. It helps answer the question: "If all sales revenues should disappear, could my business meet its current obligations with the readily convertible `quick' funds on hand?"

An acid-test of 1:1 is considered satisfactory unless the majority of your "quick assets" are in accounts receivable, and the pattern of accounts receivable collection lags behind the schedule for paying current liabilities.

Working Capital

Working Capital is more a measure of cash flow than a ratio. The result of this calculation must be a positive number. It is calculated as shown below:

> Working Capital = Total Current Assets - Total Current Liabilities

Bankers look at Net Working Capital over time to determine a company's ability to weather financial crises. Loans are often tied to minimum working capital requirements.

A general observation about these three Liquidity Ratios is that the higher they are the better, especially if the business is relying to any significant extent on creditor money to finance assets.

Leverage Ratio

This Debt/Worth or Leverage Ratio indicates the extent to which the business is reliant on debt financing (creditor money versus owner's equity):

> Debt/Worth Ratio = Total Liabilities / Net Worth

Generally, the higher this ratio, the more risky a creditor will perceive its exposure in the business, making it correspondingly harder to obtain credit.

Management Ratios

Other important ratios, often referred to as Management Ratios, are also derived from Balance Sheet and Statement of Income information.

Inventory Turnover Ratio

This ratio reveals how well inventory is being managed. It is important because the more times inventory can be turned in a given operating cycle, the greater the profit. The Inventory Turnover Ratio is calculated as follows:

> Inventory Turnover Ratio = Net Sales / Average Inventory at Cost

Return on Assets (ROA) Ratio

This measures how efficiently profits are being generated from the assets employed in the business when compared with the ratios of firms in a similar business. A low ratio in comparison with industry averages indicates an inefficient use of business assets. The Return on Assets Ratio is calculated as follows:

> Return on Assets = Net Profit Before Tax / Total Assets

Return on Investment (ROI) Ratio

The ROI is perhaps the most important ratio of all. It is the percentage of return on funds invested in the business. In short, this ratio tells whether or not all the effort put into the business has been worthwhile. If the ROI is less than the rate of return on an alternative, risk-free investment such as a bank savings account, the owner may be wiser to sell the company, put the money in such a savings instrument, and avoid the daily struggles of small business management. The ROI is calculated as follows:

> Return on Investment = Net Profit before Tax / Net Worth

These Liquidity, Leverage, Profitability, and Management Ratios allow the business owner to identify trends in a business and to compare its progress with the performance of others through data published by various sources. The owner may thus determine the business's relative strengths and weaknesses.

Return on Capital Employed (ROCE)

This measures how efficiently profits are being generated from the capital employed in the business when compared with the ratios of firms in a similar business. A low ratio in comparison with industry averages indicates an inefficient use of business capital. The Return on Capital Employed Ratio is calculated as follows:

> Return on Capital Employed = Net Profit Before Tax / Total Capital Employed

Where, Capital employed = fixed assets + current assets − current liabilities

Capital employed may be defined in a number of ways. However, two widely accepted definitions are "gross capital employed" and "net capital employed". Gross capital employed usually means the total assets, fixed as well as current, used in business, while net capital employed refers to total assets minus liabilities. ROCE compares earnings with capital invested in the company. It is similar to Return on Assets (ROA), but takes into account sources of financing.

PART F
REFERENCE/BIBLIOGRAPHY

- Ahmad, Syed. (1990) *"Adam Smith's Four Invisible Hands,"* History of Political Economy, Vol. 22 No. 1, pp. 137-44.

- Ajit S. Bhalla, Dilip M. Nachane, *"Asian Eclipse: India and China in Penumbra ?"*, (Economic and Political Weekly, September 5-11, 1998) pp. 2364

- Aksoy M. Ataman, John C. Begin, *"Global Agricultural Trade and Developing Countries"*, (The World Bank, Washington DC, 2005) pp. 1-17

- Alan S. Blinder, Robert M. Solow, *"Analytical Foundations of Fiscal Policy"*, The Economics of Public Finance, The Brooking Institution, 1974, pp. 115

- Alice Amsden, Michael Intriligator, Robert Metntyre and Lance Taylor, *"Strategies for a Viable Transition – Lessons from the Political Economy of Renewal"*, Economic and Political Weekly, December 28, 1996, p.3384.

- Alice Amsden, Michael Intriligator, Robert Metntyre and Lance Taylor, *"Strategies for a Viable Transition – Lessons from the Political Economy of Renewal"*, (Economic and Political Weekly, December 28, 1996), pp. 3384

- Altman, E.I., (1968): *"Financial ratios, Discriminant analysis and the Prediction of Corporate Bankruptcy"*, (The Journal of Finance, 23(4), 1968) pp. 558, 589–609

- Anderson T., Fredriksson T., *"Distinction between Intermediate and Finished Products in Intra-Firm Trade"*, (International Journal of Industrial Organization, No. 18, 2000) pp. 773-792

- Anthony S. Campagna, *"Macro-economics: Theory and Policy"*, (Boston: Houghton Mifflin Harcourt, 1994) pp. 301-2

- Arthur F. Burns, Wesley C. Mitchell, *"Measuring Business Cycles"* (New York: National Bureau of Economics Research, 1946), pp.16

- Atkenson Andrew, Lee E. Ohanian, *"Are Phillips Curve Useful for Forecasting Inflation ?"*, (Federal Reserve Bank of Minneapolis, Quarterly Review, vol. 25, No.1, 2001) pp. 2-11

- Aydinonat, N. Emrah. *"The Invisible Hand in Economics: How Economists Explain Unintended Social Consequences"*, (New York: Routledge, 2008)

- Ball Laurence, *"Aggregate Demand and Long-Run Unemployment"*, (Brookings Papers on Economic Activity, vol. 2, 1999) pp. 189-236

- Bernanke B., *"Non-monetary effect of the Financial Crisis in the Propagation of the Great Depression"*, (American Economic Review, No. 73, 1983) pp. 257-276

- Biplab Dasgupta, *"Structural Adjustment, Global Trade and the New Political Economy of Development"*, (Zed Books, London 1998) pp. 157

- Birthal, Pratap S., Awadhesh K. Jha, Marites M. Tiongco and Clare Narrod (2008). *"Improving farm-to-market linkages through contract farming: a case study of smallholder dairying in India"*, IFPRI Discussion Paper, No. 00814. Washington, D.C.: IFPRI.

- Birthal, Pratap S., P.K. Joshi and Ashok Gulati (2005), *"Vertical coordination in high-value food commodities: implications for smallholders"*, MTID Discussion Paper, No. 85. Washington, D.C.: IFPRI.

- Biswajit Dhar, *"Complying with TRIPs Commitment: EMR versus Product Patent Regime"*, Economic and Political Weekly, December 19, 1998) pp. 3231

- Blackaby David H., Lester C. Hunt, *"The Wage Curve and Long Term Unemployment: A Cautionary Note"*, (Manchester School of Economics and Social Studies, vol. 60-4, 1992) pp. 419-428

- Bo Soderson, Geoffery Reed, *"International Economics"*, (Hampshire: The Macmillan Press Ltd., 1994) pp. 668

- Bordo Michael D., Anna J. Schwartz, *"IS-LM and Monetarism"*, (National Bureau of Economic Research, Massachusetts, Working Paper No. 9713, 2003) pp. 5-9

- Bordo Michael D., Harold James, *"The International Monetary Fund: Its Present Role in Historical Perspective"*, (Cambridge, National Bureau of Economic Research No. 7724, 2000) pp. 36-42

- Bordo, Michael D. *"Some Aspects of the Monetary Economics of Richard Cantillon,"* (Journal of Monetary Economics, Vol. 12 No. 2 August 1983) pp. 235-258.

- Brewer Anthony, *"Cantillon, Quesnay and the Tableau Economique"*, (University of Bristol, Department of Economics, Discussion Paper No. 05/577, October 2005) pp. 4-9

- Brooman F.S., *"Macroeconomics"*, (London: George Allen and Unwin Ltd., Third Edition, 1967), pp. 288

- Callinicos Alex, *"Contradictions of European Monetary Union"*, (Economic and Political Weekly: JSTOR 1998) pp.70

- Cantillon, Richard. [1755] 1959. *Essai sur la Nature du Commerce in Général*, Henry Higgs, ed. and trans. London: Frank Cass. Page references to Cantillon (1755) are given in the following order: first, from the original French (from Higgs [1931] 1959), second, the English translation (from Higgs [1931] 1959), and third the new Brewer (2001) edition.

- Carl Eicher and Lawrence Witt, *"Agriculture in Economic Development"*, (New York: McGraw Hill Book Company, 1964) pp. 227

- Caves, R.E. (1996), *"Multinational Enterprise and Economic Analysis"*, Cambridge University Press, Cambridge, pp. 1

- Cecchetti Stephen, Stephen Krause, *"Financial Structure, Macroeconomic Stability and Monetary Policy"*, (Cambridge: National Bureau of Economic Research, NBER Working Paper No. 8354, 2001) pp. 10-17

- Charles Hanrahan and Randy Schnepf, *"WTO Doha Round: Agricultural Negotiating Proposals"*, (CRS Report for Congress, 2005) pp. 6-19

- Chirayu Isarangkun, Kobsak Pootrakool, *"Sustainable Economic Development through the suffiency Economic Philosophy"*, (Thailand: School of Development Economics, National Institute of Development Administration, 2008) pp. 5-9

- Dailami Mansoor, Paul Masson, *"The Multi-Polar International Monetary System"*, (The World Bank, Development Economics, Policy Research Working Paper No. 5147, 2009) pp. 1-9

- Danity Jr. William, Warren Young, *"IS-LM: An Inquest"*, (History of Political Economy No. 27, 1995) pp. 27-41

- Das Gurcharan, *"India Unbound: From Independence to the Global Information Age"*, (London: Profile Books, 2002) pp. 66

- Deena Khatkhate, *"Monetary Policy In India: A Command Approach"*, JSTOR Economic and Political Weekly, Vol 25, No. 33, Aug 1990, pp. 1856-58

- Deepak Nayyar, *"The Foreign Trade Sector, Planning and Industrialization in India"* in Terence J. Byres (ed.) *"The*

State, Development Planning and Liberalization in India" (Oxford University Press, 1997) pp. 362

- Deepak Nayyar, "Themes in Trade and Industrialization", (New Delhi: Oxford University Press, 1997) pp. 22

- Demirguc-Kunt, A. and L. Serven,"Are All the Sacred Cows Dead? Implications of the Financial Crisis for Macro and Financial Policies", (The World Bank, Policy Research Working Papers, 4807, 2009) pp. 3-14

- Denis, Andy. (2005) "The Invisible Hand of God in Adam Smith," (Research in the History of Economic Thought and Methodology Vol. 23-A, 2005) pp. 1-32.

- Diaz-Alejandro C., "Good-bye financial repression, hello financial crash", Journal of Development Economics 19, 1985) pp. 4-6.

- Douglas L. Kruse, Richard B. Freeman, Joseph R. Blasi (ed), "Shared Capitalism at Work: Employee Ownership, Profit and Gain Sharing, and Broad-Based Stock Options", (The University of Chicago Press, 2010) pp. 264-273

- Douglas W. Diamond, Raghuram Rajan, "The Credit Crisis: Conjectures about Causes and Remedies", (Cambridge: National Bureau of Economic Research, NBER Working Paper No. 14739, 2009) pp. 7-11

- Dunning J.H., "Towards an Eclectic Theory of International Production: Some Empirical Tests", (Journal of International Business Studies, No. 11, 1980) pp. 9-31

- Dunning, J.N. ,"Re-evaluating the Benefits of Foreign Direct Investment", (International Thomson Business Press, London, 2003) pp. 77

- Durbin E.M.F., "Problems of Economic Planning", (London: Routledge and Kegan Paul Ltd.,1955) pp. 42

- Eatwell, John, Murray Milgate and Peter Newman edited. (1987). *The New Palgraves: A Dictionary of Economics*, London: Macmillan Press.

- Economic Commission for Latin America and the Caribbean (ECLAC), *"Economic Instruments and Fiscal Policy"*, Report of the 14 th meeting of the Forum of Ministers of the Environment of Latin America and the Caribbean, October 2003

- Edward Shapiro, *"Macroeconomic Analysis"* (Harcourt Brace Jovanich Inc., Fourth Edition, 1978), pp. 454

- Einstein Albert, *"Why Socialism"*, Monthly Review (May 1949), vol. 50, no. 1

- Falk, R. (1997), *"State of Siege: Will Globalization win out?"* (Journal of International Affairs, 73, no.1, January) pp. 125

- Flowers E.B., *"Oligopolistic Reaction in European and Canadian Direct Investment in the United States"*, (Journal of International Business Studies, No. 7, 1976) pp. 43-55

- Frances Stewart, *"Technology and Underdevelopment"* (The Macmillan Press Ltd., 1977) p.12

- Frances Stewart, *"Technology and Underdevelopment"*, (London: The Macmillan Press Ltd., 1977) pp. 1

- Francisco Rodriguez, Dani Rodrik, *"Trade Policy and Economic Growth: A Skeptic's Guide to the Cross – National Evidence"*, Cambridge: National Bureau of Economic Research, NBER Working Paper no. 7081, 1999) pp. 11-17

- Frederic F. Clairmount, *"Implosion of Japanese Capitalism"*, (Economic and Political Weekly, April 28, 2001) pp. 1387

- Friedman Milton, *"Interest Rates and the Demand for Money"*, (Journal of Law and Economics No. 9, 1966) pp. 71-85

- Friedman Milton, *"The Demand for Money: Some Theoretical and Empirical Results"*, (Journal of Political Economy No. 67, 1959) pp. 327-351

- Friedman Thomas L., *" The World is Flat: A Brief History of the Twenty-First Century"*, (New York: Farrar Straus & Giroux, 2005) pp.8

- Froyen, Richard T. *"Macroeconomics: Theories and Policies"*. 6th ed. Prentice Hall, 1998.

- G. Crowther *"An Outline of Money" The English Language Book Society, Thomas Nelson and Sons Ltd., P.107*

- Galbraith J. K., "American Capitalism", (Harmondsworth, Middlesex, 1968) pp. 118

- Gomory, Ralph E. and William J. Baumol, *"Global Trade and Conflicting National Interests"*, (Cambridge, MIT Press, 2000) pp. 183-195

- Gordon A. Fletcher, *"The Keynesian Revolution and its Critics"*, (Palgrave Macmillan, 1989) pp. 290

- Gordon, Robert J. *"Macroeconomics"*, 7th ed. Addison-Wesley, 1998.

- George J. Stigler, *"A Sketch of the History of Truth in Teaching,"* (Journal of Political Economy, 81/2, Part 1,1973) pp. 491-495

- Graham E.M., *"The State of the Theory of Foreign Direct Investment and the Multinational Enterprise"*, (Economic Systems, No. 20, 1996) pp. 183-206

- Grampp, William D., *"What Did Adam Smith Mean by the Invisible Hand,"* The Journal of Political Economy, Vol. 108, No. 3 (June 2000) pp. 441-465.

- Greenway D., Torstensson J., *"Back to the Future: Taking Stock on Intra – Industry Trade"*, (Weltwirtschaftliches Archive 133/2) pp. 249-269

- Grimwade, N. (2000), *"International Trade: New Patterns of Trade, Production and Investment"*, (Taylor & Francis Group, Routledge, London) pp. 134

- Grubel H.G., Lloyd P.G., *"The Empirical Measurement of Intra-Industry Trade"*, (The Economic Record, No.47, 1971) pp. 494-517

- Gunnar Myrdal, *"The Challenge of World Poverty"*, (Penguin Books, London, 1970) pp. 229

- Gunnar Myrdal, Seth S. King, *"Asian Drama: An Inquiry into the Poverty of Nations"*, (Penguin Books, London, 1968) ed. Tim Lankester, "Asian Drama: The Pursuit of Modernization in India and Indonesia", Asian Affairs, vol. XXXV, no. III, November 2004, pp. 3-8

- Gupta S.B., *"Monetary Economics: Institutions Theory and Policy"*, (S. Chand & Co. New Delhi, 1988) pp. 356

- Gustav Ranis, *"Theories of Economic Growth in Capitalist Countries"*, (London: Macmillan & Co. Ltd., 1965) pp. 16

- Haggblade, Steven, Peter B.R. Hazell, Thomas Reardon, *"Transforming the Rural Non-Farm Economy: Opportunities and Threats in the Developing World"*, (Oxford: Oxford University Press, 2009).

- Hanchate Amresh, Dyson Tim, *"Prospects for Food Demand and Supply in Twenty First Century India"*, edited by Tim Dyson, Robert Cassen and Leela Visasria (Oxford: Oxford University Press, 2005) pp. 252-253

- Hans Singer, *"Dualism Revisited: A New Approach to the Problems of Dual Society in Developing Countries"*, Journal of Development Studies, VII, 1, (October 1970) pp. 60-61

- Harrison Mark, *"Stalinist Industrialization and the Test of War"*, (University of Warwick, History of Workshop Journal no. 29,1990), pp. 65-84

- Hayami, Yujiro, Vernon W. Ruttan , *"Agricultural Development: An International Perspective"*, (Baltimore, MD, John Hopkins University Press, 1985) pp. 386-402

- Helpman E., *"A Simple Theory of International Trade with Multinational Corporations"*, (Journal of Political Economy, No. 92/3, 1984) pp. 451-471

- Helpman, Elhanan, *"Trade, FDI, and The Organization Of Firms,"* Journal of Economic Literature, 2006, vol. 44(3,Sep), pp. 589-613

- Hill, Lisa. *"The Hidden Theology of Adam Smith,"* (*European Journal of the History of Economic Thought*, Vol. 8 No. 1, 2001) pp. 1-29.

- Hirschman, Albert O., *"The Passions and the Interests: Political Arguments for Capitalism before Its Triumph"*, (Princeton, NJ: Princeton University Press, 1977) pp. 98-107

- Hornbeck J.F., *"The Argentine Financial Crisis"*, (CRS Report for Congress, No. RS 21130, 2002) pp. 5-6

- Hull, David L. *"What's Wrong with Invisible-Hand Explanations?"* (Philosophy of Science, Vol. 64, December Supplement 1997, Part II) pp. 117-126.

- Hult Thomas, *"The BRIC Countries"*, (Michigan: Global Edge Business Review, Vol. 3, No. 4, 2009) pp. 2

- Hummels D.L., Rapoport D., Yi K.M., *"Vertical Specialization and the Changing Nature of World Trade"*, (Economic Policy Review No. 4, 1998) pp. 79-99

- Hutton W. (1995), *"The State We Are In"*, Jonathan Cape, Random House, UK, pp. 112

- IBEF, *"India: Taking India to the World, Global Agenda"*, (London: World Link Publications, 2006) pp. 35

- Ila Patnaik, Ajay Shah, *"Monetary Policy in India"*, (New Delhi: Department of Economic Affairs DEA, July 2007) pp. 2-14

- IMF (2009a), *"World Economic Outlook Update: Contradictory Forces Receding but Weak Recovery Ahead"*, Washington DC: IMF

- IMF (2009ba), *"Global Financial Stability Report"*, Washington DC: IMF

- IMF (2009c), *"World Economic Outlook: Crisis and Recovery"*, Washington DC: IMF

- Irma Adelman, *"Beyond Export-Led Growth"*, (World Development, Volume 12, No. 5, 1984) pp. 937-949

- James Arthur Ashley, *"Business Cycles – Their Nature, Cause and Control"* (Mumbai: Asia Publishing House, 1960) pp.88

- James R. Kearl, *"Principles of Macroeconomics"*, (D.C. Heath and Company, Lexington, Massachusetts, 1993) pp. 413

- Jean Dreze and Amartya Sen, *"India: Economic Development and Social Opportunity"*, (New Delhi: Oxford University Press, 1995) pp. 96 – 107

- Jere Behrman and T.N. Srinivasan (eds.),*"Handbook of Development Economics"*, Volumes III A and B (Springer Netherlands, January 1998) pp. 569-580, 2134-2157

- John Nasbitt, Patrica Aburden, *"Megatrends 2000"*, (New York: Avon Books, 1990) pp.1

- John Palmer, "The Case for Joining", M. Kettle (ed.), *"The Single Currency: Should Britain Join ?"* (Economic and Political Weekly: JSTOR 1997) pp.15

- John Williamson, *"Understanding Special Drawing Rights"*, (Peterson Institute for International Economics, 2009) pp. 3-7

- Joseph A. Pechman, Barry P. Bosworth, *"The Budget and the Economy"*, The Brookings Institution, 1982, pp. 43

- Joseph E. Stiglitz, *"Globalization and its Discontent"* (London, Allen Lane, 2002) P.121

- Kaplinsky Raphael, *"Globalization, Poverty and Inequality"*, (Cambridge: Polity Press, 2005), pp.247

- Kavaljit Singh, *"Taming Global Financial Flows"*, (New Delhi: Madhyam Book, 2000) pp.13

- Keith B. Griffin, John L. Enos, *"Planning Development"* (London: Addison – Wesley B. Publishing Company, 1970) pp. 22

- Keith M. Carlson, *"The Mix of Monetary and Fiscal Policy: Conventional Wisdom vs. Empirical Reality"*, (Federal Reserve Bank of St. Louis, October 1982) pp. 7-13

- Keynes John Maynard *"How to pay for the war",* 1940, Harcourt Brace and Company, New York, (The Annals of the American Academy of Political and Social Science, Vol. 211, No. 1, 1940) pp. 200-201

- Keynes John Maynard *"The General Theory of Employment, Interest and Money"* (Harcourt, Brace and Company, Polygraphic Company of America, New York; 2002) ch. 8, 13, 18

- Khalil, Elias L. *"Making Sense of Adam Smith's Invisible Hand: Beyond Pareto Optimality and Unintended Consequences,"* (Journal of the History of Economic Thought, Vol. 22 No. 1, 2000) pp. 49-63.

- Khan M, A. Mirakhor, "Islamic Banking: Experiences in the Islamic Republic of Iran and Pakistan", (Economic Development and Cultural Change, Vol. 38, 1990) pp. 353-375

- Kleinert Jurn, *"The Role of Multinational Enterprises in Globalization: An Empirical Overview"*, (Kiel Institute of World Economics, Kiel Working Papers No. 1069, 2001) pp. 9-15

- Kotler Philip, *"Marketing Management"*, (12 th Ed., Wharton School Publishing, 2010) pp.671

- Kynge James, *"China Shakes the World"*, (London: Weidenfeld & Nicolson, 2006) pp. 26-28

- Lal Anil K., Ronald W. Clement, *"Economic Development in India: The Role of Individual Enterprise and Entrepreneurial Spirit"*, (Asia – Pacific Development Journal, Vol. 12, No. 2, December 2005), pp. 3-5

- Lal D., Myint Y., *"The Political Economy of Poverty, Equity and Growth"*, (Clarendon Press, 1996, Oxford) pp. 48-53

- Lal Deepak, *"The Poverty of Development Economics"*, (The MIT Press, September 2000), pp.27

- Lal Deepak, *"The Threat to Economic Liberty from International Organizations"*, (Cato Journal vol. 25, No. 3, 2005) pp. 6-8

- Lal Deepak, *"Unintended Consequences"*, (MIT Press, Cambridge, Massachusetts, 1998) pp. 28

- Landauer Carl., "Contemporary Economic Systems", (Philadelphia: J.B. Lippincott Company, 1964) pp. 2

- Landes David, *"The Wealth and Poverty of Nations"*, (London: Little Brown, 1998) pp. 55

- Leo Troy, *"Business and Industrial Financial Ratios"*, (Publisher: CCH Incorporated, 2005) pp. 45-68

- Lewis Arthur W., *"Development Planning"*, (New York: Harper & Row Publishers, 1966) pp. 267

- Lewis Arthur W., *"The Principles of Economic Planning"*, (London: George Allen and Unwin Ltd., 1963) pp. 13

- Lipsey R. G., *"The Relation between Unemployment and the Rate of Change of Money Wage Rate: A Further Analysis"*, (Economica, Feb 1960), pp. 1-31.

- Lipsey Robert E., *"Home and Host Country Effects of FDI"*, (National Bureau of Economic Research, Cambridge, Working Paper No. 9293, 2002) pp. 5-16

- Llaudes Ricardo, *"The Philips Curve and Long Term Unemployment"*, (European Central Bank: Frankfurt, Germany, Working Paper Series No. 441, 2005) pp. 31

- Logue, Dennis E. and Willett. Thomas D., *"A Note on the Relation between the Rate and Variability of Inflation,"* (Economica, May 1976), pp. 151-158

- Luce Edwards, *"In Spite of the Gods: The Strange Rise of Modern India"*, (London: Little Brown, 2006) pp. 62-63

- M. Reinhart & Kenneth S. Rogoff, *"The Aftermath of Financial Crises,"* (American Economic Review, American Economic Association, vol. 99/2, 2009) pp. 466-472

- Maddison Angus, *"Contours of the World Economy 1-2030 AD: Essays in Macro-Economic History"*, (Oxford University Press, 2007)

- Maddison Angus, *"Economic Progress and Policy in Developing Countries (1970)"*, 2006, Routledge, pp. 72-83

- Maddison Angus, *"The World Economy: Historical Statistics"*, OECD (Organization for Economic Co-operation and Development), 2003, pp. 230

- Marx Karl (1887/1999), "Capital", (F. Engels, Ed. S. Moore, E. Aveling, Translated) retrieved March 19, 2008 from Marx / Engels Internet Archive: http: // www.marxists.org/archive/marx/works/1867-c1/index.htm

- Markusen J.R., Venables A.J., *"Multinational Firms and New Trade Theory"*, (Journal of International Economics No. 46, 1998) pp. 183-203

- Maurice Allais, *"The Monetary Conditions of Markets: From Teachings of the Past to Reforms of Tomorrow"*, (Jeddah: Islamic Research and Training Institute, Islamic Development Bank, 1993) pp. 34-37

- Maurice Herbert Dobb, *"On Economic Theory and Socialism"*, (London Routledge & Kegan PAUL Ltd., 1965) pp. 152

- Max Corden, *"The Logic of the International Monetary Non-System"* in Fritz Machlup, Gerhard Fels, and Hubertus Müller-Groeling, eds., *Reflections on the Troubled World Economy: Essays in Honour of Herbert Giersch* (London: Macmillan, 1983), pp. 59-74

- McNulty, Paul J. *"Economic Theory and the Meaning of Competition,"* (Quarterly Journal of Economics, Vol. 82 No. 4, November 1968) pp. 639-656.

- Messerlin P.A., *"The Long-Term Evolution of the E.C. Anti-Dumping Law: Some Lessons for the New AD Laws in LDCs"*, Mimeograph, World Bank (1987) pp.21

- Michael Mussa, *"World Recession and Recovery: A V or an L ?"*, (Peterson Institute for International Economics, Paper Presented at the Fifteenth Semi-Annual Meeting on Global Economic Prospects, April 7, 2009) pp. 2-7

- Michael P. Todaro, *"Economic Development in the Third World"*, (Hyderabad: Orient Longman India Pvt. Ltd., 1993) pp. 542

- Michael P. Todaro, Stephen C. Smith, *"Economic Development"*, (Pearson Education Singapore Pte Ltd., Eight edition, 2003) pp. 613

- Milton Friedman, *"Inflation and Unemployment"*, (Nobel Memorial Lecture, December 13, 1976, The University of Chicago, Illinois, USA), pp. 3-6

- Milton Friedman, *"The Case for Flexible Exchange Rates"* in Essays in Positive Economics (Chicago: University of Chicago Press, 1953), pp. 157-183

- Minim Di Alberto, *"Patel and Pavitt Revised: Innovation and IP Management in Multinational Corporations, 10 Years after the Case of Non-Globalization"*, (International Workshop on Innovation, Multinationals and Local Development, Catania, Italy, October 2009) pp. 2-8

- Mitchell W.C., *"Business Cycle: The Problem and its Setting"*, (New York: National Bureau of Economic Research, 1957) pp. 468

- Mundell, R. *"Financial Crises and the International Monetary System,"* (presented in Havana's International Conference on Globalization, March 3, 2009) pp. 38-56

- Nadia F. Piffaretti, *"Reshaping the International Monetary Architecture: Lessons from the Keynes Plan"*, (Banks and Bank Systems, Volume 4, Issue 1, 2009) pp. 46-52

- Natalia Percinschi, Alexandr Iscenco, *"Transnational Corporations in the World and Moldovan Economy"*, (Institute of Economy, Finance and Statistics, Republic of Moldovan, 2007) pp. 1-6

- Network Bulletin, *"BRIC Countries"*, (AXA Corporate Solutions International Network Newsletter, No. 17, 2008) pp. 2-3

- Nitzan Jonathan, *"Regimes of Differential Accumulation: Mergers, Stagflation and the Logic of Globalization"*, (Taylor & Francis Ltd., UK, Review of International Political Economy 8:2, 2001) pp. 234-246

- O' Niel Jim, Tushar Poddar, *"Ten Things for India to Achieve its 2050 Potential"*, (Economic Research Global Economics Paper Issue No. 169, 2008) pp. 3-4

- O'Neill Jim, *"Building Better Global Economic BRICs,"* (republished in The World and the BRICs Dream, Goldman Sachs, New York, 2006) pp. 14

- OECD Directorate Statistical Profile Database (New York: 1998, 2003, 2007,2009)

- Oskar Lange, *"Role of Planning in Socialist Economy"*, Oskar Lange (ed.) Problems of Political Economy of Socialism (Mumbai: Asia Publishing House, 1962) pp. 22

- Pack, Spencer J. *"Adam Smith's Economic Vision and the Invisible Hand,"* (History of Economic Ideas, Vol. 4 Nos. 1&2, 1996) pp. 253-65.

- Palat Raghu, *"Understanding Financial Ratios in Business"*, (Mumbai: Jaico Publishing House, 2005) pp. 46-78

- Parkin, Michael *"Macroeconomics"*, (Addison – Wesley, 1990), P. 307

- Patrick Baron, *"The Velocity of Money and the Business Cycle"*, An Austrian Economic View of the World, March 2010, pp.1-2

- Paul A. Samualson, William D. Nordhaus, *"Economics"*, (New York: McGraw-Hill Book Co., 1992) pp. 570

- Paul Krugman, *"The Myth of Asia's Miracle"*, (Pacific Affairs, Volume 73 (6), Nov.1994) pp. 67-78

- Paul M. Romer, *"Economic Growth"*, (The Concise Encyclopedia of Economics, David R. Henderson, ed. Liberty Fund, 2007) pp. 1-5

- Phelps E. S., *"Phillips Curve, Expectations of Inflation and Optimal Unemployment Over Time"*, Economica (N.S.) 34 (August 1967) pp. 254-281

- Phil Anderson, *"The Cantillon Effect"*, (The Educated Analyst, October 2009) pp.1

- Phillips A. W., *"Relation between Unemployed and the Rate of Change in Money Wage Rates in the United Kingdom 1862-1987"*, (Economica, Nov. 1958) pp. 283-299.

- Radhakrishna R., Manoj Panda, *"Macroeconomics of Poverty Reduction: India Case Study"*, Indira Gandhi Institute of Development Research, Mumbai, 2006) pp. 95-113

- Raja J. Chelliah, *"Fiscal Policy in Underdeveloped Countries"*, (Mumbai: George Allen & Unwin India Pvt. Ltd., 1969) pp. 51

- Ram Mohan R. Yallapragada, Alfred G. Toma, C. William Roe, *"India and China Vying for World Economic Supremacy"*, (International Business & Economic Research Journal, Volume 8, No. 2, 2009) pp. 114-115

- Rangarajan C., *"Indian Economy – Essays in Money and Finance"*, (New Delhi, UBS Publishers, 1998) pp. 59

- Robert C. Feenstra, Shang-Jin Wei (*ed*), *"China's Growing Role in World Trade"*, (The University of Chicago Press, 2010) pp. 148-173

- Robert J. Gordon, *"Macroeconomics"*, (11 th edition, Cardiff University, Wales, UK, Prentice Hall, 2009) pp. 467-475

- Robert S. McNamara, *"One Hundred Countries, Two Billion People: The Dimensions of Development"*, (New York, Praeger Publishers Inc; September 20, 1973) pp. 11

- Roger Martin- Fagg, (2000), *"Making Sense of the Economy"*, (Thomson Learning) pp. 42-53

- Rothermund Dietmar, *"An Economic History of India: From Pre-Colonial Times to 1991"*, (New York: Routledge, 1993) pp.2

- Rudinger Dornbusch, Alejandro Werner, Guillermo Calvo, Stanley Fischer, *"Mexico: Stabilization, Reform, and No Growth"*, (Brookings Papers on Economic Activity, Vol. 1994, No. 1. (1994), pp. 253-285

- Rudinger Dornbusch, Stanley Fischer, *"Macroeconomics"*, (New York: McGraw-Hill, Inc. Sixth edition, 1994) pp.78

- Sandra Lawson, David Heacock, Anna Stupnytska, *"BRICs and Beyond"*, (Goldman Sachs Global Economic Group, Nov. 2007) pp. 154-156

- Schumpeter, Joseph A. *"History of Economic Analysis"*, (New York: Oxford University Press, 1954) pp. 354-390

- Selgin, George A. and Lawrence H. White. *"How Would the Invisible Hand Handle Money?"* (Journal of Economic Literature, Vol. 32 No. 4, December 1994) pp. 1718-1749.

- Sen Amartya, *"Poverty and Famines : An Essay on Entitlements and Deprivation"*, (Oxford, Clarendon Press, 1982) pp.27

- Sen, Amartya, *"The Three R's of Reform"*, (Economic and Political Weekly, Vol. 40/19: 2005), pp. 1971-1974

- Shalabh Kumar Singh, *"Asia Pacific Economic Outlook"*, (Deloitte Research Report, November 2009) pp. 2-3

- Shirokov G.K., *"Industrialization of India"* (Moscow: Progress Publishers, 1973) pp. 72-73

- Smith Adam, *"An Enquiry into the Nature and Causes of the Wealth of Nations"*, (New York: The Modern Library, Random House, 1937) pp. 423

- Sodersten Bo, *"International Economics"*, (London: The Macmillan Press, 1983) pp. 189

- Sommers, Albert T. *"U.S. Economy Demystified".* (7 th ed. Reading, Addison-Wesley, 1998).

- Spiro, P. J. (1995), *"New Global Communities: Nongovernmental Organizations in International Decision-Making Institutions"*, (Washington Quarterly, 18, no.1) pp. 45-56

- Stanley Reed, Stephen Baker, William Ectickson and Monica Larner, *"Asian Flu, European Sniffles"*, (International Business Week, Reprinted in The Financial Times, volume IX, No. 40, New Delhi, October 4, 1998).

- Stewart M, (1986) *"Keynes and After"*, (3 rd edn. Penguin Books, London), pp. 47

- Subrata Ghatak, Ken Insergent, *"Agriculture and Economic Development"*, (New Delhi: Selectbook Service Syndicate, 1984), pp.69

- T.N. Srinivasan, *"Developing Countries and the Multilateral Trading System"*, (Yale University Economic Growth Center Discussion Paper No. 842. Yale University - Economic Growth Center; Stanford Center for International Development (SCID) - Stanford Institute for Economic Policy Research SIEPR) pp. 60

- T.N. Srinivasan, Jagdish N. Bhagwati, *"Foreign Trade Regimes and Economic Development: India"*, (National Bureau of Economic Research, Cambridge, Massachusetts, 1975) pp. 175-187

- The World Bank, *"Global Economic Prospects: Crisis, Finance and Growth 2010"*, (Washington DC: The World Bank, Report No. 53098, 2010) pp. 35-42

- Thirwall A.P., *"Growth and Development: With Special Reference to Developing Economies"*, (Hampshire: The Macmillan Press Ltd., 1994) pp.339

- Thomas F. Dernburg *"Macroeconomics"* (McGraw – Hill Book Company, 1985) p. 243

- Thomas J. Czerwinski, *"The Third Wave: What the Toffler's Never told you"*, (Institute for National Strategic Studies, Washington DC, Number 72, April 1996) pp. 2

- Thornton, Mark, *"Richard Cantillon and the Discovery of Opportunity Cost,"* (History of Political Economy, Vol. 39 No. 1, 2007a) pp.97-120.

- Thornton Mark, *"Cantillon and The Invisible Hand"*, (The Quarterly Journal of Austrian Economics 12, No. 2, 2009) pp. 27-46

- Todaro Michael P., *"Economic Development in the Third World"* (Orient Longman, 1993) pp. 499-542

- Trefler D., *"Trade Liberalization and the Theory of Endogenous Protection: An Economic Study of U.S. Import Policy"*, Journal of Political Economy 101 (1993) pp. 138-160

- Triffin Robert, *"Gold and the Dollar Crisis"*, (New Haven, Yale University Press, 1961) pp. 143-167

- UNCTAD, *"World Investment Report"*, (New York: 1997,1998, 1999, 2000, 2003, 2007, 2009)

- UNDP Report (1990), *Human Development Report,* (New York: United Nations Development Programme, Oxford University Press, 1990) pp. 10-11, 72-81

- Viral V. Acharya, Matthew Richardson, *"Restoring Financial Stability: How to Repair a Failed System"*, (John Wiley & Sons, New Jersey, 2009) pp. 29-57

- Voicu-Dan Dragomir, *"Financial Ratio Analysis: the Development of a Dedicated Management Information System"*, (Editura Economica, Bucharest, 2004) pp. 2

- Waterston Albert, *"Development Planning: Lessons of Experience"*, (Baltimore: John Hopkins University Press, 1972) pp. 367

- Weston, J., *"Essentials of Managerial Finance"*, (New York: Dryden Press, 1990) pp. 295

- William Easterly, *"The Elusive Quest for Growth: Adventures and Misadventures in the Tropics"*, (Cambridge: MIT Press, 2002) pp. 246-278

- William J. Baumol, Allan S. Blinder, *"Economics – Principles and Policies"*, (Orlando: Harcourt Brace and Company, 1994), pp. 706

- Wilson Dominic, Purushothaman Roopa, *"Dreaming with BRICs: The Path to 2050"*, (republished in The World and the BRICs Dream, Global Economic Paper No. 99, 2003) pp. 4-7

- Wilson Thomas, *"Planning and Growth"*, (London: Macmillan and Company, 1965) pp. 14

- Winters L. Alan, Yusuf Shahid, *" Dancing with Giants"*, (World Bank, Washington DC, 2006) pp. 7

- WTO Annual Report (Lausanne, Switzerland, Geneva: 1999, 2000, 2003, 2005, 2007, 2009)

- Zaim Sabah Eldin, *"Islamic Economics as a System Based on Human Values"*, (Journal of Islamic Banking & Finance, Karachi, Pakistan, Vol. 6, No.2, 1989) pp. 13-21

DOWNTOWN CAMPUS LRC

J.S. Reynolds Community College

3 7219 001636011

HB 171 .T75 2011
Tripathi, Ashutosh.
Economics

DISCARDED